A MATTER OF
CRIME

A MATTER OF
CRIME

New Stories from
the Masters
of Mystery & Suspense

VOL. 2

Edited by
Matthew J. Bruccoli and Richard Layman

A HARVEST/HBJ ORIGINAL

HARCOURT BRACE JOVANOVICH, PUBLISHERS

SAN DIEGO   NEW YORK   LONDON

Requests for permission to make copies of any part of the work should be mailed to: Permissions, Harcourt Brace Jovanovich, Publishers, Orlando, Florida 32887.

Editorial correspondence should be directed to the editors at: Bruccoli Clark Layman, Publishers, Inc., 2006 Sumter Street, Columbia, SC 29201.

ISSN 0892-9416
ISBN 0-15-657720-8
Designed by G.B.D. Smith
Printed in the United States of America
First Harvest/HBJ edition 1987
A B C D E F G H I J

Contents

Joe Gores:
An Interview

Joe Gores is the only writer to have won Edgar Awards in three categories (first novel, short story, and teleplay). His latest novel, *Come Morning* (which was excerpted in *New Black Mask #2*), was nominated for a 1987 Edgar. In addition to his much-admired DKA Agency novels, he wrote the novel *Hammett*.

Gores lives in Marin County, California, where he juggles work on books, screenplays, and TV scripts.

AMOC: From the vantage point of your experience as a private detective, do you find that you cringe at the inauthentic material you read in other private-eye novels?

Gores: The problem with the private-eye novel is that the guy with the bottle in the drawer and the blonde secretary he doesn't sleep with—if he ever existed—sort of stopped existing in real life about 1935. The detective today can't be a bum who wakes up one morning with nothing else in his life working out so he decides to be a private eye. In almost every state of the Union, you have to have three years of experience as a P.I. or as a cop; you have to put up a $25,000 performance bond; and you have to pass a rigorous written exam on legal matters and on investigative techniques. If you start with this as a base point, you can knock off an awful lot of "private-eye" fiction today. I still enjoy reading a lot of it, but I read it as fantasy, not reality. A guy like Loren Estleman, now: I find his detective, Amos Walker, very believable. I enjoy Robert B. Parker very much, though he's not really after a detective novel: he's after a definition of what it is to be a man in our society. I have a descending scale. I start with Hammett. We won't get into how good or bad a writer he was—a lot of his stuff was not incredibly great writing, but it was incredibly good detection work. He's a base point of reality; but then you've got to remember that even his reality was growing out of Carroll John Daly's Race Williams, an early Spillane precursor. It was only because Hammett happened to have been a detective that any reality came into the field in the first place. Then Chandler poeticized the detective and gave him the soul—which in itself is not too realistic, believe me. Next came Ross Macdonald—whose work, especially the early stuff up to *The Galton Case*, was excellent—and suddenly it's the detective as sociologist. Sociology doesn't necessarily make a bad detective novel, but it doesn't guarantee a realistic one. I'm not sure that the hard-boiled private-eye novel can exist today except as a conscious evocation of the past or a pastiche, unless you accept the fact that reality has changed and go on from there, as I try to do with my DKA novels.

AMOC: When the amateurs, the outsiders, the fakers, fall down, in what areas do they tend to fail most frequently?

Gores: Very few fictional detectives investigate. I don't even see them pick up a cross-phone directory. I don't see them use credit checks. I don't see them having bought somebody in the cops, in the phone company, in the utilities company. This is the reality of a detective's life. I like to see some of that in a detective novel. Your fingerprints are on file; you can't go breaking into people's houses; you can't hit people in the nose and get away with it unless they don't know who you are. I used to say when I was a detective that we'd commit a felony a week, but you made damn sure nobody saw you doing it, and you made very damn sure the police didn't see you doing it. Your readers have to have the feeling that the writer and therefore the detective know this stuff, even though it might be glossed over in the writing.

AMOC: What was the turning point in your career as a detective that made you give up the business?

Gores: I became a detective knowing that I wanted to be a writer. But I got very, very deeply into detective work and was spending seventy-five, eighty hours a week at it. I was writing thousands of reports, but I wasn't doing any fiction writing. My breakaway started in 1957, when I quit for a year and went to Tahiti. I went on an old freighter that took two weeks. In Tahiti I got a little house out in the country and lived there for a year. I did a lot of skin diving and a lot of writing. I came back to go into the army— I was drafted. When I got out of that in 1959 I went back into detective work, and in 1960 my former boss, Dave Kikkert, who's now dead, broke away with me and three others from L. A. Walker Company to form David Kikkert and Associates. I used DKA a few years later when I started writing short stories about a fictional agency. During all this time I was trying to be a writer. I just couldn't make a living at it. At that time I didn't have any ideas about screenwriting or television. The break became inevitable, because doing detective work is like trying to shoot off a cannon a little bit at a time. You just can't do it part-time. So in 1962 I went off to Africa for three years. When I came back at the end of '64, I ended up managing the DKA Oakland office—which I hated because I liked field work. By mid '66 I'd reached the point where I really didn't give a damn anymore about agency work. I was jaded with the givens: The business had changed; the laws were getting tougher and tougher; it was getting harder and harder to practice your profession; you got sued every week. I wasn't having a whole lot of fun, and I was losing my guts. I was not that wildly happy anymore to be out in an alley somewhere at three in the morning with some son-of-a-bitch chasing me with a hammer. Plus, the urge to write a novel was growing in me. I'd only done short stories up until then. So in August '66 I resigned and never went back full-time, even though I did pickup work for the agency on an hourly basis when I was broke up until the mid '70s. One of the early dates I had with Dori, my wife, was to repossess a car from Weasel Fratianno, the mob hit-man who wrote a book about his experiences after he turned federal informer. We stole it from a house party. They were all in the pool. It was the damndest car you ever saw, a Cadillac with a big pair of Texas longhorns on the front. Dori was very cool. I just put her behind the wheel and said go, and she went, and they didn't even know we took it. We did it two o'clock on a Sunday afternoon. That had to be in '75, so even then I was still doing occasional jobs through the agency as I needed money or as they would suddenly come up short of a field agent. But I was really very deeply into writing then, and that's all I wanted to do, so I was sort of easing myself out even though I retained my stake in the company. I wrote *Hammett*, the novel, in '73 and '74; it was published in '75. Detective work was very much in my mind then; the book tried to get at the feeling of loss that I had and imagined Hammett must have also had when he got away from detective work. Even though you love the writing much more, sitting at a typewriter writing about it is not the same as being out there and doing it.

AMOC: In the last several years, with the exception of *Come Morning*, you've been writing more for television and the movies than for the printed page. What are the attractions of this kind of writing?

Gores: First, money. Let's say the average novelist today can command a $10,000 advance on a book, or even $15,000. It's usually half on signing, half on delivery. Let's take $10,000. You get $5,000, and you're supposed to live on that for a year while you write the book. Then you deliver it and you get another $5,000. It's a year before the book gets published, and it's a year after publication before your royalties start coming in. If you get a paperback sale, your hardcover publisher keeps half of that. Unless you get a movie deal out of it, the book just isn't going to keep you until you can write another one. There was a time when a $10,000 advance—well, hell, anybody could live off that. That was terrific. Now $10,000 a year . . . it just won't reach. You don't make a lot of money on any given book at any given time. It's a cumulative thing. But meanwhile, what do you live on while the foreign money and book clubs and royalties and the like are accumulating? If you write four or five books a year, you're okay. But most of us can't write that many books. Second, I got into film and TV because somebody asked me. In 1975 I got a phone call from a man named Jack Laird, who was the supervising producer on *Kojak*. He had read *Dead Skip*, and he said, "I like the way you write dialogue. Have you ever thought of writing for television?" I said, "I haven't, but I'd love to." Jack nursed me through the whole process of submitting story lines and giving ideas. The first three or four or five that I sent him, he said, "This doesn't work. Send me something else." Finally I hit with two in a row, and they became the first two *Kojaks* that I wrote—"No Immunity for Murder," which won an Edgar, and "Bad Dude." A couple of movie producers saw "Bad Dude," which had Rosey Grier in it and was about a black bounty hunter and a black vice lord in Harlem. They called the network and got my name—they'd tuned into the show late and had missed the credits—and called my agent and said, "We want Gores to write a movie for us." That was how I did my first feature script. The point is that film and TV money is immediate. With television, the rules say forty-eight hours after delivery. Which for writers is blessed bread. Films are not that fast, but even so, if you're going to write a feature movie script you work on a step deal and might get $17,000 or $18,000 when you sign. That's going to take care of you while you write your script. So you write your script, with some money left over to work on other things. During my long hiatus between published novels I wrote seven feature scripts for hire, a lot of episodic TV, the novel *Come Morning*, and half of another novel, *Wind Time, Wolf Time*, that

I will be finishing up in the next three or four months. Mainly during those years I was trying to learn the screenwriting craft. It is really very different from novel writing but equally difficult. Not as deep but more fun. It's a collaborative art, which is a pain in the butt sometimes, but at least you have somebody to talk to every now and then.

AMOC: Do you find having no final authority over your work frustrating?

Gores: Unbelievably frustrating.

AMOC: They can change it; they can junk it; and you have nothing to show for it. At least with a book you've got black marks on white paper.

Gores: Recently I have been trying to get to the point where I don't have to do any more hour television scripts as a free-lancer. They change everything you do; staff guys put their names on your scripts; you're always in arbitration with the guild; and it's all a tremendous crapshoot. Which is why I have come back to the novel and the short story: those little black marks on paper you mentioned, which after all is what got you in this business in the first place. That feeling of accomplishment. But I refuse to knock script work. I enjoy both kinds of writing. There is a great thrill in writing an original script. An excitement. The novel is more satisfying. It's *yours*. Nobody can screw it around on you. A script is just the first step in an enormous process that too often goes nowhere. But both have their attractions. It is seductive to write scripts, and I have no intention of stopping them. I just want to do more novel work. I have nine novels outlined to write in the next eight or ten years.

AMOC: Would you be willing to detail your long

and not always happy involvement with the *Hammett* movie script?

Gores: I'd love to. A long and as you say not always happy, but usually quite funny, involvement. It started in '74, when Francis Coppola bought the rights to the book from the manuscript and hired me to do the first-draft screenplay. Nick Roeg was going to direct it; he's of Dutch extraction but is a British citizen and has done *Walkabout* and *Don't Look Back* and *Performance* and *Insignificance*—all very, very idiosyncratic and beautiful films. Nick was an incredible guy to work with. Francis was in the Philippines shooting *Apocalypse Now*, and so Nick and I had his apartment in San Francisco to work in. All inlaid wood, the penthouse in the Flat Iron Building at the top of Columbus and Kearny. Nick and I had the run of the place. We would sit up there with gallons of tea, go through the book, and fight over what this should be and what that should be. I would write the stuff and then bring it in. We'd argue a lot and laugh a lot and cuss each other out; we had a grand, grand time and produced what an awful lot of people have told me was the best script they ever read. Truffaut said it was the best script he'd ever read by an American. So of course it was never used. Nick eventually quit because they couldn't solve a casting problem. He wanted Freddie Forrest, who eventually did play Hammett, but at that time Freddie had no credits so the money people wouldn't go for him. Nick, in frustration, quit and did a bunch of commercials in New York. About a year later they brought in Wim Wenders, the well-known young German director who'd just done *An American Friend* from one of Patricia Highsmith's Ripley novels. Wim was completely different from Nick. There wasn't that volatility; he loved to put three-by-five cards up on a corkboard on the wall. We plotted out a new script because he didn't want to use the one that had been done for a different director. I'd done two versions for Nick; I did three more versions for Wim. Writing the last one was like a Keystone Kops comedy. While waiting for Wim's reaction to script number two, I was working also on a script for Paramount that was supposed to be for Richard Gere. I was in Las Vegas researching blackjack players, and from there Dori and I were going to Mexico to see our son, who was in summer school in Guadalajara. Wim got hold of me in Las Vegas and said, "Ve haf to vork on the script." I said, "Well, Wim, we're going down to Guadalajara." He said, "I vill meet you there." We were at the Fenix Hotel in Guadalajara. Wim showed up, and he and I were locked in a hotel room in one of the upper floors of that hotel for three or four days while Dori and Tim, our son, got to do all the sight-seeing. I was writing the script on yellow legal pads in longhand, and as I finished each page I'd give it to Wim. There was only one typewriter in the whole hotel, one of those ancient Underwoods down in the office. He would run downstairs and type up the page on the office machine. We were doing this day and night. At night after the office closed, Wim would check people in and out of the hotel. There was a disco up on the roof, and by the second night he was selling tickets as people came in to go dancing. I finished that one, and the powers-that-be at Coppola's wanted new directions. They started talking a framework story—open in the '50s with Hammett looking back. I was committed on several other projects, so I bowed out.

AMOC: How many months had passed at this stage?

Gores: I sold it to Coppola in '74; this was '78. They brought in a guy named Tom Pope, and he did two scripts with Wim. They didn't please everybody. So they brought in Dennis O'Flaherty. He started writing scripts as Wim started principal photography. He's writing scripts and Wim's shooting film. When the smoke cleared, he'd done seventeen different versions. So I'd done five; Pope did two; O'Flaherty did seventeen. At that point Francis finally got back from the Philippines, and Fred Roos, the line producer, who was also producing *Black Stallion*, got back from Malta. They took a look at the footage Wim had shot, about 80 percent of the picture, and they closed it all down. It was gorgeous footage, it really was; but Wim and his scriptwriters had gotten themselves into Hammett the man and they'd lost their story line. All of a sudden all that footage wasn't about anything. By this time, they had spent $10 million, and Francis felt it was unusable as a suspense film. Several more months went by and then they hired Ross Thomas, the novelist, who I think is one of the best writers in America today, to jack up this footage and put a new story line under it. He went back to the novel as much as he could, and they built an elaborate set down in L.A. at the old Hollywood General Studios, which at that time was Zoetrope. There they shot about 40 percent of the film over again to go with the 80 percent they already had. Ross did eight more scripts during this shoot. They replaced Brian Keith with Peter Boyle for the character of the Op, and they had Freddie Forrest as Hammett. It is an interesting and entertaining little film, being only remotely connected to my book. In the Zoetrope computers they have thirty-two scripts for *Hammett*. Thirty-two scripts and two directors and $13 million, and you've got a movie that Warner Bros. wouldn't put into general release, only a number of platform and festival showings around the country. Overseas it was number one in London for a week, and number one in Paris for I think three weeks. It did well in Seattle, and it ran for about a year in Portland, one of these weekend after-midnight deals like the *Rocky Horror* thing. It has the potential to become a cult film, I guess, like much of Wim's work. It's not a bad film. It just isn't the film it should have been.

AMOC: What would you give it? B? B-plus?

Gores: B-plus, yeah. And I think it could have been an A-plus. It could have been a home run. In a way, it's nobody's fault. In a way, it's the fault of the industry itself.

AMOC: As you have been pointing out, the big frustration with writing for television screen or theatre screen is that you have no authority over your work. Everybody interferes.

Gores: Everybody interferes. Everybody can change it. When I was writing *Kojak* scripts, there were nine different offices or individuals who had to okay a script. I was told a story a few years ago by a guy on the staff of a show called *Shannon* that didn't last very long, starring Kevin Dobson as a San Francisco cop. He had turned in a script that was about a cop who had cancer and as a result killed himself in such a way that it would look as though the mob had murdered him. That was his way of pinning something on the mob and making his inevitable death meaningful. A very dark story. When it aired on TV, it was about a fashion model in jeopardy. No connection at all between what they bought from him and what they put on the screen. The trouble is that relatively few network or studio execs are creative people themselves. They don't know what makes a good story. They only know what worked last week.

AMOC: Have you had much trouble with book editors?

Gores: Very, very little. When I turned *Come Morning* in to Otto Penzler, he asked for about eight or ten single-word changes, and two paragraphs to change. Less than a page in the whole book. The DKA File novels went through without any changes whatsoever.

AMOC: So you've never had the experience of working with a collaborative editor?

Gores: I did on *Hammett*, yes. The first draft of *Hammett* that I turned in to M. Evans, the original publisher on that project, wasn't really working yet. So they brought in Jeanne Bernkopf. Next to my wife, she's the best hard line-editor I've ever known. Jeanne did a line-by-line on it. I never really had any arguments with her. I felt that what she suggested was reasonable and helped the book.

AMOC: You just mentioned the editor you live with. At what stage does Dori get into the process? After the first draft or chapter by chapter?

Gores: Dori's the only person in the world who ever sees my stuff as it comes out of the machine. At the first-draft stage she makes a lot of suggestions and even will often turn the page over and rewrite a scene on the back. Her literary judgment and her commercial sense are both impeccable; her understanding of what is right for story is almost always 100 percent. If I'm not fighting a deadline, if I have any time to let things sit for a couple of weeks and then come back to them, I instantly see what she's talking about and go along with it. Otherwise I sometimes argue and kick and scream, but in the last analysis I make her changes and never regret doing so.

AMOC: Fortunate man.

Gores: Tell me about it.

AMOC: Do you see the crime/detective/suspense novel moving in any direction, evolving anywhere?

Gores: I don't know. I find myself, maybe because Dori and I travel as much as we can, much more interested in suspense, intrigue novels that move around the world than I used to be. Also, I find myself interested in reading and in writing a larger book. Books of more depth, more thought, more characterization. I find myself moving away from the strictly hard-boiled. It's a limiting kind of story, because it is the story of an alienated person with few relationships. These can be wonderful—gosh, it's hard, and it's tough; it's mean; it's tight. But you know, there's not a lot of meat on those bones. I find myself more and more interested in that meat. Now whether this is a trend in the field . . . it seems to me it is. We look at a Mary Higgins Clark or a Jonathan Kellerman or a P. D. James—these people who are selling extremely well are writing relationship books. Sure, great, gripping suspense novels that have you on the edge of your chair, but books in which you have to be able to really identify with the person in jeopardy. It isn't enough anymore to admire their stoicism or their ability to handle pain. You want to walk down their road with them. I believe the mystery-suspense novel is being taken closer to mainstream fiction. It can be done. Look at the sheer brilliance of something like *Mirror, Mirror on the Wall*, by Stan Ellin. A psychological novel with great penetration, which is at the same time a marvelously tricky challenge, a puzzle novel. So you can have it all in the field if you're willing to work hard enough at it.

AMOC: Do you have a sense that in the last five years the kind of novel you write is enjoying a very strong revival, even a renaissance?

Gores: Yes. It is. The whole field. I mean from the cozies and the English tea gardens right through the hard-boiled or the hard suspense novel.

AMOC: For a while it looked as though the British spy novel was wiping out the American detective novel.

Gores: Not just the *British* spy novel. Bill Granger, who lives in Chicago, writes marvelously good espionage books. The *November Man* series is terrific. I've always read Le Carré and Deighton and Gavin Lyle. They have their conventions too, which can be irritating in minor hands. I don't know where the private-eye novel per se is going, but the hard-type suspense-thriller-noir kind of novel is very healthy. What's important is that involvement, that menace, those mean streets. The private eye will always be with us, but I'm not sure he's going to dominate the field as he did in the early years.

AMOC: Given your year in Tahiti and your three years in Africa, are you contemplating an international thriller?

Gores: I've written a couple of dozen short stories with foreign settings, as well as two adventure novels which would need revision to work in today's market.

The one I'm working on right now is a suspense novel about a presidential campaign. Another novel, set in Africa, deals with a search for the Ark of the Covenant. Lucas took care of that for a few years with *Raiders*. Another is about a multi-billion-dollar international swindle in the commodities market. I'm working on another DKA, *32 Cadillacs*, where they're chasing Gypsies all over the country, even into Mexico. I've been doing research for a novel about an African hunter set in Kenya in the '60s and have started prereading for a novel about pre-man. A long-term project is a suspense novel about Shakespeare and Kit Marlowe.

AMOC: What about Bonecrack Krajewski and his possible reincarnation as a series hero?

Gores: When you asked me to do a short story for you guys, I had the "Smart Guys" plot lying around over there in a corner of my mind. I hadn't hit on a hero yet; then I read in the newspaper that people who snore aren't as bright as people who don't snore, and that title just came to me, "Smart Guys Don't Snore" I thought to myself: Who snores? Usually a guy who's big, who's overweight. An overweight hero didn't really appeal, but what about a hero who's just big? A big ex-sports figure. It was during the football season, and I heard John Madden remark during a game he was calling that the real guts of a football team is the noseguard. He's the guy who's down there in the trenches; he's the guy with blood on his thighs. Bonecrack Krajewski was born. I played noseguard on defense during my football years—though the blood on my thighs was usually my own. So I made Bonecrack a noseguard. I made him ex–Notre Dame because Notre Dame has put more players in the pros than any other school, and because I went there myself. I follow the 49ers and the Raiders, so I made him an ex-Raider. I fell in love with him as I was writing the story for you guys, so I have already started a second one, "Fat Guys Aren't Funny."

AMOC: We want an option.

Gores: It starts with a disquisition on how Caspar Gutman in the *Maltese Falcon* wasn't really a master criminal after all. Then we have three guys in masks coming in and holding up a warehouse. That's as far as I've gotten.

Smart Guys Don't Snore

JOE GORES

Joe Gores, past president of the Mystery Writers of America, is one of the most respected writers in the mystery-suspense field; his work has a quality of authenticity that derives from twelve years as a San Francisco private eye. Although best known as a novelist, Gores has published some seventy-five short stories. "Smart Guys Don't Snore" is the first in his projected series of stories about Bonecrack Krajewski, a pro-football player turned detective.

I was calf-deep in the ivy outside Eric Goldthorpe's bedroom window, listening to him snore like a semi-load of scrap iron going over the Grapevine into L.A. When I'd arrived seven minutes earlier, a tall, skinny guy in a loud sports coat too big for him and a hat too small, wearing shades at 11:48 P.M., was just letting himself out the front door.

He moved easy but looked husky enough to take candy from a baby only if the baby hadn't started teething yet. After the phone message I'd gotten, however, I'd had to check that Goldthorpe was okay inside his converted one-story carriage house. Hence, Krajewski among the nightingales.

The snorer creaked the bedsprings rolling over, then started again. I backed away before the vibrations brought down the slate shingles. Hell, I wasn't even really hired yet.

Back on the nighttime San Francisco street in my Toyota, I opened my thermos of tea and listened to the crickets and tree frogs. No mosquitoes; Pacific Heights was out of their price range. Down the block where the skinny guy had gone, an auto started, then a black Lincoln limo with personalized plates whispered by, a blonde with long, shimmering hair driving.

I ran a mental checklist. Goldthorpe was inside, snoring safely away. I had the front covered, and I'd hear anyone trying to come over the chain-link fence at the back. Eight in the morning, as suggested in his phone message, would be time enough to find out who was trying to kill my soon-to-be client, and why.

But at 3:29 A.M., a prowlie from a cruising black-and-white pointed his Police Positive at me through the window. I stepped out, hands in plain sight, and assumed the position. Pacific Heights isn't Beverly Hills, but even so, all that growth capital makes cops tense.

After patting me down, they told me the sort of thing cops tell a six-foot-seven, 289-pound man they catch with a gun in Pacific Heights at three in the morning. I told them the sort of thing I always tell cops. None of them has ever actually tried to do it, but I keep suggesting and hoping.

An insomniac neighbor had "happened" to see me—hanging off the drainpipe by her fingernails, perhaps?—and had phoned the police. We finally went to wake Goldthorpe so he could confirm he'd called me. We found the front door unlocked and

Goldthorpe in bed where I'd heard him snoring three hours before.

Except that now he was dead.

Homicide Inspector Red Delaney, a lanky, sad-eyed guy with freckles and carroty hair gone gray, was in the barrel that night. I figured him for an easy lay, since I had only the truth to tell on this one; and besides, he'd remained a diehard Raider fan even after the switch from the Bay Area. But then his boss showed up, not quite as wide as a barn door nor ugly as a griffin, but in that league.

Delaney looked surprised. I looked surprised. Damn few homicide chiefs turn out for the routine stiff at dawn.

"I'm Captain Pritchard," he snapped.

I batted my eyes at him. "Peekaboo," I said.

He turned to Delaney. "Who is this clown?"

"Thaddeus Krajewski. They called him 'Bone-crack' when he was with the Raiders because—"

"I've heard all about you, Krajewski. Big mouth, bitty brain. I'm not taking any crap off you, understand?"

"Does that mean I'm under arrest?" I trilled. To Delaney, I explained, "He likes to say 'Peekaboo' at the perps before he claps the nippers on 'em."

Actually, "Peekaboo" came from his days on the dicky-jerk patrol, busting flamers in downtown men's rooms: Straights coming in for a whiz were outraged at being offered three minutes of true love by a guy with dusty knees. Word was that in those days if you were prominent, married, with a lot to lose, Peekaboo might mislay the tape of your transgression—for a kill fee.

19

"Okay, Krajewski, by the numbers," he said in a tired voice. "Just for drill. No conjecture."

An electronic flash splattered white light around the bedroom. A man with no more chin than Barry Manilow was lifting prints off the bedside table onto clear plastic rectangles. I yawned abruptly; it had been a long night, getting longer, but I was suddenly wide awake, impatient to get back to my office.

"I came off a case last night at ten-thirty, checked the answering machine at my office and—"

"What case?"

I shook my head. "I might tell a grand jury. Not you." He was silent. "An Eric Goldthorpe had left a message that his life was in danger and maybe he wanted to hire me. He told me to come around to his house at 8:00 A.M. He didn't say whether he was looking for a bodyguard or an investigator, so—"

"I want that tape!"

I just nodded. "Since he said his life was in danger, I thought I'd maybe not wait for morning. The lights were out, but this other man came out of the house." I described him. "I heard Goldthorpe still snoring, so—"

"Why couldn't the skinny guy have been him?" asked Delaney.

"Goldthorpe's trust fund was something like the gross national product of Canada," I said. "Poor bastard had to do the society whirl on just the interest and the coffee-import company he also inherited. Such men may not be dangerous, but they get their picture in the papers a lot. He would have outweighed the skinny guy by a hundred pounds."

The phone rang. It was the M.E. with a preliminary on cause of death. Red Delaney listened, taking notes, nodding every now and then and grunting. Finally he said, "Thanks, Oscar." and hung up. He grinned at me.

"Saved from the chair, Bonecrack. Natural causes. Looks like Goldthorpe died of apnea."

I screwed up my face in obvious puzzlement. "Apnea?"

"Respiratory problem in some overweight men. Their throat closes down as they sleep, so they quit breathing for periods ranging from a few seconds to a couple of minutes. Can happen a couple of hundred times a night."

Goldthorpe had quit snoring for quite a while before he rolled over and started again. I said so. Red shrugged.

"See? Sometimes they just don't start again, period."

Peekaboo said suddenly, "I've heard that snorers get dumber as they get older—brain damage from oxygen starvation. Anything in that, Krajewski?"

"I don't know, I don't snore," I said with great dignity.

He jerked a thumb at the door. "Come in tomorrow to make a formal statement—and bring that phone-machine tape with you."

At my office in Coppola's flatiron building, I ran a copy of the Goldthorpe message. He had a chewy, indistinct voice, as if he were eating caramels, but his words were clear enough.

"Eric Goldthorpe, 2544 Jackson Street. I might need a private cop and somebody gave me your name. Ah . . . somebody's maybe trying to kill me, so just for drill, maybe I want to hire you. Here. Eight o'clock tomorrow morning."

21

I put the copy into the phone machine, the original that Peekaboo wanted for the police file in a desk drawer, and lay down on my seven-foot office couch to think about it. Why, if the death was by natural causes, was the skinny guy wearing a coat that was too big and a hat that was too small?

On the other hand, what the hell business was it of mine? My client was dead before I was hired. If at least two different people were playing games, was an ex-Raider lineman smart enough to figure out who and why? Wasn't he maybe just smart enough to stay out of it?

I wrestled with such cosmic questions for fifteen seconds and then fell asleep. Actor Victor Mature'd had the couch custom-made in the '40s because he was so big and liked to lie down a lot; I'd bought it secondhand in the '80s for the same reasons.

"You sure snore loud. I thought the elevator was breaking down while I was on my way up here."

The blonde had her back to the curved bow window with WE NEVER SLEEP backward on the glass. WE NEVER SLEEP had been a good joke when I'd opened the office three years before, to avoid becoming the local TV sportscaster that ex-football players are supposed to be when they grow up. Now its rich humor had paled; who likes to get caught snoring on the office couch?

"The door was open. Honest." She had a little-girl voice in a big-girl body, like sexy little fingers on your spine. When I didn't say anything, she added, "Anyway, I read in the *Chronicle* that people who snore aren't as smart as people who don't."

That joke was getting a little old too. I grunted and sat up on the edge of the couch to look her over

22

frankly. It bothered her as much as a swimmer bothers a shark. Long and lithe. Gleaming hair almost to the small of her back. Skirt slit all the way to whoops, as they say in the columns, showing a lot of leg. Sheena of the Jungle, Penthouse Pet of the Year.

"I snore and I played pro football for eleven years," I told her. "That sort of argues your case, doesn't it?"

At the sink in the corner I splashed water on my face, whuffling and blowing like a grampus. When I turned back, she was stalking me like a cat, hand in her purse. Watching her gliding tread clicked something inside my head. On TV she would have taken out a nickel-plated .22 and shot me in the duodenal ulcer I wasn't going to live long enough to develop. In real life, she took out a roll of hundreds heavy enough to drive a tent peg.

"My name is Judi Anderson-Powell. I want to hire you."

"My lucky day. One client dies in the night, another shows up in the morning. *Très* convenient." I gave her my sexy grin, the one compounded of equal parts of lust and greed that somehow seems to never get me a score. "As Mr. Kerouac was fond of saying, Wow, gee whiz, and whew!"

She giggled. "You talk funny."

"You ought to hear me when I'm awake."

But fun time was over. Her eyes got very round and serious. "I *always* forget to pay bills and things, and now the bank has repossessed my husband's company car. He'll just *kill* me if he finds out it was taken." She wiggled her assets around. "It's worth a thousand dollars if you get it back for me."

Every private eye ever born is bright enough to

23

take a thousand bucks for a couple of hours' work. I got the details from her, the money to bail out the car, and my thousand—all in cash. Plus the Marin address where I was supposed to deliver the car. She'd run me back to town.

Alone, I had a quick shower and shave and re-checked the phone machine copy of Goldthorpe's call. Yeah. It figured. *Somebody* wasn't letting me drop this case. I ran the address she had given me through the Marin County crisscross directory that lists by addresses as well as names, then called SRS in Sacramento, which runs licenses, autos, and individuals through the DMV, to ask for a check of Eric Goldthorpe; there had been no car parked by the carriage house. Finally, I called the Stanford Sleep Center for a chat about apnea.

I considered my findings with a buffalo sandwich and a Pauli Girl at Tommy's Joynt, a garish, red short-order emporium that has been on the corner of Van Ness and Geary since 1922 and has some of the best food, beers, and characters in town. My first pro-bowl year, a couple of hotshot publishers from back East had bought me lunch there while trying to convince me I should write a book about pro football. When I decided to retire, they decided to shelve the book. I didn't object. As Ovid said, *Leve fit quod bene fertur onus*: Get screwed cheerfully.

I went through the Hall of Justice detectors at the Bryant Street entrance of the cold, gray concrete shoebox and up to homicide to dictate my statement. Peekaboo came in as I was finishing. He'd decided I was human after all; he said he'd just come from watching Goldthorpe get sliced up.

"The autopsy turn up anything?"

He gave a grunt of what could have been derision. "Exotic poisons? Rare drugs? The bite of a deadly South African mamba?"

"I'd settle for the utterly ordinary: the curare-tipped nib of a goose-quill pen thrust between the second and third ribs and into the heart."

"No contusions, no punctures. No results yet on drugs and poisons, but everything is consistent with death by apnea. Where's that tape I asked for?"

"I forgot to bring it."

"Forgot? Or erased it by mistake?"

I looked sheepish. "You know how it is, Captain."

"You screwed up and erased it! Well, what the hell did I expect, ten years of three-hundred-pound guys sitting on your head?" Then he shrugged. "Oh, hell, when the coroner's report comes in we'll close the file anyway—death by natural causes."

"Then I'll be on my merry way," I said. "I've got a nice dirty buck to make."

"Dirtier than most," Peekaboo allowed judiciously.

The repo outfit was at 340 11th Street, a midblock, two-story brick building that had been a laundry when I'd been playing left tackle for Lowell. This was a commercial district turning lavender, with a gay bar on the corner and a bathhouse down the street that was probably hurting for trade since AIDS.

A couple of agency field men were making out a condition report on a new T-bird run up across the sidewalk, its nose poked in between the heavy, slid-open doors of their storage garage. When I came up they stopped working with identical wary stances.

"Nice car," I said.

The shorter one unobtrusively picked up a tire iron from the open trunk and gave me the sort of grin you see on the skulls in anatomy labs. "Yours?" He was plum-black, very wide in the shoulders and narrow in the hips. Always beware of well-conditioned men whose necks are as wide as their heads.

"You don't know?"

"We didn't stop to chat with the registered owner when we grabbed it."

"Not mine."

He relaxed fractionally. The tall one said, "We thought maybe you'd come to tuck it under your arm and take it home."

He was white, about six feet, rangy, almost too pretty at first glance for the business; but the cold blue eyes above his hawk nose said he was able to carry the weight. He was Ballard, the other one was Heslip. I said I was Thaddeus Krajewski.

"Hot damn, Bonecrack Krajewski," said Heslip. "Nose tackle for the Raiders. Before that, All-American at Notre Dame."

Ballard said, "Forty-niner games, you spent so much time on top of Montana I thought you guys would get married."

"Fickle bastard gave back my ring when I retired." I recognized Heslip then. "You used to headline fight cards at the Cow Palace."

"I was gonna be middleweight champ of the world, but I quit the game when I had to start banging my head against the wall in the morning to get my brain started."

The car was a black Lincoln limo with only 11,000 on the clock, smoked rear windows, and a personalized license plate, IMPORT. I caught up the bank's payments and all charges, which weren't too heavy. It had been a voluntary turn-in; they'd found it parked outside that morning with the keys through the mail slot. They gave me a champagne case full of personal possessions that had been in the car, which I stuck in the tire well. I took off, leaving my Toyota in their fenced parking area overnight.

The Lincoln was quite a boat, with a mobile phone I used to call Sacramento to get my rundown from SRS on Goldthorpe's car. Yeah. As I'd thought. Waiting in rush-hour traffic on the Golden Gate Bridge approach, I tried to figure out if the personal effects had any hidden or extended meaning: A box of Kleenex, seven packets of rock-hard bubble gum, three three-pound cans of coffee, a flashlight, a *Nurse Romance* comic book, a charge card receipt for a case of Dom Perignon and ten pounds of dry ice, and two spent .44 Magnum shell casings.

Not immediately illuminating, not unless you posited an allergic bubble-blower who broke a tooth on the over-age gum, tried to keep his mind off the discomfort with a *Nurse* comic book and ice-cold champagne when he couldn't get the coffee open, finally despaired and shot himself with a .44 Magnum.

Conjecture, like statistics, can be vastly overrated.

I crawled across the bridge into Marin with the rest of the rush-hour ants. Forget about peacock feathers and yuppies and hot tubs and dope dealers who weigh their money by the pound: It still doesn't get any better than Marin County. Civic Center has sold out to the builders, but for a few more years you'll still be able to find open country, sweeping vistas, and an individual life-style not dependent on the national whim. Southern Marin can go the distance with Beverly Hills any day; outlying areas still have not only some hippie enclaves, but even a few shaggy unregenerate beats whose jeans haven't seen soap since 1955.

It was dark by the time the winding blacktop off Route 1 took me up Mt. Tamalpais toward the address the blonde had given me, in one of the little residential pockets above Mill Valley. I could smell the dusty pollen of the Scotch broom that was taking over the mountain. When the other car came up too fast in my rearview, about a half-mile short of Judi's turnoff, I hit the window button just in time.

Something stubby that looked like an Israeli Uzi poked out of their open window. Muzzle flashes illuminated their intent, brown murderous faces. Would-be murderous; the slugs sparked and whined harmlessly against the Lincoln's Kevlar plating, ricocheting off the armored glass windows.

Fuck them. I was in three tons of steel. I jerked the wheel over, hard. There was the shriek of metal on metal, and the sedan soared up and out, already turning in midair as it went over the rim of the road and out of sight. I could picture it, crashing sideways down through the stand of trees in a burst of shiny eucalyptus leaves like an injured koi swimming on its side through a cloud of silver scales. I didn't bother to stop. Anyone tough enough to walk away from that one was tough enough to find his own way home.

Man, they were not near my conscience; they made love to that employment.

The house clung to the hillside by concrete fingernails above a sheer fall of greasewood, sage, and broom. There was a sporty new Mustang ragtop in the carport on the roof; the bedrooms were in the basement, and the view out the living room picture-windows was a stunning one-eighty of the distant city and sprawling bay, black-and-white in color.

Judi seemed genuinely glad to see me; she gave me a big hug when I came through the door, then stepped back with a puzzled look on her face. "You're trembling. Are you all right?"

Three men are dead. Are you all right?

"Nothing that a glass of champagne wouldn't fix."

She clapped her hands in delight. "I have some Dom Perignon on ice because . . ."

She let that drift away as if it led into an abrupt mental cul-de-sac she didn't want to enter. While she went to the wet bar in the corner, I admired the view. Her see-through point d'esprit lace chemise showed that she had a great deal to see, and her short red silk robe, edged in black lace and left carelessly open, did very little to obscure the sights.

"Expecting your husband?" I asked in a husky voice. The deaths of the three killers and my concomitant survival had left me as tumescent as a snort of ground rhino horn. In the midst of death we are in life.

"He was due home this evening but . . ." she shrugged as she set a bottle of Dom Perignon on the countertop. "But he's away."

"Far away?" I was feeling a little hoarse.

"Overnight away."

I cleared my throat. "You said he would kill you if he knew you'd let his car get repossessed." I paused dramatically. "I just killed three guys getting it back

29

for you." She started to give me that little-girl giggle, then stopped at what she saw in my eyes. I gestured. "Go look at your car."

I stood at the picture window pretending to look at the view. In the heat of pro-football combat you say, even do, a lot of destructive things. But most of that is deliberate intimidation, or a tactical ploy to get the other guy mad so he'll foul you in front of the ref and draw a penalty.

This was three men *dead*. Yeah, they'd planned to kill me, and hadn't succeeded only because the Lincoln was armor-plated and because professional athletes are trained to act first and think afterward. But just maybe they were nearer my conscience than I'd thought in my first flush of continued existence.

Judi's hands were on my arms, turning me from the window. Her hungry face was against mine, her little-girl's voice was saying, "Poor darling! Don't think about it . . ."

The silk robe was just a crimson flame on the rug at our feet; the black lace dissolved between my fingers like spider webs. Her flesh was feverish to the touch. For a little while there was no thought, no conscience, nothing but thrust against yielding thrust, raking nails, and finally her soft cries of completion to bring me to my own.

Afterward we sat on the couch drinking icy Dom Perignon and looking at the view. I told her about the attack. She shook her head in the semidarkness, her pale hair shimmering with the movement like ripe cornsilk. It had smelled of herbal shampoo when my face had been buried in it.

"But who would want to follow you and . . . try to kill you?"

"Probably somebody who thought I was your husband. What does he do that he has to drive around in an armor-plated car?"

"He's a gemstone importer. He's in Europe right now. . . ."

"Yeah. Somebody thought he was just coming back from Antwerp or Rotterdam with a pocketful of uncut diamonds."

As if chilled by the realization that she was a married woman who had just broken her vows on the floor of her living room with a man she had met that morning, she got up and started pacing the room with fluid, gliding grace.

"When I looked at the car," she said as she moved, "I didn't see . . . oh, I had some groceries and—"

"Those damned repossessors!" I exclaimed. "I'll go back and get the personal possessions from them tonight."

"No! Please!" Then the urgency departed her voice. "Don't bother. All of it can be easily replaced."

I told her I'd better take the Lincoln when I went to report the attack. She agreed. There was an awkward moment when we parted; we were suddenly back to what we really were, two strangers who had met, connected, now were shearing off again. What we'd needed from each other we'd gotten.

At Tam Junction I wiped all the places I had touched inside the bullet-pocked limo, retrieved the personal property from the trunk, and left the car in the parking lot under the freeway. I also called the cops, leaving no name, to say it had been involved in the shoot-out in the foothills. They'd have a lot of fun tying the bullet-acned Lincoln in with the three dead men, especially when the registration checked back to another dead man.

After the bus ride into the city, I couldn't sleep.

It felt like the night before the Super Bowl. I got up and heated a cup of Red Rose tea in the microwave, turned on MTV, and tried to analyze what was bothering me. .

Yeah! The receipt for the champagne and the dry ice. It came back from some forgotten chem course. Dry ice! Plain old carbon dioxide. An odorless, colorless, incombustible gas. Found in natural springs or processed from coal or natural gas through carbohydrate fermentation. Some .03 percent of the atmosphere at sea level. Produced in the human body at varying rates during exertion by the burning of blood sugar, then liberated from the venous blood into the lungs and exhaled. Used in carbonated soft drinks and in fire extinguishers and, when called dry ice, to keep things cold.

Finally I could sleep.

When I retired from football I dropped 22 pounds from my playing weight of 311, and I work hard to keep it off. I have a slantboard and a rack of dumbbells at the apartment for quick workouts when I'm on a case. I did a concentrated forty-five minutes and after my shower called a cab, then Red Delaney at the Hall of Justice. By luck he was in.

"I know Goldthorpe is supposed to have died of natural causes," I said, "but indulge me. In the postmortem lab work were there any traces of—"

"What do you mean, supposed? *Did* die of natural causes."

"Fine. Were sedative traces found in his blood workup?"

I heard pages turning. "Yeah. Probably ten milligrams of something like Dalmane. But with an alcohol level of only point zero-zero-one, definitely not enough to affect cause of death, if that's what you're thinking."

"I'm not thinking anything."

"Your usual state."

"Just a little old headpiece filled with straw. Come to think of it, that's the trouble with this whole damned scenario—too many people think that smart guys don't snore."

My cab honked down in the street. I hung up and went out. I found Heslip and Ballard in one of the back rooms at the repo agency, knee-deep in an incredible jumble of possessions—old clothes and flashlights and tool kits and letters and payment books and road maps and magazines and boxes of condoms and, by contrast, an unopened package of Pampers as big as a trash bucket.

"A burglary of the personal-property storage lockers, can you *believe* that?" demanded Ballard glumly.

I had expected it, the final figure in my equation. I now was sure of *who* and *how*—I just didn't know *why*. Yet.

"What'd they get?"

"Who can tell?" said Heslip. "The personal possessions in a repo don't generally make me want to grab them and take off for a country with no extradition."

When I got to Goldthorpe's coffee-import offices and warehouse in China Basin off Third Street, there was the Mustang convertible. Of course: the old asp-in-the-bosom scenario. I played Twenty Questions with a couple of yardmen who had gotten the idea I was a cop. No, Goldthorpe's death hadn't really interrupted much. Coffee prices being what they were, the business was going down the toilet anyway. He'd spent most of his time in South America, buying coffee. Better talk to Judi Anderson.

I kicked a tire of the Mustang convertible. "This hers?"

"Yeah." The young one had a dusting of acne across his chin and a dirty laugh. "Not that she paid for it herself."

"Shut up, Harry," said the older one, much too belatedly.

I left them glaring at one another and crossed the warehouse with its burlap bags wearing bonded warehouse seals and a heavy aroma of roasted coffee beans. A hallway went past the rest rooms to the front offices. Here functional gave way to front: hardwood walls, original oils, heavy-legged furniture to suggest an old-line firm. I kept poking my head into doorways and saying "Pardon me" until I found her alone behind a fancy hardwood desk.

The shimmering blond hair was tucked up into a sort of bun at the back of her head, giving her an old-fashioned look, and her perfect features were either without makeup or with makeup so artful that it looked like none. She had a lot of different looks. Her eyes popped wide when she saw me. She flowed out of her chair and across the room toward me.

"Thaddeus! What . . ."

I gave her my biggest, dumbest grin. "Hey, it's okay that you lied to me about being somebody's wife when really you were Goldthorpe's girlfriend. What else could you do, right?"

She looked around nervously. "Oh, Thaddeus, we can't talk here, but I desperately want . . ." Inspiration flooded her face. "My place again? Tonight? Then I can explain everything."

I said that was swell. She put her hands on my upper arms, as she had when she'd turned me away from the window the night before. Her face was ashamed.

"I . . . didn't know what else to do. I . . . I had to get the car back, and I was afraid that maybe those men . . ."

"Hey, sweetie, I said it was okay."

"I'm so scared and I just . . . I want someone to tell me what to do so I'll be safe. . . ."

"Sure." I almost licked my lips. "Like last night."

She cast another quick look up and down the hall, then went up on tiptoe to kiss me. It wasn't a peck. "Yes!" she breathed into my mouth, then added fiercely, "Like last night!"

Heading home, the afternoon *Examiner*'s headlines about the dead guys in Marin and Goldthorpe's bullet-pocked Lincoln stopped me. They had been Colombian nationals. Colombia is where the coffee comes from, and Goldthorpe had been a coffee importer. Obviously, a hit over whose coffee was the richest kind.

Like hell.

Watch a man minutely examining something unknown and—creationists be damned—you will see a risen ape, not a fallen angel. We are suddenly chimpanzees turning over rocks for the grubs beneath. I call it the Chimp Trip. I got the champagne case from where I'd stashed it and laid everything out on my kitchen table. The flashlight was a most promising place to hide something, but it proved a bust. The coffee made a mountain on newspapers spread across the table, but without treasure inside.

Would I know what I was looking for even if I

found it? Something worth paying me a thousand bucks to recover. Something worth three brown-faced men, dealt out of the action, waiting in ambush for whoever might show up in the dead Goldthorpe's car.

Then I got smart. If it was conceivable that someone could secrete something inside a can of coffee and reseal it afterward, how much easier with a packet of stale bubble gum? It was anticlimactic, it was so mundane.

In one package, the Giants baseball card wasn't a baseball card. It was a claim check.

The bus station on Seventh off Market was its usual self: big, noisy, echoing, barren, cold, filled with people whose best years were behind them or, in a few cases, yet to come. Minorities, the elderly, servicemen, the unemployed and the unemployable, the third-generation welfare recipients. And of course the rapists and muggers and pimps, sliding through the crowds seeking warm meat to feed their varied psychoses.

The woman behind the counter handed me a large gym bag, the sort that will hold your sweats and Reeboks and two pair of sweat socks and a towel and a jump rope and your Heavy Hands grippers. Whatever this one held still smelled of coffee. And I remembered a feature of coffee: A beagle would go baying right by a rabbit that hid in a bin of the stuff.

I opened it down on Townsend Street, where I had unused railroad tracks on one side, empty warehouses on the other, and could pour sweat unobserved. I thought I knew what was in the bag, but there were, after all, four people dead. Better not add half a city block of shoppers. But what was inside was like that verse in Isaiah: The valleys were exalted, the hills were made low, the crooked straight, and the rough places plain.

I knew it all, then, except how he had met her. I didn't have to wonder how she had gotten him to go along with her: She could have gotten an archbishop to rifle the poor box.

Peekaboo wasn't available, but I found Red Delaney in the low-ceilinged, gloomy cafeteria under the Hall of Justice. He swore a lot but in the end got me her rap sheet. Not much, but enough: material witness in a murder case three years before. Never charged with anything. We talked seriously then. I seemed to keep doing things to Red's coloring; his face had become as gray as his hair had by the time I left him.

Then I talked to Peekaboo. He was, after all, captain of homicide. I made a few remarks to loosen him up and, poor sport he, got back a visual *mano nera* from his cold fish-eyes.

"One of these days, Krajewski, I'm going to have you in an alley all alone. And then, just for drill—"

"Just for drill, you're gonna bruise my knuckles with your nose. I know. But first, I'm going to make you look silly at the same time that I give you a big, juicy Murder One bust. . . ."

Judi threw open the door dramatically and kissed me on the mouth, breathless, eyes sparkling, bringing the warmth and smell of a hardwood fire with her. She backed into the living room, leading me with my paws in her hands. The lights were out; the fire cast moving patterns of light and shadow across the floor and walls; and the slow-seething vapor settled around a big ice bucket on the white fake-bearskin rug.

"What have you got in there? Rocket fuel?"

"Something more potent. Dom Perignon."

"What're we celebrating?"

She let go of my hands and whirled around in the middle of the floor, the long tails of her white silk tailored blouse billowing out like a miniskirt. She fell against me giddily.

"Being rich. Being free." Her eyes, suddenly enormous, sought mine. In her little-girl voice she added, as a question, "Being safe?" Then with urgency, "If you'll be loyal to me, Thaddeus, then I know I'll be safe."

"Hey, was Sam loyal to Brigid? You can count on me, kid." She snuggled into my arms again. I tried to keep my head when all about me were losing theirs. I said, "Your burglar at the repo agency last night didn't find the personal possessions out of Goldthorpe's armored limo because I took them with me."

She smiled up into my face lazily. "What did *you* find?"

"A claim check." I stepped back to take a square of cardboard out of my jacket pocket. "I haven't had a chance to pick up whatever Goldthorpe checked on it, but . . ." I paused. "But I think we've just become partners."

She didn't speak. She kissed me.

"Then that's settled," I said with a big, dumb grin. "Let's go find out if it's what I think it is."

"First, champagne!" she exclaimed.

The Dom Perignon had two long-stemmed champagne glasses stuck down into the dry ice beside it. General Sternwood had said champagne should be drunk cold as Valley Forge, and this was. Time—and bottles—passed for us, side by side on that silly rug. Dom Perignon I don't get every day. Sometimes I poured, sometimes she poured. It started to get stuffy in there. The firelight played mysteries across her flawless features.

"What do you think we'll find, Thaddeus?"

"A lot of uncut cocaine," I said drowsily.

Her eyes got very big. "Cocaine! You mean Eric was—"

"Now, sweetie," I chided thickly, "we gotta be hones' to each other. It was you got him to do it, after the interest of daddy's trust fund wasn't enough anymore. . . ." She was silent for a long moment, then found a smile. It was small and tentative, like a kitten coming out from under a strange bed. "It was easy, you had a Colombian connection. I 'membered your picture from the newspaper. . . ." So I was lying, so I'd seen it in her rap sheet. "Some drug murders . . ."

"You're a rather clever man, darling."

"He could bring it in easily—the smell of coffee throws off the drug dogs at customs. The real danger would be in the transfer of the coke to the distributors. The Colombians."

I peered at her again in the candlelight. The smile had gotten more sure of itself, like the same kitten a day later.

She said, "The repo idea was my contribution."

I nodded. "It's cute and devious." I had a distinct impression I was slurring my words. "He stashes the drugs at the bus depot left-luggage. After he's been

39

paid, he leaves the claim check in a pack of bubble gum in his car, which he makes sure is repossessed. The Colombians redeem it, get the claim check and the coke. Anything goes wrong, he's not tied into it."

"I think it was a very good plan," she said a little defensively. I laughed heartily and held out my glass.

"Sure, f'r you."

She poured. I spilled most of mine on the rug. I laid down on my back, the glass balanced on my chest. She smiled.

"Not for Eric?"

"Ol' Eric, he dies right on time, you get the money he's already collected. Then you offer a guy 'way too much money to redeem the car before the Colombians do. You get both the dope *an'* the money. . . ." She was an indistinct black cutout against the flickering firelight. I was definitely stumbling over words. "Didn't 'spect me being outside that night, hadda leave wearin' Eric's sports jacket and hat. Jacket too big, hat too small—'cause of all that hair coiled up underneath it."

She said softly, "Eric died from apnea."

But I was on a roll. "I saw you drive by in his limo *without* your shades an' hat. Persh . . . personalized plate: IMPORT. Same car I 'deemed th' next day." I yawned suddenly. "Whassa difference, an'way? We go get the coke, we're rich. . . ."

My head dropped back on the rug. All of a sudden I was snoring. After about a minute, she said, softly, "Thaddeus? Honey?" I grunted and rolled around and didn't breathe for twenty seconds. Then I started to snore again. She'd doctored my champagne with Dalmane, but it was easy to fight: I had a lot of muscle tissue to absorb it.

I felt her hand slide into my pocket for the claim check.

"Goodbye, fool," she said softly.

Even with my eyes shut, I could follow the sounds of her quick movements. Taking her glass out to the kitchen to wash it. Sloshing water into the bucket as if ice had melted there, leaving it near me on the rug, along with the empty champagne bottles. Setting the big clump of dry ice beside my head.

Dry ice. Pure carbon dioxide. Colorless, tasteless, odorless. A heavy gas, displacing the air as it melts, settling as a layer around Goldthorpe's head, around my head. You're asleep, lightly sedated. You breathe carbon dioxide instead of oxygen. At 3 percent, 100 times normal, respiration doubles. At 6 percent, you're panting. If you're awake, you're confused. At 10 percent, you thrash and gasp, but it's too late for you.

Because at 30 percent, you're dead.

Meanwhile, the dry ice would melt away, the free gas dissipate. Everything gone. Carbon dioxide, unlike water, does not leave a wet spot. Tests of the blood from your corpse show only high concentrations of carbon dioxide—as death by apnea does.

Case closed.

The front door closed quietly. I already was breathing heavier than normal from the gas. "Not such a fool," I said aloud. The net would close around her any moment.

A gun went off outside!

I jumped to my feet, ran out and up to the carport, stopped to stare at Judi, crumpled beside her open Mustang door. I went down on one knee beside her. No pulse. I looked up at Peekaboo.

"You shot her," I said stupidly. "You weren't supposed to shoot her."

He still had his service revolver in his hand, a shocked expression on his face. "I . . . I told her to stop. She went for something in her purse, I thought . . . it was a gun. . . ."

I stood up slowly. She'd murdered one man, put me in a position where I killed three more; she'd planned to kill me. . . . I didn't know what I felt, except self-disgust. Some smart guy! I should have seen it coming.

"Probably a claim check," I said dully.

"Yeah. I know that now." He held it up. "Evidence."

I shook my head. "The trouble is, Peekaboo, people really do think big guys are dumb." I felt the anger grow in me. I let it. I liked it. "We hulk around; we have fingers like sausages; our voices are too deep and our chins too blue. Fat guys can't be tragic; big guys can't be smart."

I took a step toward him.

"But ever since I was a kid, bigger than anybody in my class, I had to be smarter, too. *Had* to be. How come the cops rousted me outside Goldthorpe's house? I'd parked where nobody could see into my car. So the report that brought them was a phony. Why? When we found him dead, I knew it was because I'd been supposed to show up the next morning and find the body."

Peekaboo's big, harsh face was puzzled.

"You're telling me Goldthorpe *didn't* call you?"

I gestured at Judi's dead, deflated body. The anger, blunted by talk, spurted again. "Of course not. She and her partner needed him dead—but found quickly so his death by natural causes would be established and the case closed. No matter what some P.I. without any proof might say about threats."

He shook his head, amused, perhaps, if we hadn't been standing over the corpse of a woman he just had killed.

"I gotta give you that she's a killer—though I thought you were nuts earlier when you said so. But a partner? C'mon."

I nodded. "You, Peekaboo."

"*Me*? I never even met—"

"Interrogated her two years ago in connection with the drug bust of a Colombian—I killed him on this mountain last night. It's in her rap sheet, Peekaboo, but I didn't need that to know it was your disguised voice on my phone tape. First you show up at Goldthorpe's, not even on duty, and then—"

"You're nuts, Krajewski!"

"And then, just for drill, Judi comes and erases the tape in my phone machine the next morning before she wakes me up. That afternoon you didn't give a damn if I gave you the tape or not—because she'd already told you she'd erased it."

His eyes had gotten bleak. "Did you say, 'Just for drill'?"

"Yeah. Not a common locution. You say it, too often. The voice on the tape said it too."

He chuckled nastily. "Well, without the tape to run voice-print comparisons off of . . ."

To show how smart I really am, I kept talking. "Oh, I've got that. Judi just erased a copy I left in the machine—"

He shot me.

The slug took me high on the chest near the collarbone, nonlethal, because I already was moving even though my conscious mind didn't know he was going to shoot. It felt about like a blocker's elbow when you're rushing the passer, but, always articulate, I said something like "Arghhhh!"

He got off two more shots, both wild because my big paw already was pulping his hand around the revolver. He screamed, then I had him bent backward over the hood, choking him, not caring which shattered first, his neck vertebrae or his spinal cord. I was liking this work; I was liking it fine. Just like they always say, the first killing is the hard one.

But then some fool was yelling and bouncing a gun butt off my skull. "Bonecrack—*no!* He has to stand trial! No!"

I went down. Peekaboo was on his face and knees beside me, making retching noises, his face purple. I tried to kick him in the temple but was too tired. I peered up at Red Delaney. Blood running down my face youthed him, made his hair red again instead of gray. He crouched beside me, revolver still in hand.

"How bad is that shoulder?"

"Like a dumb mouth it doth ope its ruby lips."

He stood up. "Jesus you're an asshole, Bonecrack."

Peekaboo groaned and rolled onto his side and drooled a little blood.

I said hopefully, "Let me finish him so he can't figure out some way to get off."

"If they let him off, I'll do it myself."

And such sudden hot rage suffused his features that I knew it was going to be okay. He meant it. Red Delaney played cop the way I'd played nose tackle. No compromise, no quarter. No pity. The bastard started to laugh.

"Let him shoot you, when you *knew* he was guilty! Hell, he was right about brain damage after all. Smart guys *don't* snore."

I tried to tell him to go screw himself, as I always tell the cops to do, but I was already asleep.

Not snoring, dammit!

Linda Barnes:
An Interview

Linda Barnes is a former high school drama teacher. After winning prizes for her one-act plays, she published her first novel, *Blood Will Have Blood* (1982), introducing actor-detective Michael Spraggue. She has since published three more novels about Spraggue.

A transplanted Detroiter, Barnes is a graduate of the Boston University School for the Arts and lives in Brookline, Massachusetts. Her extracurricular interests include folk music, film noir, and wine—the last of which she "married into."

AMOC: Did you take creative writing courses before you commenced authoring?

Barnes: No. My writing career is a tale of two contests. I won a National Council of Teachers of English writing award at the age of seventeen and promptly gave up writing in the belief that anything one could master at seventeen must not be worth much. I pursued a career in acting and did not write again until pressured to write a play for a high school theatre contest. We won, and I began writing again.

AMOC: After winning prizes as school playwright, you turned to the novel. What moved you to switch to the novel form?

Barnes: My school moved to a new building that didn't have a theatre. I took that as a subtle hint they no longer required my services. I couldn't get another teaching job. The prevailing philosophy was "back to basics," and drama was considered a frill. I prefer to write plays for a company of known actors, and once I'd left teaching I no longer had such a company. I didn't see much future in running off to New York in the naive hope of finding a company in search of a playwright. New York is filled with starving playwrights. I started writing mysteries. It's something you can do alone.

AMOC: Why mysteries rather than bodice-rippers?

Barnes: I wrote what I like to read. Mysteries had always been my escape from theatre—which leaves me fairly far removed from reality.

AMOC: Did you attempt to model your work on any mystery writers you admired?

Barnes: No. I think that what I was trying to do was to find a mystery that spoke to me. I was not content with the traditional British mystery. It didn't seem to come from my world at all. Nor was I content with the hard-boiled American mystery, which I love but which treats women rather badly. So I thought that perhaps I could write what I call the mid-Atlantic murder mystery. That I could create in Michael Spraggue an American with some of the British sensibilities and some of my own feminism.

AMOC: Do you think of yourself as a feminist writer?

Barnes: I think of myself as a writer, and I am a feminist—by my definition a person who expects to be treated as such without benefit of assumptions about my sex.

AMOC: Do you see your novels as conveying a feminist message?

Barnes: I see them as conveying a human message,

and I guess that any message in a novel is what the writer sends but also what the readers perceive. Many readers do perceive my novels as sending a feminist message, so who am I to quibble with that? I'm not sure that I do any more than reflect life as I see it. I don't consciously say to myself, "Let's write a feminist mystery here."

AMOC: Do you feel that there are limitations placed on females who write detective fiction?

Barnes: Perhaps there are, but I don't accept any of those limitations, if they do exist. I write what I write, and no one can control that except in publishing or not publishing my work. Writing is an activity that one does alone, and as such I hoped would prove an escape from sexism. Black-and-white words on paper look the same whether they are written by a man or a woman. I would like very much to believe that the work is evaluated in the same way, whether it's written by a man or a woman. I'd like to believe that, but reality sometimes stands in the way. At the last convention I attended, several men, supposedly mystery fans, informed me that they never read mysteries written by women.

AMOC: One of the facts of literary history is that women writers have been far more successful in the field of detective and mystery fiction than in any other genre, putting aside the gothic romances. The all-time list of the great mystery writers would be heavy with women. Do you have any explanation for the preponderance of women among successful detective writers?

Barnes: No, but it certainly provides a nice role model. The women who come to mind are British, and I think you would have to work hard to find

American women who are at the top of the heap. The British have always seemed far less rigid about what men can do and what women can do, and I think that to some extent when one woman has the phenomenal success of an Agatha Christie it opens the door for a lot of others. Part of the great list of British women mystery writers is a reaction to: "Well this is an area in which I can excel." There is opportunity there, and I think that writers are influenced by that.

AMOC: You wrote your first mystery novel, and by God you got it published. How?

Barnes: I'm still not certain. I sent it in; I found an agent; and she sold it. It was all over in what seems now a blinding flash and what seemed then a tediously lengthy process. I never expected not to be able to publish a novel. When I wrote my first play, a man in the audience came up to me after a performance and asked if he could publish it. I guess I expected that to happen with my novel. Imagine my surprise. I think now that if I had known how difficult this business is, I'd never have had the nerve to write that first book.

AMOC: Has your theatrical experience provided more than background for your novels? Do you think you learned anything about plotting and structure from playwriting?

Barnes: Very much so. It's more than a coincidence that many people who write mystery novels also write plays. There is an immediacy about both theatre and the mystery novel. You have a certain amount of time to get the reader hooked in a mystery; you have a certain amount of time to interest your audience in a play. The tightness required by a modern two-act play benefits the mystery novel. My theatrical background has also helped in developing characters. Through acting I learned or tried to learn as much as I could about people and what made them tick. I have a wealth of characters I've tried to experience. When I was an acting student we used to have various assignments following people on buses and trains, trying to imitate a walk or a look or a voice. And now I find that in developing my characters I use a lot of that acting training.

AMOC: If you need a character that you can't dredge up from memory, do you go out and hunt for one on the streets, in the MBTA?

Barnes: It's seldom that conscious, but when I'm out on the streets, when I'm taking the MBTA, I notice people around me, and I store them up. So that I'm very rarely at a loss for a character.

AMOC: Most of the reviewers of your books have commended your strong plotting and fast pace. Do you work out detailed outlines of your plots before you commence writing, or do your stories grow organically?

Barnes: I do a great deal of plotting and outlining beforehand, but my outlines are never engraved in stone. I find that perhaps the most pleasurable part of writing is when the outline disappears and suddenly a new twist, a new turn, occurs that you had never seen before but that seems wonderfully right. I always go with the impulse and worry about the outline later.

AMOC: According to the literary grapevine, you have dropped Spraggue after four novels. Why did you make that decision?

Barnes: Let's say he's on sabbatical. It's not so

much that I've dropped Spraggue, but that I have become enamored of another character. My game plan was always to do four books with Spraggue and then to look around and see if I was still satisfied with him. Because he is a character I created when I truly did not know much about writing, I found that I had made decisions about him that I could not undo and that I was uncomfortable living with.

AMOC: Now you are talking about the problems of a series character.

Barnes: Absolutely. I had to keep him true to the books I had already written, and yet I wanted to do more and found that the best way to do it was with another character. I was very apprehensive about the change and decided to audition my new character with a short story.

AMOC: Why have so many good, even great, mystery writers gotten themselves locked into a series character? Could it just be that readers expect a successful hero or heroine to be repeated?

Barnes: There's pressure for a repeat. People think in terms of series. Once you have established your name in conjunction with a character's name, the question people ask is: "When is the next Spraggue coming out?" As if from now until eternity that is what you are going to do. Knowing that there is a market for another book with that character, it's difficult just to say, "Well, that's not what I want to do right now." The ground shakes a little bit underneath you. I worry that people will look at the new Linda Barnes novel and say, "Wait a minute, where is Spraggue?" But I think they will prefer Carlotta Carlyle.

AMOC: Are you going to do four Carlottas?

Barnes: I don't know. I know that I am doing at least two Carlottas. I'm excited by her, and I think that she has a lot of potential.

AMOC: Any chance of bringing Carlotta and Spraggue together in some future novel?

Barnes: I don't know. They live close by and could conceivably run into each other. Right now I doubt that they would even speak. All they have in common is their height; they're both six-foot-one.

AMOC: Spraggue had an incarnation on the television screen. How much did you have to do with that, and how did you like it?

Barnes: I had nothing to do with it.

AMOC: Nobody asked your advice about anything?

Barnes: Well, no one listened to my advice about anything, and I was not pleased with the result. And, yes, I might do it again.

AMOC: Given your theatrical background, have you given any thought to writing directly for television?

Barnes: I would prefer to write directly for a theatrical film because I think that you can do more, that it's not quite as disposable. I am interested in writing screenplays. I normally begin writing in dialogue and find it extremely relaxing. Dialogue moves very quickly. I enjoy writing it. I would like to try my hand at screenplays sometime, but right now I'm more interested in establishing Carlotta in novels. You learn so much more about people in novels. Perhaps later she will make a transition to the screen. I think her first outing, *A Trouble of Fools*, coming out in the fall from St. Martin's Press, would make a good movie.

AMOC: What have I failed to ask?

Barnes: I'd like them to know a little more about my change of characters. In switching from Spraggue to Carlotta, I'm going from a Ross Macdonald type of detective—a man so thin he disappears in the story, a remote, distant man who keeps an actor's distance from life—to a committed, active, born interferer of a detective. I'm going from third-person removed to first-person live wire. It's fun to do something so different. In Spraggue I tried to create the mid-Atlantic detective. In Carlotta I'm trying to make a viable American female detective, a responsible, adult woman with a different voice than the typical American male hard-boiled detective. For Carlotta, relationships are important and the maintaining of relationships is one of her goals, rather than the achievement of some cold peak-of-the-mountain justice.

A Trouble of Fools

LINDA BARNES

A Trouble of Fools is Linda Barnes's first novel
about detective Carlotta Carlyle, introduced in
the Anthony-winning story "Lucky Penny" (*New
Black Mask #3*). This excerpt from the novel to
be published by St. Martin's Press in the fall in-
dicates that Carlotta has staying power.

If Margaret Devens had told me the truth right off
the bat, things might have turned out differently. Or,
as my mom used to say, in Yiddish or English, de-
pending on the situation, "If your grandmother had
wheels, she would have been a truck."

I never met my bubbe, my grandma, the source
of all my mother's Yiddish proverbs, but thinking
about it now, I guess I wouldn't mind if she'd been
a ringer for Margaret Devens—stubborn, smart, and
crafty behind the sweet-old-lady façade.

"Congratulations, **Mr. & Mrs. Thomas C. Carlyle** . . ." the letter began cheerily. The stationery
was thick and creamy, sharply creased, names typed
in boldface, the way they are in those "personal"
computer-generated mailings.

I read on. No such couple existed.

The vacuum cleaner hummed pleasantly. If you've
never considered your Hoover's voice soothing, you've
probably been shoving it across a high-pile carpet.

From the right distance, propelled by other hands—in this case the paint-smeared hands of Roz, my tenant cum new-wave-artist cum sometime assistant—vacuum cleaner buzz could make the lullaby obsolete.

Roz gets reduced rent in exchange for basic household chores. As a cleaner, she's a great artist. My spice rack is color coded, my knickknacks adroitly arranged. Books and papers are stacked in tidy piles at attractive oblique angles. My floors have never been filthier, but then Roz doesn't have much time for nitty-gritty cleaning. She dyes her hair a new color every three days, and that takes up the hours. I like Roz.

A firm of Omaha lawyers was pleased to inform me that the above-mentioned Carlyles were the lucky recipients in their GRAND GIVEAWAY. After a courteous tour of a "luxurious time-sharing condominium resort," located someplace I'd never want to visit, much less live, I—or rather Mr. and Mrs. Carlyle—could claim the Grand Giveaway First Prize of (take your pick): a trip to Italy for the entire family, all expenses paid, or twenty thousand bucks.

I searched for the fine print that said "valid until yesterday," or "provided you make a ten-thousand-dollar donation to the United Church of Holy Poverty." I didn't find it. I read the whole thing again. It said trip to Italy, all expenses, twenty thousand dollars.

Claiming the prize was going to be a problem.

I know Mr. T. C. Carlyle pretty damn well. The T. C. stands for Thomas Cat, aka Tom Cat. Right. A good sort, Mr. Carlyle, but definitely of the feline persuasion. Sleek and black, with a white right forepaw that looks like he dipped it in a dish of cream, he has a disposition you could describe as independent, which I prefer, or surly, which is closer to the truth. He is not your eager three-piece-suit-and-tie type. I have trouble getting him to wear a bell around his neck, a necessary indignity that keeps him from dumping dead sparrows on my doormat, which in turn prevents the parakeet from going bonkers.

I list my home phone under Thomas C. It's okay with him. He loves getting calls from admirers of the late essayist, survey takers, anyone at all. I didn't want to put my name in the book, first because women get crank calls, and second because ex-cops get crank calls. So I listed Tom, since he's the only male I share the place with regularly. And what do you know, he started getting letters. Begging letters from charitable organizations and pleas from campaigning congressmen. Credit card offers and magazine subscriptions. He subscribes to the *New York Times Book Review* and *Mother Jones*.

As far as cats go, Tom's a prize, but I didn't see how I could get him married off in time to claim the trip to Italy or the cash.

The doorbell sounded over the vacuum hum, the way it does when you're wearing ratty sweatpants and have your mouth half full of Swiss cheese and roast beef on rye. I waited, hoping for three rings. Three rings means Roz, the third-floor tenant.

The bell rang twice, stopped.

"Hang on!" I yelled, swallowing fast.

The bell rang again, twice in rapid succession.

It isn't that I have far to travel from the dining room to the hall. It's that I have about five locks on my crummy front door. Filing burglary reports has

56

replaced baseball as my neighborhood's prime pastime.

It was slightly past noon on a late September Sunday that had no business being so cool, and I wasn't expecting anybody. I squinted my left eye shut and pressed my right one to the peephole. If I had been expecting someone, it wouldn't have been the cozy old lady who perched on my front stoop like an inquisitive bird. As I struggled with the last deadbolt, always sticky, she turned up the collar of her woolly pink coat and got ready to hit the buzzer again. She wore white cotton gloves. I haven't seen a pair of white gloves in ages.

"Coming," I yelled, forestalling the buzzer.

She was too old for a Mormon missionary, so I steeled myself for the Jehovah's Witnesses pitch. She had sparse white hair, like powdered-sugar frosting on her pink scalp, and a round face that must have been cheerful when she smiled. Her skin was crosshatched with fine lines. Deeper ridges creased her forehead and carved channels from her broad nose to her small, anxious mouth. Her almond-shaped gray eyes, unsettlingly steady, stared gravely at the peephole.

The lock gave, and I yanked open the screen, apologizing. She didn't respond like a proselytizer or a fund raiser.

"Margaret Devens," she announced hopefully. "Miss," she added, "Miss Margaret Devens, spinster." I smiled at the quick glint of humor in her eyes, at the outmoded term and the clean white gloves, but the name meant nothing to me. She stretched her small mouth into a grin, and nodded as though it should.

"And you," she continued, giving me the once-over with a nice touch of disbelief, "are Miss Carlyle, the investigator?"

Now I admit I have looked better. My sweats had seen their heyday long ago, and most of my right knee was visible through a tear. My shirt was slightly more reputable, an oversized bright-red pullover. I don't wear it much because, to tell the truth, it doesn't go well with my coloring. I've got red hair, really red hair, the kind that beggars adjectives like "flaming," and Mom always told me to wear blues and greens, but every once in a while I break loose. For the rest, I was barefoot, and I hadn't even thought about makeup. I go barefoot a lot because I'm six-one and I wear size 11 shoes. You may not realize this, but for all practical purposes, women's shoes stop dead at size 10. Much of my life is spent shoe shopping. I hoped I'd brushed my hair before I plunked it on top of my head and stuck in the hairpins.

Probably I had. I mean, I don't always remember brushing my teeth in the morning, but I do it. With my hair under control, I almost look my age, which is on a different side of thirty than most people suspect.

"I usually work by appointment only," I said, not so much to discourage her as to excuse my appearance.

"This is not a usual matter." Her voice was soft and quavery, with the charming hint of a brogue.

With a caseload so light I was reading the cat's mail, I figured I ought to welcome any nibble, so I ushered her inside and draped her coat on the rack in the foyer. My nose twitched with the smell of mothballs and lavender. Underneath, she wore a blue flower-print dress of such high-collared respectability that she must have come straight from church. The woolly coat had given her an illusion of bulk. Without it, she was so thin I could see the sharp shelf of bone between her shoulders.

She opened her mouth to speak, but nothing came out except a small, dry cough, so she closed it again and spent some time fiddling with her gloves, rolling them together in a tight ball and depositing them in the pocket of her coat. My clients are a nervous lot, on the whole. Most of them would rather have root canals without novocaine than discuss their troubles with a stranger. I offered coffee to break the uneasy silence.

She nodded gratefully and took her time crossing the living room. I couldn't tell if she moved slowly because of her age, which I put in the high sixties, or because she was checking out the decor. Her eyes lingered on the furnishings, and she clucked and murmured as if she approved.

If she was using the living room furniture as a clue to my character, she was making a big mistake. Mostly it's the way Aunt Bea left it when she died. I even kept her dumb parakeet, but I moved the cage to one side of the bay window so it didn't block the light. Old Fluffy squawked indignantly for a week. The living room's not my style, but I don't mind it. The oriental rug's a little threadbare, but it looks terrific when the sunlight pours in, like some glistening ruby-and-sapphire brooch. The sofa velvet is worn around the wood scrollwork, and I don't polish the mahogany the way my aunt did. Neither does Roz. Her idea of cleaning is a halfhearted flick of the feather duster here and there, but then she's got her thoughts on higher things.

Margaret Devens went unerringly for Aunt Bea's favorite rocker and settled her narrow backside against the embroidered cushion with a satisfied sigh. She fit the chair like the missing piece of a puzzle. I half expected her to yank out her knitting and clatter away. I hadn't realized how I missed that sound.

I fetched coffee, a cup for myself, too—cream and two sugars—and crammed a quick bite of sandwich into my mouth. Chewing steadily, I rolled a few chocolate chip cookies onto a plate. By the time I got back to the living room, Miss Devens was rocking steadily, staring straight ahead, chin high. She looked like a woman who'd made up her mind, bitten the bullet, and disliked the taste.

I sat on the sofa, which creaked to let me know that while it hadn't collapsed under my weight, it was only a matter of time. I steer plump clients away from the couch. No danger with Miss Devens. She touched her coffee cup to her lips and gave the cookie plate a welcoming reception.

"You know, I'm only here because my brother's gone," she said between bites, as if we were continuing a conversation instead of starting one.

"Gone?" I wasn't sure if she was using a euphemism for dead or what.

"You handle that kind of thing, do you?"

I don't handle communication with the dead, so I assumed she meant just what she said. Gone, as in vanished. I wondered if she'd seen my ad in the yellow pages. I wondered if anyone did. I paid extra for fancy red print. "If you're talking about a missing persons investigation," I said gently, "the police are the place to start. More personnel, more clout. Step number one: File a missing persons report."

She bit her lower lip and looked helpless. "I wouldn't like to involve the police."

"Any particular reason why not?"

She examined her hands as if she expected to see the right answer written on them. "Well, you see, I'd hate to embarrass my brother, you know. He's younger than I am and a bit foolhardy still. But a good man, you understand, a good man." There was something almost defiant in her insistence. She started another sentence, gave it up. Her hands fluttered.

I eyed the pile of past-due bills next to the cat's mail on the dining room table. Had to keep T.C. in Tender Vittles until I could figure out how to collect his twenty grand. Of course, I could always take in more tenants. I've got rooms galore, and students will kill to be within walking distance of Harvard Square.

"What's your brother's name?" I asked.

"Bless you," she said, "bless you."

"Whoa. I haven't decided anything yet, Miss Devens."

"Oh, of course." More fluttering of hands. "Well, you haven't decided against it, have you?"

"I need a little information. Like your brother's name."

My tone must have gotten sarcastic. The lady's lower lip trembled, and I felt like I'd kicked my unknown grandmother downstairs. My tour of duty as a cop did not do much for my manners or my vocabulary. The sleazebag bastards I dealt with did not go in for "please" and "thank you."

"Take your time, Miss Devens," I muttered. "More coffee?"

"Thank you," she said, beaming as if I'd just given

her a present. The smile faded quickly from her eyes and she pressed her lips together, as if embarrassed that they'd been caught tilting up. "My brother is Eugene Paul Mark Devens." Again, I had the feeling that she expected more of a reaction from me than she got. I wondered if she always gave his full baptismal name.

"How long has he been missing?"

"All of ten days," she said, not trying to keep the worry out of her voice. "And he's lived with me for sixteen years, ever since his wife passed on."

"And?"

"That's it. It's hard to imagine, much less say, but one day he was there, and the next day he wasn't."

"You, uh, had some kind of quarrel?"

"I'm not much of a fighter, Miss Carlyle." She patted her white hair and rocked gently back and forth. "Truly, I'm at my wit's end."

"What about work?" I asked. "Does your brother work?"

"Sure, he's a driver, nights mostly, for the Green & White Cab Company. That's why we don't talk as much as a brother and sister should. The hours, you know. I'm a busy woman myself, with my volunteer work and all, and our hours didn't—our hours don't coincide."

Green & White. Bingo. Lightbulbs lit over my head. That's where the name Devens came from. I had only the faintest recollection of the guy's face, but I remembered those smelly cigars of his. His term at G&W had overlapped mine on both ends, but the part-time drivers, especially the ones labeled "college kid" like me, didn't mix much with the lifers.

Green & White. That answered the referral question. G&W's dispatcher, the formidable Gloria, was always good for a boost. Someday one of my old cop buddies would tip someone off to my existence. I wasn't holding my breath.

"A cab driver." Miss Devens pursed her lips and shook her head sadly. "He could have done better for himself, no doubt about that. If ever there was a boy with all the advantages, well, that was Eugene. I can't say he was lazy, but he had a mind of his own always, and no will to follow the plans of others. Not his mother, not his wife, not his big sister, surely. . . . But that's no matter now, is it? I saw my brother last on Wednesday, September 10th, before he went off to work. And then I haven't seen him since." Her hands clutched each other for support. "Should I write that down for you, now?"

"I'll remember. I have a good memory." Once it's jogged.

"I did too," she said, "once upon a time."

I said, "What do you think happened to him?"

"I don't know."

"You said he was married. . . ."

"Could have done better for himself there, too. The story of his life. Could have, should have, might have. But he married the first girl. . . . His wife, Betty . . . well, she wasn't our kind of people."

"Irish?"

"Oh, she was Irish, all right, I'll give her that." Miss Devens used the word *Irish* the same way my Dad's relatives, lace-curtain Irish all, used it when they talked about the folks they called shanty Irish. "It wasn't what you'd call a happy marriage. I think, when she died, it was a release for him. But who am I to judge? What do I know about it, love and marriage, happy or not?" She smiled ruefully. "I could have joined the convent for all I know about it."

"Your brother have children?"

She sighed, and the smile faded. "The union wasn't blessed. In many ways."

"Could your brother be staying with a friend?"

"I'm afraid I—I don't know his friends as well as I might."

"Does he drink?" Considering cab drivers I have known, I thought I'd better get that one out of the way.

"Some. At an Irish pub."

Ah, now I knew where to look. There are two hundred Irish pubs in Boston. Maybe another hundred in Cambridge.

"To excess?" I inquired, putting it as politely as I knew how.

"At times," she answered cautiously. "You know what men are."

I ignored that one. "Has he gone off on benders?" I asked. "At times?"

"Well, I can't say no. After Betty died, he'd go off once in a while. He'd get, well, bleak looking, and then he'd be out a night or two. But it's been years now. And he never stayed away so long. Never."

I bit into a cookie. "Did he take things with him?"

"Things?"

"Did you check his room? Did he pack a bag?"

"If he had I wouldn't be here, would I? If he'd taken a trip, I'd know where he was. My brother and I are close, truly we are." She fumbled in her lumpy handbag. "I brought his picture," she said, and when she looked at her brother's photograph, her face melted. She tried to smile, but the corners of her mouth quivered, and tears welled up in her eyes.

"May I see it?"

She offered it with a shaky hand.

If there ever was a man with the map of Ireland on his face, Eugene Paul etcetera was it. I recognized him from the cab company, remembered him vaguely, a cheerful, red-faced man with unruly hair. He looked a bit like his sister with a fuller face, minus most of the worry lines. He looked like he knew how to have a good time.

"How old is he?" I asked.

"Fifty-six. Doesn't look it, does he? Baby of the family and all. Spoiled."

He seemed a lot younger, boyish even. Charming.

When my Aunt Bea looked at you in a certain way, you knew all was lost. She knew you hadn't done your homework. She knew you'd failed that history test. She could see clear to the back of your soul and plumb the depths of unworthiness lurking there. Imagine my surprise when I glanced up and found Margaret Devens peering at me with eyes like that—determined, purposeful eyes.

Quickly, she turned away and made fluttery motions with her hands, distractions that came too late. I'd recognized her.

No, I didn't know her from some other time or place, not personally. But I have known women her age, women of steel who grew up in an era when feathers and fans and batted eyelashes were the name of the game. The smart ladies learned the score, played along. I recognized Margaret Devens's silly gestures and flowered dresses and woolly pink coats and white cotton gloves for what they were: camouflage fatigues.

She might have slipped past me if she hadn't been sitting in Aunt Bea's chair. Aunt Bea's shawls and scarves and bangles and hats were armor plated, every one.

"What exactly do you want?" I asked. "To know where he is? To talk to him, to see him? Do you want him to move back?"

"I want you to find him," she said, smiling and nodding and dithering away. "That's all."

"Women?" I asked.

"Possibly." She blushed demurely, and for a moment I wondered if I'd imagined the whole thing. I mean, she *was* sitting in Aunt Bea's chair. Maybe I'd had some kind of flashback. Certainly there was nothing in her demeanor now to suggest anyone but a dear old biddy come from church to set her mind at rest about her brother.

So I didn't mention the dire possibilities—the hospitals, the refrigerated drawer in the morgue—because of the blush, out of deference for her age, because of the look on her face when she saw her brother's photo. I don't have a little brother, but I've got sort of a little sister, and I have the feeling that when I look at Paolina's school photos, I get a goofy expression on my face too.

"How much do you charge?" she asked.

I glanced down at her shoes. My full-price clients are mainly divorce lawyers with buffed Gucci loafers. Margaret Devens wore orthopedic wedges with run-down heels, much worn, much polished, shabbily genteel. My pay scale started a downward slide.

"I'm not a charity case," she said firmly. "You tell me the same price the rich ones pay. I've plenty of money. What do the wealthy pay you?"

"Three hundred a day plus expenses," I said, knocking a hundred off the top. "But with missing persons cases, I generally take some expense money up front and charge a flat fee on delivery. Maybe I'll find him with one phone call. Maybe I never will."

"Will a thousand do for a retainer? Or an advance—whatever you call it."

I nodded. It wasn't the cat's twenty K, but it would sure help pay the bills.

I waited for her to pull out a checkbook, but she took a fat leather change purse out of her handbag. She crowded it behind her purse, trying to block my view.

By sitting up tall, I had a perfectly clear view of a huge wad of bills. She peeled off ten hundreds, squared the edges neatly, and placed them on the cookie plate.

So, don't get me wrong. I'm not saying I didn't think something was fishy right from the start.

The Motive

MICHAEL COLLINS

Michael Collins has a distinguished record of stories devoted to thoughtful experimentation, to which "The Motive" can be added. His new novel, *Minnesota Strip*, has just been published by Donald I. Fine, who claims it is "an important blockbuster that will blow away" other books about sexual exploitation of adolescents.

You never know what's going to solve a case, what you'll have to do, who's going to help you. Later, Lieutenant D'Amato admitted the cops would never have known the old man's motive without me and Alice Connors, but after a week I wouldn't have given myself much chance of doing any better than the police.

At the end of that first week I drank a cold Beck's in Alice Connors's Queens apartment and waited for her to come out of the bedroom. She'd appeared in my loft on a Monday night with Marian Dunn, sent by Jim Flood of Your Family Friend Loan Company in Queens. Alice worked at Family Friend, and I'd done skip-tracing for Flood. Marian Dunn had stared at my empty sleeve. Alice hadn't. I'd liked her right then.

"The police asked us over and over about Bruce and Mr. Dunn and the old man," she'd explained. "I just don't remember Bruce ever saying the name, or talking about any old man." There were tears in her eyes. "Why did he kill Bruce?"

Not a pretty girl, but you didn't notice that. You noticed the dark eyes, her vulnerability. Twenty-five, olive skinned, shy, the nose too large. Well groomed. Black hair in a wild cut that said there was something inside her she wanted to let out but that had been stopped by something or someone.

"The police don't know why they were murdered?" I said.

"That's what they say," Marian Dunn said. She was a big woman, soft and uncertain. The kind who whispers nervously to the children as she urges them along behind an irate husband. "My son says some lawyer'll get that old man off, say he's crazy or something." She shook her head in despair. "I've got four kids at home, Mr. Fortune, not much insurance. We never took a dime off nobody, except Paul's dad a couple of times. Now he's gone. Forty-two. Alice and Bruce was going to get married. Bruce was twenty-six. You find out why that old man killed our men."

I got what little they knew about the murders, took their retainer, went down after they'd gone and put it in the bank. All but forty bucks I blew on dinner and Beck's at Bogie's. With a nice glow and money in the bank I got a good night's sleep, rode the subway to Queens next morning.

Sam D'Amato was CO of the precinct detective squad. I'd worked with him a few times over the years; he knew me. He also knew Marian Dunn and Alice Connors.

"We'd like to know the motive too," he said. "We'd like to know almost anything."

"I thought you had the killer."

"The killer, yes. The motive, no." D'Amato glowered at his wall. "Looks like he never even met them before that night."

My missing arm began to ache. "How about the details?"

He tossed me a thin manila folder. The two victims had been working late at Steiner Nissan on Northern Boulevard. Paul Dunn was service manager, Bruce Henry a front-end man. Joseph Marsak walked into the salesroom and asked for Dunn and Henry by name. The salesman sent Marsak back to the service desk in the garage, heard Marsak ask if they were Paul Dunn and Bruce Henry. Someone laughed, shots exploded, no time for an argument.

The old man walked out the side garage door. No one tried to stop him, no one could give a real description. The police were stymied. Then they found the gun in a yard a block away. A 9-mm Luger they traced in half a day. It had been issued to Joseph Marsak by the army forty-three years ago, never turned in. They found Marsak's address in the phone book. The witnesses all identified him.

"He said, yes, he shot them," D'Amato said, "and, yes, he'd come with us, and that was and is all."

Marsak lived alone on Social Security and a pension in a room in an apartment off Roosevelt Avenue. He'd been a history professor in California, retired to New York. He'd lived alone in California too. His naturalization said he had been born in Russia in 1906 and that he'd served in the U.S. Army in World War II.

"Witnesses, ballistics, and a confession. Isn't that enough to put him away?"

"Sure," D'Amato said, "but where? Without a motive his lawyer grins all the way. Senility, insanity.

Creedmoor tops, maybe as low as probation and psychiatric treatment."

"Can I talk to him?"

He made a call, and we drove into Manhattan in his squad car, parked at the Tombs, and went up to a modern interrogation room of the renovated jail. Marsak's lawyer was waiting for us, a tough-looking type in an expensive blue pinstripe suit. The old man had someone on his side. I tried a direct approach.

"What business were you and Paul Dunn in, Mr. Marsak?"

The old man's head turned slowly like a tank turret traversing toward a target. His almost colorless eyes stared at me.

"Must I speak to this man?"

He had never been tall, but he had probably been solid. Now he was skinny, almost emaciated. His neck emerged from his shirt without touching the collar, his face was pale, and his thin hair and full mustache were white. His hands were pallid and bony. They hung limp, without strength or even interest. As if the years had washed more out of him than color.

"You don't have to talk to anyone," the lawyer said.

"No one murders without a reason," I said to the old man.

"He doesn't remember why he did it," the lawyer said. "He had no idea what he was doing."

"They were bad men," the old man said.

"Bad?" I said. "How?"

The old man said nothing. He had an accent. Slavic, yet something else too. A different accent mixed with the Slavic.

"Where else did you live besides Russia?" I asked.

"I have lived many places."

"Why do you carry a gun, Mr. Marsak?"

"I do not carry a gun."

"You had a gun that night."

"I have a gun since the war."

"And you took it to the Nissan agency to shoot Paul Dunn and Bruce Henry. No accident; not a matter of chance."

"I kill the enemy," the old man said.

The lawyer rubbed his hands happily. "Crazy as a loon."

I said, "Paul Dunn and Bruce Henry were your enemies?"

"They are the enemy."

The lawyer was almost dancing, but I didn't think the old man was crazy. He spoke in a firm, calm voice. Literally, the words sounded paranoid at least, but I didn't think Marsak was being literal. He was telling the truth, but not the facts.

Outside, the lawyer laughed. "Not even an indictment."

D'Amato didn't contradict him as he left still grinning.

"Who's paying the lawyer?"

"Marsak's old army buddies."

It was late afternoon when I came out of the Tombs, headed uptown for my loft/office. Four potential clients had left messages on my answering machine. None panned out. I went to Bogie's for some beers and thought about why an eighty-year-old man would kill two total strangers.

In the morning I rode the subway out to Queens and the loan company. *Tired of bank red tape? No house to mortgage? Own a car? Come to your Family*

Friend and walk out with cash. Alice Connors was going to lunch.

"Bruce took me to lunch twice a week," she said. "That's the kind of man he was. Now—" She wiped at her eyes.

"Want to talk at lunch?"

In the Peking Restaurant I had moo shu pork. She ordered kung pao chicken.

"How long had you known Henry?"

"You make him sound like a stranger." She sipped tea. "He was the nicest man I ever met. He took me into New York. We had fun. Before I met Bruce I lived with my folks. I got my apartment so we could be together. Now I'm alone in it."

That was when I heard the shadow in her voice. Something held back inside her beside the passion. Something she didn't want to tell me, maybe didn't want to tell herself.

"Why couldn't you be together where Bruce lived?"

"His mother was old and sick, so he lived with her."

"Was?"

She nodded. "His mother died four months ago. That's when Bruce asked me to marry him. It was going to be in August."

She broke then. I let her cry. I guessed that Bruce Henry had been the first man to pay any attention to her beyond trying to get her into bed on the first, and probably last, date.

"How long have you worked at the loan company?"

"Six years, nearly seven."

Her first job after high school, and she still had it. Ninety percent of young girls from Queens work in

73

offices in Manhattan. More money and more men. Local jobs went to older women who'd tried Manhattan and given up. An unconfident girl, lonely now, and a little lost.

"How long *had* you known him, Alice?" I asked.

"Two years. Two wonderful years."

There was defiance in her voice and eyes. Something about those two years had not been wonderful.

When I took her back to her office I watched her run in. Seven years and she still rushed back to work scared. Not the kind of woman who married the kind of man who got murdered. Either she was a different woman than she seemed, or Bruce Henry had been a different man than she said.

I took her for drinks after work all the next week while I got nowhere on the killings. Tonight we'd gone to dinner. Now I waited for her to get comfortable. When she came out of the bedroom she wore a purple robe zipped up to her throat.

"You've never told me how you lost your arm," she said.

She sat on the small couch of the neat little living room and tried to smile at me. She was being bold, her bare foot out from under the robe. Her eyes were up now, and I saw her nakedness in them, her awareness of her naked body under the robe.

"I was seventeen," I told her. "We were looting a ship. I fell into a hold, crushed the arm. Except for that I'd have joined the gangs and been dead by now. Instead I got away, saw the real world. When I came back to Chelsea I wanted to do more than be a big wheel in the world as it was."

I was talking too much. It was the bare foot beneath the hem of the robe, her dark eyes trying to be bold. As if she had to answer some question about me, or about herself.

"After Henry's mother died, where did he live?"

"He got an apartment near where he worked. He'd become a full mechanic for Mr. Dunn. He could afford his own place."

She was evading what I was asking.

"Why didn't he move in here, Alice?"

"We weren't married yet."

She looked at the floor and I saw that shadow inside her.

"You never slept with him, did you?"

She sat there, her toes protruding from under the long robe. I waited. She would tell me in her own time. I drank my beer and thought about her and Bruce Henry and Paul Dunn and his nervous wife and all I hadn't found in a week of hard footwork.

I'd started at Steiner Nissan. It was the usual showroom where salesmen hovered like gigolos meeting the tourist train in Venice. The garage for shining up trade-ins and fixing lemons was in back. The sales manager talked about Joseph Marsak.

"He wasn't any customer. We all compared notes."

"Were Dunn and Henry working on anything unusual?"

"Routine all the way. The cops checked every work ticket the last three years. *Nada.*"

"Could they have been operating a sideline?"

The manager licked his lips, his eyes bright. "You mean maybe crooked? Illegal? Dope or something?"

"Maybe moonlighting. Working on stolen cars?"

He shook his head. "Paul hated anything illegal

75

or immoral except one thing, right?" He gave me the fraternal wink.

Was jealousy a motive for an eighty-year-old man who lived alone? I know at least two octogenarians who married women half their age, and they aren't sleeping in twin beds.

"Is there anywhere the two victims hung out?"

"Over in Ryan's every lunch hour and after work."

"What about weekends?"

The manager shook his head again. "Paul moved out to Little Neck; I don't know anything about what the hell Bruce did."

Across the street, Ryan's was a neighborhood saloon with a kitchen, an old shuffleboard along the right wall, and booths in the rear. At 11:30 only a few morning regulars were in—the kind who would be there for closing at a far-off 2:00 A.M. and had learned to pace themselves. The bartenders were glad to see me. I had a Beck's, asked about Dunn and Henry.

"Ain't safe nowhere today," one barman said. "If Arabs don't hijack a ocean ship, some old nut walks up and plugs you right on the goddamn job."

Neither of them knew Joseph Marsak, neither had noticed Dunn or Henry meet anyone, buy or sell anything.

"Paul got in plenty of arguments," one said. "He didn't take shit from no one, liked the women, but that's all."

"What did his wife think of his interest in women?"

"Wouldn't of worried Paul. He used to say a man brought in the dough and did what the hell he wanted."

"Bruce too?"

The bartender snorted. "Talked big, but never saw him make a move. Tagged along after Paul."

76

"Either of them have any particular woman in here?"

The bartender hemmed and hawed but finally admitted that Paul Dunn and Grace Callas had been chummy. He gave me an address in Jackson Heights, and I got a taxi. It turned out to be the top half of a semidetached on a shaded block of maples and oaks. There was no answer. I went to meet Alice Connors and take her to lunch.

After lunch I walked to the apartment house where Joseph Marsak lived, climbed to his second-floor rear apartment. There were voices inside. I knocked and a square little man opened the door. He said he was Joseph Marsak's landlord.

"My wife died, I got too many rooms and no one to talk to so I sublet. Marsak been here five years. So he's moody, who ain't got trouble, right?"

"Moody about what?" I said.

"Who knows? Maybe something out in California, maybe a long time ago. He's too damned quiet. Sometimes I think he ain't home, I go into his room and there he is sittin' in the dark."

Marsak had no visitors the whole five years, didn't even have a telephone in his room, went out to a movie, to eat, to the library and maybe the cleaners. Laundromat once a week like everyone else. Only everyone doesn't take a gun and calmly shoot down two men who seemed to be total strangers.

"You want to see his room like the cops done?"

The single room was bare and Spartan, except for a large, modern stereo. Shelves were filled with records, tapes, and compact disks, and the bookcase was crammed with books in many languages. Above the bookcase were framed photographs of a family on a picnic; in a boat on some lake with mountains and pines; on the streets of an old city with stone buildings and cobblestones; in front of a country house with white walls and dark beams and a thatched roof. Two adults, two girls, and a boy. The woman was in her mid-twenties, dark haired. The man was short, stocky, and mature. The photos were old. The man could have been a young Joseph Marsak.

When I left, the landlord was hunched in front of his television set, talking to it. "Watch that guy!"

I left him with his friends, checked with D'Amato, who had nothing, tried Grace Callas again with no luck, and gave up for the day. In my office I had a call from a lawyer with a client, wasted the next morning in the lawyer's office waiting for the client who never showed. I got back to Queens that afternoon. Rock music played inside Grace Callas's apartment. I knocked. A curtain moved.

"Don't you cops get tired? I said I don't know nothing about Paul's damn business." The music went up louder.

I shouted, "I'm a private detective hired by Dunn's wife."

The music stopped. The door flung open.

"Don't go trying to hang anything on me! I didn't know he was married."

"Sure you did," I smiled, "but that's your business. All I'm interested in is why the old man killed him."

She looked me over. A big woman. Paul Dunn had liked big women. Grace Callas was as tall as Mrs. Dunn, but there the resemblance ended. Callas was angular and athletic. The kind who would stride out, head high and hair in the wind.

"Want a manhattan?"

She'd been lying on the couch, all the curtains and shades drawn, drinking manhattans and listening to the stereo.

"Too early for me," I said.

"I work nights. I hate to drink alone."

"Why do it then?"

"I do a lot of things I hate. At least this gets better."

"You have a beer?"

"Does the mayor like his picture taken?"

She brought a can of Coors, lay down on the couch again, and sipped her manhattan. I sat in an armchair with my beer.

"Did Paul Dunn like to drink in the afternoon?"

"He liked to screw in the afternoon." She drank. "No, he liked to walk out of Ryan's to screw in the afternoon. He liked to leave his buddies to screw in the afternoon. He liked to haul me to his car to screw in the afternoon."

"If he was like that, why pick him?"

"You seen the other guys in Ryan's?"

"Why do it at all?"

"Why do I get up in the morning?"

"I don't know. Why?"

"I don't know either."

She went to make another manhattan. I drank my beer. When she returned I asked her about Joseph Marsak, but she'd never heard of him. Paul Dunn didn't come there to talk, and if he did it was all about his service empire at Nissan. She didn't know of any sidelines but wouldn't have put anything past Dunn.

"He was starting to be a pain," she said. "I was just to show his buddies what a big man he was. Time I had a new guy." She nodded to my beer.

"No more for me." I didn't want to take Paul Dunn's place.

"Suit yourself." She looked at my empty sleeve. "It might've been fun."

I left her thinking about all the fun we might have had and found Alice Connors again. She knew nothing about Grace Callas; Bruce Henry had never mentioned her. She was shocked to think of Paul Dunn like that and begged me not to tell Marian Dunn.

Now, a few days later on a hot Queens night, Alice Connors sat in her living room and looked down at her bare toes visible under the hem of the purple robe as she talked about Bruce Henry.

"He wanted us to wait until we were married. He was like that. His mother was real narrow, hated any girl he took out."

"So you never . . . ?"

"No." She reddened, smoothed the purple robe over her lap. "At first I . . . I was scared. I fixed it so we never had a real chance. Then I wanted to, got this place. My father was mad, but I didn't care. Then Bruce said we should wait. He had too much respect for me to do anything before we were married."

Men like that could be on the increase again with the sexual backlash, but the Bruce Henry who drank at Ryan's didn't sound like he respected women any more than Paul Dunn did.

"He said he wanted our marriage to be the most important moment in our lives." She looked up at me. "I didn't want to wait. He said I was only saying that because I thought he needed sex but he didn't. He got that apartment and would never let me go there. Then he started taking me home early, saying good-night downstairs, showing up late for dates, even breaking them sometimes. Was there another girl, Dan? Is that why he was killed?"

"Paul Dunn had a woman, but . . ."

She wasn't listening to me. Her dark eyes were large and wide and fixed toward me. "What's wrong with me, Dan?"

"There's nothing wrong with you."

She sat and stared at me in the living room above the quiet Queens street in the warm night. Then she stood and walked toward the bedroom, her bare feet showing under the robe at each step. She looked back, the need in her eyes. I followed her. There was nothing wrong with either of us once she dropped the robe in the dark bedroom.

Afterward she went to sleep curled close to me as if she needed a mother more than a lover. I didn't go to sleep. It was too early for my sleep clock, and I didn't need a mother. I lit a cigarette, thought about the rest of my long week.

The day after Grace Callas and Marsak's apartment, I had to testify in an old case, didn't get the LIRR out to Little Neck until afternoon. Marian Dunn lived in a big, shabby frame house. A teenage girl answered the door, stared at my missing arm.

"Yuk, I hate cripples."

I leaned down close to her face. "Honey, tell your mother Dan Fortune's here or I'll spank you with my stump."

There are those who think the maimed, the sick, and the poor aren't really human, not people the way they are. Most of us have it civilized out of us before we're the age of Paul Dunn's teenager. Kids tell you a lot about their parents.

"Mr. Fortune?" Marian Dunn dried her large hands on an apron. "Did you find out why . . . why . . . ?" Her hands fluttered helplessly without a husband.

"Not yet, Mrs. Dunn. Can we talk about your husband?"

Her face collapsed, she sat down on a chair in the entrance hall. "Paul was a good man, Mr. Fortune. Made good money, never missed work, didn't drink too much or gamble. Nice to the girls, always taking the boys fishing, bowling. He worked ten, twelve hours a day, six days a week. Service manager before he was forty. Brought us out here after the blacks started moving into the old neighborhood. A good husband, Mr. Fortune. Now—"

"Did you know about Grace Callas, Mrs. Dunn?"

She sat for a time, then stood and walked into a large, run-down living room. The girl who hated cripples sat watching TV with a stocky youth in marine green and a younger boy. Marian Dunn spoke low to the marine.

"Okay, out," the marine ordered. "Me 'n' Ma got business."

The kids looked at me with directionless anger. Marian Dunn smiled at the marine, grateful for his taking charge. She sat on the seedy couch. The marine stood.

"They know why that old man killed my dad?" the young marine said. "I get him he hangs by his bare balls."

"Don't swear, Paulie," Mrs. Dunn said. "Your dad never—"

"I'm getting a different picture of his dad, Mrs.

Dunn. A man who did what he wanted when he wanted."

"A real man, my dad," the marine grinned.

Marian Dunn reddened. She knew all about Paul Dunn's women. She would probably say that made him a real man too.

"That old kike gunned him without no warning," the marine said.

"What about Bruce Henry?" I asked Marian Dunn. "Did he have a woman on the side too?"

"I don't know," she said. It didn't surprise her that Henry, about to marry Alice Connors, might have had other women. I was getting a clearer picture of life with Paul Dunn. "He was a good husband, Mr. Fortune, he—"

"I know," I said. "Hardly drank at all, didn't gamble, paid the bills. Nice to the girls, a pal to the boys. But he was late to dinner a lot, took long lunch hours in Ryan's."

The voice came from the open archway, low and angry. It was an older girl I hadn't seen before.

"Tell him the truth, Ma! Tell him Grace Callas wasn't the only one. Tell him about Joey!"

Marian Dunn said, "Your father never lied, Agnes. Some men got to be that way."

"He drove Joey from the house. His own son."

"Joey's a fucking fag," the marine, Paul, Jr., said.

"Joey's a gentle boy who hated everything Dad stood for the same as I do." The girl crouched in front of her mother. "Ma, he's gone. You should thank that old man. We all should."

The marine moved as if to hit the girl. I caught his wrist. Under the uniform he was still a boy, and I've got a lot more strength in my one arm than most people expect. The marine was pale, unable to break free without using both hands, and that wouldn't be manly.

"Mr. Fortune, stop!" Marian Dunn said.

I let the boy go.

"Paul was a good husband, Mr. Fortune. The children are too young to know, and other people are all fools and atheists."

I got the next LIRR train back to Woodside, but Alice Connors had her dance class, so I made a date for dinner the next day and walked to the apartment house where Joseph Marsak lived.

"So?" the landlord said. "The cops was here again too. You still got no answers?"

"I haven't even got questions," I said. "You said he was a man with trouble. Money? A woman? Old? New?"

The square little man thought. "The kind of trouble you got it so long it's part of you like your skin."

"But he acted like everyone else?"

"Just an old man lives alone."

"Was there anything about him not like everyone else?"

The landlord shrugged. "That crazy modern music he listened to, I guess. Maybe that girl downstairs."

"Girl downstairs?"

"A nutty kid plays her guitar too loud, got a whole rock band down there. Her and two other girls in the garden apartment. Sit out in the yard in those bikinis; they should be naked it wouldn't be no different. Marsak'd sit in his window and watch her down in the yard and talk to her."

I described Paul Dunn and Bruce Henry, asked if he'd seen them with the girls. He hadn't.

"What's the name of the girl downstairs?"

"Janice Stevens."

I went down to the apartment below. Janice Stevens wasn't home, but a roommate was.

"Jan? Murder? God, come on in." She talked all along the hall. "I'm Madge. You got the wrong person. Jan wouldn't hurt a fly. She's the kind that takes in stray kittens, you know?" In a small kitchen she worked over a pie, putting on a layer of walnuts. "You like walnut pie? I die over it. Who got murdered?"

I told her who had been murdered, described Dunn and Henry.

"Never heard of them. No one like that ever around Jan."

"How about Joseph Marsak? Have you heard of him?"

She stopped laying walnuts on the pie. "You mean the old guy upstairs? What's he got to do with anything?"

"He killed Paul Dunn and Bruce Henry."

"That old guy? You're crazy! Why would he kill anyone?"

"That's what we don't know, Madge," I said. "What's his relationship with Jan Stevens?"

"Well," she frowned even more, suddenly wary for her friend. "The old guy sits in his window and watches Jan practice guitar in the yard and they talk. Sometimes he shows up when we do a gig, watches us, buys us drinks on breaks. He just likes Jan, I guess. I mean, he even likes our music, you know?"

I got nothing more. It was time then for my dinner date with Alice Connors. A date I hoped would be more than dinner.

It turned out to be a lot more than dinner, and when she woke up again around 2:00 A.M., maybe more than I could handle for long. At my age she was a little frightening. This time she didn't go to sleep afterward. We talked.

"Did Bruce ever mention a Janice Stevens?"

"No. Was that the other girl he had?"

"Maybe."

"I hate him! For her and for all the time I wasted!"

She was more than ready to go on making up for the lost time, but I had the case on my mind and she had to work the next day, so we both eventually went to sleep.

I was still thinking about Janice Stevens when I woke at seven. I slipped out of bed, dressed, and went out for some breakfast. Over three cups of coffee, I thought about what else had changed in Bruce Henry's life in the last four months: He'd been promoted to full mechanic for Paul Dunn, a man who liked to impress barflies by shacking up in the afternoon. Could Marsak, and Dunn or Henry or both, all have been after Janice Stevens?

I walked to the saloon across from Steiner Nissan, Ryan's. The bartenders had never heard of Janice Stevens, had never seen Dunn or Henry with a young girl. At Steiner Nissan I got a different answer.

"Sure," the sales manager said, "she worked here. Switchboard girl. Big boss let her go two weeks ago. Made too many mistakes, always playin' that damn big portable tape deck."

"She worked with Paul Dunn and Bruce Henry?"

"Hell no, the kid was strictly front office."

I headed for the old apartment house off Roosevelt

Avenue. Janice Stevens had worked in the same place as Dunn and Henry, had lived in the same place as Marsak. A tall girl with intelligent eyes opened the apartment door. She stood with a hand on her hip. It was a nice hip in black tights, white Cossack-style shirt, and low white boots. I told her who I was.

"Want to talk about Joseph Marsak?"

She walked into a living room jammed with electric guitars, amplifiers, an electronic keyboard, a drum set, microphones, and a four-track tape recorder. Wires curled in a maze on the floor. There were two open suitcases and some empty stereo boxes.

"Going somewhere?"

She shrugged. "It's go home or starve."

"Why'd you get fired?"

"How the hell should I know!" Her dark eyes raged at me. "I was good at that job. They never even warned me!"

"Anything to do with Paul Dunn or Bruce Henry?"

"I didn't even know them."

"But you know Joseph Marsak."

Her face became sad. "I don't know why he shot them. I couldn't believe it. He's such a nice old man."

"How well do you know him, Janice?"

She gave me a cold, disgusted stare I guessed she used often on eager young men. A stare of contempt that sent them slinking away. I don't slink that easily.

"Don't try to tell me it didn't cross your mind."

She sat down. "All right, I wondered at first. He was so damned nice, so interested in all of us. Then he seemed to fix on me. He'd sit up there at his window and watch us practice. He came to our gigs, bought us drinks. But he never made a pass, and I know from passes, believe me."

"You never went out with him? Nothing ever happened?"

"Never and nothing."

"And you didn't do anything with Paul Dunn or Bruce Henry? They didn't make passes, try to make dates?"

"They never talked to me, for God's sake! I barely knew who Dunn was, and I didn't know what Henry looked like!"

"What happened the day you were fired?"

She shrugged. "I finished work on Friday night. The boss told me not to come in Monday, I was through."

"What did you do?"

"Went out and got drunk. What would you do?"

"Was Marsak around when you got drunk?"

"Not that I know."

"He killed two men who worked where you did. There was no reason for him to kill them. Then why did he?"

"How should I know? What do I know about him or them?"

I left her looking glumly at her instruments, cabbed to the Woodside LIRR station and rode out to Little Neck. Marian Dunn was at home alone, had never heard of Janice Stevens. Paul Dunn had hated rock music. I rode the empty noontime train back to Grace Callas. She wasn't alone, let me know I'd missed my chance, knew nothing of Janice Stevens, and the two men were waiting below her stairs. In coats and hats. One of them had a gun, the other got my lone arm and hustled me behind a garage.

"We want you to leave Joe Marsak alone."

"Let the police and the lawyers take care of it, Fortune."

They knew what they were doing, but they breathed too hard and their moves were stiff, out of practice. Their speech was too good for hoods, and I saw gray hair under the hats.

I said, "You're the old soldiers who hired his lawyer."

"He was a damned hero, let him alone. You hear?"

"Let the lawyer work, Fortune. We won't kill you, but we'll put you in the hospital."

They left, a car drove away. I went to talk to D'Amato. He was out. It was five when he got back, looking as tired as I felt. I told him about Janice Stevens and the old soldiers.

"No girl like that shows up around Henry or Dunn. An old man sits in a window and ogles a young girl. Where's a motive?"

"Unless he did more than ogle, and she's lying about Dunn or Henry," I said. "What about the old soldiers?"

"He was a hero. OSS behind the lines with Soviet partisans. They say they don't know why he shot those two, but it had to be a war flashback. The lawyer loves them as witnesses."

I left. Last night had been nice, Alice Connors expected me back, but it had been a short night and a long day, so I took the subway home. I'd call Alice, tell her I got too involved, make it up to her tomorrow. I should have known better.

She'd waited a long time to break out, was waiting on the stairs in front of my door. We went inside. She had her clothes off before I locked the door.

A lot later I told her about talking to Janice Stevens and Marian Dunn and Lieutenant D'Amato. Suddenly she started to cry, her whole body shaking with a kind of grief.

"What happened to him, Dan? He was so gentle, so attentive. Then his mother died, he got that apartment, and he was horrible!"

"Horrible?"

"I didn't want to tell you. You'd laugh at me, think I was just another neurotic female." Her face was against my good shoulder. "One night a month ago he got real drunk and started acting like waiting was all my idea, he was tired of my little-girl crap. He scared me, so I said no. He threw me on the floor and I thought he was going to rape me, but he was so drunk he couldn't do anything. I got into the bedroom, locked the door, and heard him staggering around half the night. In the morning he was gone and didn't call for three days."

In the dark of my loft with the early-morning sounds of Eighth Avenue outside, I sensed the start of a picture of what had happened to Bruce Henry. "He called me less and less. He'd say he'd call, but he didn't. Almost like he wanted to see me, but after that night when he tried to rape me he couldn't."

She pressed tight against me. I said, "His mother died and he got an apartment. He went to work under Paul Dunn, started hanging around with Dunn, drinking with Dunn." I had half an answer, but where was the other half? "Alice, did Bruce talk about a switchboard girl who got fired at Steiner Nissan?"

"No." In the dark beside me she moved closer. "Mr. Dunn was trying to fire a man who wouldn't take orders, but nothing about a girl. Bruce was going to get the man's job, but someone warned the man and ruined it. Mr. Dunn was furious, was going to get even with whoever told."

Joseph Marsak had murdered two men he didn't know. The enemy. Not "enemies," but "the enemy." And in my mind I saw the photographs on the wall of Joseph Marsak's room.

He was a big, grizzled black with the years of working on greasy engines ground into his large hands. His name was Walter Davis, and he sat in Ryan's with his back to the bar.

"Yeh, they was out to get me. I knows too much 'bout cars I gonna let Dunn tell me how I gotta work."

"Could he have gotten you fired?"

"He was working on it. I was drinking too much. He could get younger guys as good. I was bad for morale, all that shit."

"But you were warned, and you didn't get fired."

He grinned. "I'm at Steiner twenty years longer'n Dunn. I tol' the boss I wasn't doin' nothin' 'cept not let Dunn push me around, wasn't drinkin' no more'n ever, was the best mechanic in town, an' Honda wanted me if he didn't. That always gets 'em."

"Janice Stevens warned you."

"Nice kid, likes things clean an' fair. She heard Dunn and Henry talkin' on the phone about me. She heard Dunn tell Henry he'd get my job. They laughed about it, so she told me."

"And got fired for it."

"I talked to the big boss all that next Monday. He said it wasn't my business. Dunn and Henry had nothin' to do with it. She just wasn't no good at the job, listened to music all day."

"What do you think?"

"They got her for sure. The boss threw her to them

91

to make up for keepin' me. Can't prove it. Really lose my job I try."

"Yeh," I said.

Janice Stevens was at her apartment with her two roommates. They were finishing her packing; none of them looked happy.

"Tell me the real story of the night you got fired."

She turned away. "My dad's coming in ten minutes. The new roommate's coming. I don't feel like talking, okay?"

"Not okay. You left too much out. You know why Marsak killed those two men."

The blonde, Madge, said, "Hey, you're crazy."

"Leave her alone," the other roommate said.

I said, "Start with that Friday night, with what Marsak heard when he sat up in the window."

After a time, Janice Stevens started to talk in a low voice. "The big boss gave me my check, told me not to come back on Monday." Then she was crying. "I needed that job. I was only there two months, I'd spent all the money on the apartment and paying the agency fee and making payments on my guitar. If I lost that job I'd have to go home. I begged him not to fire me. I asked him what I'd done wrong. He said I wasn't fast enough, I didn't have enough experience—all that bullshit—and none of it meant anything but I was fired and he wouldn't even tell me why!"

She raged and cried, paced the living room, smashed one hand into the other. She was going through that night again, the pain and the defeat. Her first job, her first apartment, her first break from parents who told her she couldn't survive on her own. She had done it in spite of them. Had come to New York, gotten a job, joined a band, had an apartment. Then in an instant it was gone. The loss of her dreams, the loss of everything.

She wiped at her tears. "I just sat there on the floor. I couldn't stop crying. I wanted to smash everything, but all I could do was sit on the floor and cry. Then I heard them."

The doorbell rang. A roommate opened the door. A girl came in, and behind her a graying man in a suit. The new roomer and Janice Stevens's father. Janice didn't look at either of them.

"They were just outside the office in the garage. Dunn and Henry. They were laughing. Laughing and smirking. Laughing at me! They saw me crying and they just laughed and laughed, and I got up and ran out and ran all the way here. I knew why I was fired. They'd lied to the boss, told some story, gotten me fired, and then they'd laughed at me."

She started to cry again. The roommates looked at her in silence. The new roomer looked like she wanted to cry too. The father looked uncomfortable.

"You came home," I said, "went out in the backyard to cry and tell your roommates exactly the way you've just told me. All about why you were fired and how they laughed at you when you cried. And Joseph Marsak sat up in his window and heard it all."

She wiped her face. "I don't know why he did it, but I know he'd tried to help me, and I didn't want anyone to hurt him."

She was the kind who took in stray cats, pulled thorns from the feet of battered dogs. She'd tried to help a black mechanic and had her world destroyed for it, and when she knew what Joseph Marsak had done she had tried to protect him by saying nothing.

"We better talk to the police," I said.

"I hated them," she said. "I liked the old man. I was glad they were dead, and I didn't want him hurt."

"I know," I said.

"I wanted to kill them myself, crush them, blow them away! Blow all the mean, laughing goons away!"

"It's in all of us," I said, "but we fight it. That's what civilization is supposed to be."

Her father said, "I'll drive you to the police."

At the precinct, D'Amato listened to her story with a dazed look on his face. He looked at me.

"Marsak shot them because they got a girl fired? A girl he barely knew? I mean, a girl young enough to be his granddaughter who lived downstairs and was lively? Christ, he *is* nuts."

"Not because they got her fired," I said. "Because they laughed. Because they watched her suffer and laughed."

D'Amato was silent.

"You remember the accent he has, the accent that isn't Russian? It's probably German. You remember he said he lived in many places in Europe? How he worked behind the Nazi lines?"

"Paul Dunn was just born then. Henry's *father* was a kid."

"You remember the pictures on his wall? The family before the war? How he's lived alone ever since the war?"

D'Amato drove us down to the Tombs, took me and Janice Stevens into the interrogation room. They brought Marsak in a few minutes later. When he saw

94

Janice Stevens he stopped, then he sat down. He looked at me.

"You are a good detective."

D'Amato said, "Can we see your arm, Mr. Marsak?"

He shrugged. "There is only a small scar. They removed the tattoo in the OSS; it would have been too obvious."

I said, "Your family?"

"My wife and son. My two daughters. I escaped, they did not. I watched the Nazis laugh while my wife died, while my son died, while my two daughters died. They killed them and they laughed. Those two laughed at the pain of Janice, at her suffering. I have heard those laughs all my life. I took my pistol and went there. They laughed at me, too. I shot them."

D'Amato was pale. "You didn't even know them. Dunn had a wife, a family. Henry was going to get married."

"I know them," the old man said. "Family men, dog lovers, beer drinkers, but they are who make Auschwitz possible. They build Auschwitz; they staff it; they permit it. Leaders cannot exist without followers. They are the enemy."

"They could be changed, Mr. Marsak," D'Amato said.

"I saw their eyes. I know those eyes. They do not change. I am an old man, I do not matter. They must be stopped."

I got up and walked out. I lit a cigarette and was smoking when D'Amato and Janice Stevens joined me. D'Amato was still pale. Janice went to her father.

"I'll be back, Mr. Fortune. They won't beat me."

95

She would be. D'Amato watched them go.

"The DA'll faint," he said. "The mayor'll run screaming. It'll make that subway vigilante mess look like a cakewalk."

He was stalling before he went to tell the DA he would have to prosecute an eighty-year-old man who had lost his whole family in the Holocaust, risked his life against the Nazis, and killed two men he didn't know because they had laughed at the pain of a girl. I only had to report to my clients, but I needed some beers before I went out to Little Neck.

The marine opened the Dunns' door. "Get lost."

"A chip off the old block. Call your mother."

He turned red, but he was still a boy, uncertain. He'd grow up, and then he'd be certain.

"The cops called," he said sullenly. "She's in church."

He slammed the door in my face. The church was three blocks away. Marian Dunn was kneeling at a small shrine with a hundred burning candles. She'd been crying again.

"That old man killed my Paul for nothing. He wasn't the best husband; he wasn't even such a good man; but he was my lawful husband, and a woman should love her husband."

She started to pray for Paul Dunn, and Bruce Henry, and Joseph Marsak, and her daughter, and even for me. She prayed for forgiveness for thinking bad thoughts about her lawful husband.

I rode back to Woodside. Alice Connors wasn't home. I went to my loft. She was there waiting for me. She cried a little for Bruce Henry, but mostly for Joseph Marsak, and then we made love in the late afternoon. Later we talked.

"What will happen to him, Dan?"

"A lot of loud talk about law and justice. Then declare it delayed pyschotic trauma and put him in a mental hospital. It's probably the right answer, even the truth."

We had a good month. Then she got a better job in Manhattan, met a younger man with two arms and flew off to the Bahamas. She would always be grateful for what I'd done. She was just starting in life, and, thanks to me, she knew she was going to be okay. She even kissed me good-bye.

Indian Poker

CURTIS E. FISCHER

Curt Fischer was born in Jamestown, North Da-
kota, grew up in Sacramento, California, and lived
in Nebraska, Illinois, and Minnesota before arriving in 1979 in Sheboygan Falls, Wisconsin, where
he teaches and writes.

"Been twenty-five years now, ain't it, Sheriff?" old
Miles Haskell asked me the other day over at the truck
stop during lunch. His eyes had drifted over to the
stools at the lunch counter that the local folks kind of
avoid. Now and then a stranger in town who don't
know no better sits there, but nobody local does.

"Yeah, Miles, twenty-five years next Tuesday," I
said, wiping my mouth with a paper napkin.

"Biggest thing that ever happened in this town,"
Miles sighed with a shake of his head. "Twenty-five
years. Seems like yesterday, in a way. Lord knows,
a lot's happened to Plum Creek since then."

Yeah, a lot's happened. Interstate 80, cutting
through the heart of Nebraska, had relegated Plum
Creek to "Gas—Food—Lodging" status on a sign
out by the cloverleaf. Most of the downtown area
had become barren, even the Sears catalog outlet
had folded. And St. Andrew's College, once the town's
primary source of income, had closed three years
before. If it weren't for the fact that Plum Creek was
the county seat, it probably would have died alto-

gether. But the population had stabilized at 3,700, half of its all-time high in '66. Twenty-five years before, the day it happened, Baumann's Truck Stop, right on what was then the main highway, was the prime eatery, and it was always full. Today, outside of me and Miles, there were only two others, a couple of young kids, in the whole place.

I put enough money down on the table to cover my tab, left Miles contemplating his choice of candy bars under the glass by the cash register, and went to my car. To the south a storm was brewing. One always has to be wary of twisters in July, so I checked to see if my binoculars were in the car and proceeded to the bridge west of town, my favorite vantage point. Standing by the open car door, with my elbows resting on the roof, I scanned the horizon, looking for a tell-tale funnel cloud. For a moment, in a particularly dark spot in a swirling mass, I could've sworn that I saw Emil Tyne's scowling face. It hadn't changed in twenty-five years.

That night I awoke, cold and sweaty, as, in a hellish dream, Tyne's eyes had searched mine as they had on that long-ago date he had had with eternity. It had never happened before. For twenty-five years, the only sleep I had ever lost was when my wife had up and left me. Up till then I had managed to rationalize away that afternoon in the truck stop so many years before. I had never felt guilty; I knew I didn't feel guilty now. At least I knew I didn't feel guilty about what had happened, but maybe it was about time that everyone knew the truth about why it had happened. Maybe that was it. Maybe I felt guilty that I had kept the truth inside for so long.

Tuesday came too soon. I was out on patrol when noon rolled around. I thought about driving over to the north side of town to the old bowling alley for a bite, but Tuesday was Mexican food day at the truck stop, and I hadn't missed a Tuesday there in many a year. To miss on this particular Tuesday would've looked, well, funny, you know? So I parked out by the two dilapidated Texaco gas pumps that hadn't been used since old man Baumann had died in '76, went in, and took my normal booth from where I could see the door, the register, and the road. If nothing else, what had happened twenty-five years earlier had taught me not to leave myself vulnerable.

"The usual, Sheriff?" Sophie Gehrke asked as she managed to stop at my booth for a moment. Tuesday's Mexican special and Friday night's fish fry were about the only times that the stop was busy any more, and workin' by herself ran poor Sophie ragged. At least she could rest up the remainder of the week.

"Yeah, sure, Soph," I said with a weak smile. "But bring me the weaker sauce for the tacos today, okay?"

"What's the matter? Ulcer kickin' up again?"

"Somethin' like that," I lied, looking at the Plum Creek Bank calendar hanging over the cash register. As she moved away, I spotted Miles Haskell driving up with Bobby Clementson sitting next to him in the cab of his truck. They parked next to my tan, flasher-bedecked cruiser, and I saw Miles motion to it as he walked toward the café, as if to say, "See, told you he'd be here." Bobby looked sick. I had a feeling he didn't want to be here today any more than I did.

"See, told you he'd be here," Miles said, as they approached my booth. I smiled involuntarily at how he had verbalized my thoughts, but Miles, seizing the moment, took it as a sign of welcome and slid into the seat on the other side of the booth. Bobby hesitated and then slid in next to him. "Went out and picked Bobby up from offen his farm. Figured I'd buy lunch for such an auspicious occasion."

"Auspicious?" I asked. Somehow the word hit me wrong.

"Sad day when we lost Emil Tyne. He was a great sheriff." Miles was being sincere, but he suddenly realized that I might be offended at this praise of my former employer. You know, like I might feel he wasn't givin' me my due. "Hey, Sheriff, not that you ain't, you are—but Emil. . . ."

I shook my head. "It's okay, Miles, I know what you mean," I said to calm his fears.

Suddenly Bobby blurted, "I don't. I don't know what he means."

I tried to silence Bobby with my eyes, but the arrival of Sophie with my lunch and her taking of Miles's and Bobby's order did more than I could to quiet him.

After Sophie had left, Miles had to go and push the issue. "What did you mean by that last comment, Bobby?" Miles's forehead was furrowed. It had suddenly occurred to him that twenty-five years' worth of rumors and gossip might have some truth to them.

Bobby looked over his shoulder uncomfortably and then back to me for support. I became impassive. Not getting any help from me. "Look, Miles, I really didn't want to come in here with you, but I didn't want to hurt your feelings, okay? But don't sit there and sing the glories of good old Emil Tyne, all right?"

Miles sat forward. He didn't say anything for a bit; he just watched me eat my first taco, which I was having trouble getting down. "Sing the glories of old

Emil Tyne? Is that what you said?" he finally asked Bobby. Without waiting for an answer, an answer it was obvious that Bobby wasn't going to give him anyway, he plunged on. "I don't have to. Sing his glories, I mean. They're on a plaque at the courthouse, on this date every year the weekly paper does a memorial on him, and the new jail is named after him. Seems to me that somebody thought he was a great man."

"That's what they thought, all right." The voice was like an echo. Haunting. It was my voice. When I snapped back to reality, I found Bobby and Miles staring at me. Bobby was smiling. All of a sudden, feelings that I had repressed for twenty-five years found their way to my tongue. "Emil had fooled a lot of people. Few knew that he was a bully, a cheat, a liar, a—"

"He was mean. Ugly mean. Rotten mean." Bobby had joined the litany.

Sophie brought their orders. I had lost total interest in mine.

When Sophie left, Miles snorted an angry laugh and sat back, his thumbs hooked in the suspenders of his bib overalls. He looked the both of us over for a bit and then issued his scalding judgment. "Wonderful. Just wonderful. I can just see the headlines now. 'Local Hero Smeared by Friends.' You were, weren't ya? His friends? His best friends? His deputies? Didn't you ride beside him on his rounds? Play cards back at the station with him? Drink with him?"

"We were kids, Miles. Deputies? What a joke. We were kids he could keep in awe of him and jerk around. I was twenty. Bobby here was nineteen. Deputies? Emil even took a cut of our pay as compensation for putting up with us. But like everybody else, we thought Emil Tyne was something special. He was the law. He was the power. He was everything we could hope to become. We idolized him when he scared some drunk high school kid half to death when we caught one weaving down County trunk X. We thought he was doing the kid a favor by making him bring ten bucks a week to the station instead of ticketing him for the full fine then and there. It never occurred to us then that the money went straight into Emil's pocket. When he'd beat up the tramps down by the old depot with his nightstick, we believed him that they had it coming and that that was the only way to deal with them." I stopped to take a breath. A few in the café had noticed my agitation, but I had managed to keep my voice down. "We honestly thought Emil's way was the right way. Oh, we were big shots, working for Sheriff Emil Tyne. Didn't it ever occur to you or any of the other adults that Emil couldn't keep older deputies? Didn't it seem strange to you that older guys always quit on him?"

"Why should it? The pay was lousy. You young bucks, on the other hand—"

Bobby cut him off. "Some of 'em tried to tell you why they were quitting, but by then you had made such a god out of good ol' Emil, you turned a deaf ear."

Miles picked at his burrito. He still hadn't taken a bite. His position in the booth had ironically placed him in a position without an escape. When he spoke, his voice was tight. "You trying to tell me that Emil Tyne, my neighbor, the man that we all played poker with three nights a week, the man on my bowling team for six years, the man—"

"Was scum," I supplied. "You mentioned poker . . ."

"He was a great poker player. He won near every night we played. Even you traitors gotta admit that."

"Oh, yeah, he always won all right," admitted Bobby.

"Wanna know how he won?" I prodded.

Miles looked me in the eye. His eyes were angry and defiant. He didn't answer.

"Did you ever notice that one of us deputies always had to sit out whenever you and the rest of the boys played? Ever wonder why?"

Without thinking, Miles shook his head no.

"So we could move about the table and signal him, that's why," Bobby volunteered. "We'd signal him with our eyes. He told us it was a joke and that it was to teach you guys a lesson seeing that gambling's illegal. He said cops had to stick together like that. We believed him. We didn't understand things like ego, especially his. We were impressionable and stupid."

"In awe," I mumbled, repeated myself from earlier. "Remember Indian Poker? That was his favorite game, especially if he didn't have one of us free to move around the table. Remember? Everybody got one card face down. Then you lifted it up to your forehead." I lifted my right hand to my forehead, using my thumb to demonstrate. "You could see everybody else's card but not your own."

"I remember," Miles stated flatly.

"It took a real poker face to win that one. But Tyne always did, didn't he?"

Miles and Bobby both nodded.

"As we'd look around at each other, evaluating our chances, Tyne would look only at us. By shifting our eyes up and to the right, we'd be signaling that he had the highest card we could see, while down and to the left would be the opposite."

"We were really the only ones he had to beat," Bobby finished, "and he could figure the odds on beating us from what he could see."

Miles said nothing, but disbelief lined his weathered face.

"You know, just before he died . . ." I had trouble getting out the rest. "I found out that girls he'd catch in backseats with boys he'd blackmail for sexual favors. He was a real dirtball." I looked into Miles's gray eyes. Eyes that were turning sadder by the minute. "You know," I continued, "if they wouldn't do what he asked, he'd threaten to tell their folks what he had caught them doing. And us dummies, me and Hal Zwick and Bobby and everybody—including you, Miles—we'd sit there in the radio room while those girls, three . . . four a month, would come over to the station and Emil would take 'em into his office and close the door. 'For counseling,' he'd say. And we all thought it was just another example of what a great guy Emil Tyne was." I paused for a bit. Then I said it. I'm not sure why. Maybe it was my way of saying I was sorry to her. "My sister, Cindy, she got counseling from Emil. Remember? And there I sat, just next door. . . ."

Miles hadn't taken his eyes off of me. "When was it that Cindy left Plum Creek?" he asked quietly.

"About twenty-five years ago . . . just before Emil," I responded simply.

"You never heard from her? She never wrote or nothin'?"

"Never."

Miles sat there with his head down for some time,

stabbing meaningless little holes in his burrito. He sighed once, but he didn't speak.

Bobby took a sip of his Pepsi, his eyes searching mine. I think we were both wondering if we shouldn'ta let sleeping dogs lie.

Finally the awkward stillness at our table was broken. "I don't believe you," Miles said bluntly.

It was a challenge. We had taken liberties with the memories of an old man. We had taken history as he wanted it and turned it into a battle of conscience. It wasn't just because Emil Tyne had been his friend. He took it personal. It meant that his whole generation had failed to see the truth. It meant a whole chapter of his life had been written wrong.

"You don't believe us, or you don't want to?" asked Bobby.

Miles became louder. "He died a hero! You can't deny that! I was here that day when that crazy kid from the college came in here and threatened all of us."

"All of us? He got the one he was after," I said.

Miles's face went blank. "What do you mean? The kid went out into the parking lot after he did it and blew his own . . . Nobody could ever figure . . . We all thought that ol' Emil just happened to be in the wrong place at the wrong time. Now you're saying he deliberately singled out the sheriff?"

"I was there. I heard him," I said.

"And I know why," added Bobby.

"Huh?" was all that Miles could utter.

"Tell him, Bobby. Tell him everything," I prompted.

Bobby pushed his untouched plate to the center of the table, crossed his arms, and leaned forward.

He reached up with his hand and massaged the back of his neck. "It all started on the previous Friday night," he began, but he was interrupted by Sophie.

"Should I take your plates, fellas? I mean, you haven't even touched your food. Was it bad? Is there a problem?"

"No, no, Sophie. We're just overcome by nostalgia," I said, bending the truth. "Today's a special day. Go ahead, you can have mine."

"Mine too," said Miles, and Bobby assented with a wave of his hand.

When she had gone, he continued. "On the previous Friday night, Emil and I were patrolling the perimeter farm roads. You could usually catch some underage drinkers or a couple making out. At the time, I thought it was a real kick to scare hell out of 'em. So did Emil. Well, anyway, we came up on this car parked on the shoulder with a St. Andrew's sticker on the bumper. Lord, was there ever a scramble in that car when we hit it with the spotlight. I thought Emil was going to split a gut. When we got up to it, the girl was still buttoning up her blouse. 'No need to do that, little lady,' Emil said. 'I got a little game we're going to play.'

"I thought I knew what he was talking about. We had done it before to other couples to scare them. Usually we'd threaten to turn them in to the college dean, but this time was different. He made the girl get out of the car and get next to the driver's-side door where the lights from the patrol car were hittin'. Then he opened the back door on the kid's car and sat in. 'Now, here's the game, little girl,' Emil said. His voice was different. It was crueler . . . sick. 'I'm going to sit back here with my gun on your boyfriend.

You start taking your clothes off. All your clothes. If you don't, I'm going to blow his head off. Resisting arrest, you know? I can do it. I'm Emil Tyne, sheriff, and I'm one mean son-of-a-bitch. Just ask around.' Then he leaned forward and growled into the kid's ear, 'And you, young man. You can stop it. Just turn around and ask, ask pretty like. If my gun's out, I blow your head off. If my gun's holstered, you two can go.'

"The two college kids couldn't believe it. I couldn't believe it. They looked at me. I looked at them. I just stood there." Bobby stopped his story to reach for his water glass and take a sip.

"That was Emil," I said. "The real Emil. Not the one the rest of you knew."

"Anyhow," Bobby continued, "after a few more threats from Emil, the girl started to strip. All the while, Emil kept taunting the boy, telling him that he had the power to put a stop to it. The kid's knuckles got white on the steering wheel. His girlfriend kept looking at him, begging for him to do something. She was hysterical before she even got her blouse off. When she got down to her undies, she couldn't take any more. She ran off into the cornfield. The boy broke down. When we drove off, he was pounding his steering wheel, sobbing, and Emil Tyne was laughing so hard he was holding his sides. That was the last time I saw Emil alive. I was so ashamed— of him, of my own cowardice—when I got home, I called him," Bobby said, motioning to me, "told him about it and about the other girls that I knew about, packed a small bag, went to Omaha and enlisted in the navy. I didn't hear about Tyne's death till after boot camp."

"That's why you weren't there that day," Miles

stated. "You know, for the longest time, we all said that if Deputy Clementson had been there, that kid couldn't have gotten the drop on the sheriff."

"Since Bobby had called me, I knew why the kid had come up behind Tyne with that revolver that day. I saw his face. He had been humiliated. He probably had spent a couple of days questioning his own manhood. He was the picture of hate. I knew he hated enough to kill. I heard what he said. 'Now it's your turn, Sheriff. Turn around. If I've got a gun, you're dead. If not, you're a hero. Come on, Sheriff, don't you want to play?'

"Tyne froze. His face went pale. The coward's eyes darted about until they finally rested on mine. We looked at each other for an eternity. His eyes begged to know. 'Indian Poker,' his lips mouthed. I could see whether the kid had a gun or not. He knew I could see. All I had to do was signal as to whether or not he was beat."

"I remember," Miles intoned solemnly. "I was here. A couple of us at the back booth saw the kid come in and wave the gun. We saw Emil look at you. Then he whirled—"

"—and got his head blown off."

"And you sit there and tell me he wasn't a hero? Knowing that crazed kid really did have a gun, he turned and tried to take it, and you call him a coward?"

I stood up and took twenty dollars from my billfold to pay all three checks. "You still don't understand, do you, Miles? Emil Tyne never acted unless he knew he had the upper hand—in anything."

"But, you signaled him," insisted Miles.

"Yeah, I signaled him. And for twenty-five years, I've lost only one night's sleep over it."

A Cup of Coffee

STEPHEN A. RUDLOFF

During a twenty-year career as a naval flight officer Stephen A. Rudloff attained the rank of
commander and amassed over 2,300 hours aboard
jet fighters. A veteran of 295 combat missions,
he spent the final year of the Vietnam War as a
prisoner in Hanoi. "A Cup of Coffee" is his first
published piece of fiction.

On the first of September, when major league teams
are permitted to expand their rosters to forty players,
most clubs bring up their best minor league prospects
for that last push during the pennant drive or to get
a glimpse of what they hope will be a prosperous and
unencumbered future. Unfortunately, very few of
these farm phenomena attain even a modicum of
success, so that this one autumnal enterprise is the
only taste of the big time that some of these rising
stars will ever get. In baseball jargon these young
hopefuls are said to have come up to the majors for
a cup of coffee, the connotation being that they spend
only enough time on the top rung for a sip of java
before their talent seeks its own level at Ogden, Jack-
sonville, or some other way station on the return trip
to oblivion.

I'd long since found a level of my own, in the
supposedly glamorous world of the private eye. I was
doing background investigations for local firms and

keeping tabs on various Lotharios and Jezebels at the request of suspicious consorts. Not exactly the kind of business that conjures up images of Bogie, fat men, and falcons, but then paperback novels and late-night movies promise us only dreams, not the real world. I won't say that I was content doing somebody else's dirty laundry but to tell the truth, I was probably right where I ought to have been. With the equivalent of a class-C fastball and a curve that wouldn't last a month in a rookie league, I didn't belong with the big boys. The trouble was, I not only got called up to the majors ready or not, I had no idea who I was playing with until I was in so deep I couldn't just walk away. I guess there are some pretty colorful expressions to describe guys like me, but the word *overmatched* is about the kindest I can come up with at the moment.

It was Tuesday, April 28, and the weatherman had promised some cloudiness, with continued cool temperatures and a high in the 50s. Not ideal baseball conditions, especially for a night game, but I'd already planned to catch the Dodgers–Reds contest, a chilly wind notwithstanding. We'd taken two out of three from the Giants over the weekend, and we trailed a red-hot Phillies club by only three games. The Phils had won eight straight, but everybody knew they were playing way above themselves and had to come down to earth soon. I'd made the trip over the bridge for each of the games against New York, and the fever was upon me. It would not subside until the leaves turned in the waning days of October.

I was seated at the desk in the living room of my apartment, which also serves as my business office, relaxing over the morning's first cup of coffee and inhaling the sports section of the *Mirror*. The probable pitchers for tonight's game were listed as Raffensberger and Erskine, but rumor had it that Preacher Roe would make his first start of the season that night for Brooklyn. He'd won thirty-three games for us over the past two seasons, so Dodger fans were anxious for his return to the rotation. With no pressing business to attend to I was looking forward to a leisurely day as I turned to the details of the De-Marco–Savoie fight which had taken place in Montreal the night before. Since I live on the second floor of a two-story building, access to which is guarded by a long flight of uncarpeted wooden stairs, I was able to discern an intrusion long before I heard a knock on the door. When it came I half-hollered, "Come in. It's open."

The door swung open, and from over the top of my paper I could see a slightly disheveled man of about forty, fumbling with a black fedora and briefcase that he tried to balance in the hand that wasn't occupied with the door handle. Releasing the door and kicking it shut behind him, he inquired, "Are you Charles Endicott, the private investigator?"

"Yes I am." I took him in as I answered. He was about six feet, reddish-brown hair, fair complexion, with a look of harassment about him. I figured him for a tormented accountant or a henpecked husband, or both. He looked like a stiff breeze would carry him away.

"Please . . . sit down. What can I do for you?" He hesitated, his jaw working silently as he tried to foster the courage to tell a total stranger about Hildegarde or Prudence or whatever her name was slipping in late at night with flushed cheeks or caught embracing the local barber at the last Rotary Club dance. Another domestic entanglement was all I could foresee, and my interest was already wandering back to Paddy's unanimous decision over Savoie.

Ignoring my invitation to sit, he just stood there, as though trying to decide if I was a worthy recipient for the intimate family secret about to be revealed. Finally he blurted, "Someone is trying to kill me, Mr. Endicott, and I don't know who it is or why."

My mind did a double take. When your life revolves around spying on cheating spouses, chasing delinquent alimony donors, or tracking down the juvenile record of some teenager who wants a summer job as a runner on Wall Street, attempted murder doesn't exactly fit into your daily repertoire. I took another look at the man who had just thrust me into the world of Spade and Marlowe. He was still six feet, still needed about forty pounds to fill out his frame, but that harassed look I'd been so sure about was closer to the fear I'd seen on the faces of some of my comrades in Korea.

"Hold on," I said. "Why don't you sit down and tell me the whole story, beginning with your name?" I hoped he couldn't hear my heart pounding in my chest. If he knew that for me excitement was having the toilet back up and not being able to locate the plunger he might just take his business elsewhere. How or why he'd settled on me I didn't know and couldn't have cared less.

"I'm sorry," he answered, grabbing hold of a straight-back chair I kept near the desk and seating himself directly in front of me. His thin face mirrored the rest of him, and once he'd deposited his briefcase on the floor and his hat on my desk, I could see his thin fingers working nervously in his lap. They were mottled with stains and blotches ranging from deep purple to pale yellow.

I'd long since given up trying to determine my clients' professions based upon their appearances. I know Sherlock Holmes could do it, but my deductions more often than not rivaled those of Dr. Watson. In fact, the only time I'd ever come up with the right one was in the case of a doctor. That he'd come into my office carrying a black bag with his name emblazoned on the side in gold lettering and followed by the elucidative M.D. was, of course, of considerable assistance.

"My name is Alfred Riegel," he began. "I work for the firm of Jacobsen and Dunlop, over on Third Avenue. I'm employed there as a master printer, and up until yesterday morning I'd led the most uneventful, serene life you can imagine. That's when it began, yesterday morning," he repeated, then continued on in a voice that sped through his narrative as though he were afraid he'd run out of time before he finished. He'd have won a fortune on *Beat the Clock*.

"I live uptown, on East 77th Street to be precise, and every morning I walk two blocks to the 77th Street station. From there I take the subway downtown to work. Yesterday, as I do every morning, I bought the *Times* at the subway newsstand and began reading it as I waited for my train. I was leaning against the side of one of those large steel beams that support the ceiling, or roof, or whatever you call it of the station. Those beams are indented on two sides, so you can actually lean in a bit, and I suppose that's what saved my life. As I said, I was leaning against the beam, reading my newspaper, when I heard the roar of the train as it entered the station. Just as I raised my eyes I felt someone push me forward, and the next thing I knew I had been spun diagonally toward the edge of the platform. It was only a few feet from where I'd been standing to the track, but I managed to reach out and grab the lip of the beam, and that kept me from falling off the platform and into the path of the train. There were a few gasps and someone muttered, 'Hey, watch it, buddy!' but I'm sure everyone thought I'd just slipped trying to be first on the train so I'd get a seat. Anyway, I was quickly forgotten, and since I was too shaken to get on the subway I found myself virtually alone on the platform less than a minute later.

"Now, I know it was crowded, it being rush hour and all, but I've been jostled before in a crowd and I can tell the difference between that and a direct shove; and I was pushed, no doubt about it! When I'd sufficiently recovered my wits I looked around the station and saw a transit cop. I went over to him and explained what had happened, but it was obvious that he didn't believe me. He told me to run along. I caught the next train, and by the end of the day I'd more or less convinced myself that what I knew had happened hadn't, that I'd let my imagination get the best of me."

He stopped to catch his breath, but the fingers that kept fidgeting with each other while he spoke did not rest. Neither did his eyes, which would fix on me for a few moments, then dart down to make sure the hands were performing their ritualistic movement. I took the opportunity to interject a question.

"Did you get a look at the man you think pushed

you, or anyone else who was standing behind you when the train pulled into the station?"

His eyes met mine once again, but his face took on a momentary look of . . . what? Disbelief? Scorn? I couldn't tell. All the fictional detectives can read faces and eyes like they were cue cards. I'm lucky if I can read a guy when he flips me the finger.

"No." A pause, followed by, "I didn't see anyone. I got on the platform just as a train was leaving and immediately started to read my paper. Except for a continuous low murmur from the growing crowd I wasn't aware of anyone. After I'd been pushed it took me a few moments to regain my composure, and, as I told you, by the time I did everyone was rushing past me to get on the train. Whoever tried to kill me either got on the subway or went back up to the street. But that was yesterday; let me tell you what happened just a few hours ago, and you'll realize I'm not just being overly dramatic about the events of yesterday morning.

"I think I told you that I walk about two blocks to the subway every morning?" he asked by way of continuing. "The station is on Lexington Avenue, and my apartment is just off Second Avenue. As I started down the street just after seven I caught sight of an automobile out of the corner of my eye just as I heard a loud bang, like the backfire of a car. I turned my head toward the street and a bullet struck the hood of a parked car that was between me and the one driving down the street. It wasn't speeding down the street like the ones you see in the movies. In fact, it was moving rather slowly. I immediately hurled myself down onto the ground, using the parked auto as a shield. After what seemed like forever, I heard the motor being gunned and the car speeding away.

I stayed on the ground, afraid that someone might have gotten out of the car. I didn't move until a number of people began to gather around me. Most of them had been on their way to the subway, just like me, and saw or heard the whole thing. This wasn't my imagination, and neither was the bullet hole in the hood of that parked car. Someone tried to kill me, Mr. Endicott, just as sure as I'm sitting here in your office!" Beads of perspiration had begun to form above his upper lip, as though this were July and the heat was on.

I gulped at my lukewarm coffee just as he finished his narrative. "Okay, Mr. Riegel, just take it easy," I said a bit too excitedly. "I don't doubt your story, but let me make sure that I've got it all straight up to here. Now you say you were walking on 77th toward Lexington Avenue, so that means you were heading west, correct?"

"Well, I guess so," he responded.

"Fine; 77th is a one-way street, if I'm not mistaken, and being odd numbered, the traffic should have been going in the same direction as you. Which side of the street were you on?"

"The right side; I'd come out of my apartment, turned right, and walked maybe twenty or thirty paces when I saw the car and heard the shot."

"Were you aware of a car starting up, either as you turned into the sidewalk or while you were walking down the street?" I was trying to get a clear picture of what had transpired, but also trying to gather my wits about me so that I didn't say or do something stupid that would lose me the case before

I ever got it. I'd been expecting that nice, big curve-ball named Prudence, leaning over the plate and sitting on the break, but old Alfred had slipped me the high hard one right under the chin when he'd mentioned attempted murder. My mind was just stepping out of the batter's box while I regained my composure.

"No, the first thing I was aware of was this movement out of the corner of my eye. As I turned my head the shot rang out." He wasn't much on elaboration.

"All right, then, you turned your head to the left and saw the car. First, can you describe anyone in the vehicle?"

"No." He shook his head as he spoke, as if to add emphasis. Seeing that it still wasn't enough, he added, "I only got a glimpse of the car before the shot. Then I threw myself onto the ground."

"Okay, let's go to the car, then. What can you tell me about it?"

"Not much, I'm afraid. It was a sedan, black or dark blue. It, uh . . . well, that's all I can recall, really." His forlorn expression pleaded for compassion on the question of automobiles, but I pressed on. I was drawing confidence from his meek countenance.

"Well, how about a hood ornament? Anything?" This last imploringly. I was getting desperate.

"No, at least not one that I noticed. I'm not very good with cars. I don't even own one myself," he said by way of excuse. "It was the same with everyone who was there. No one could remember very much about the car except what I just told you . . . and yes, that it was new. Somebody said he thought it looked new."

What an observant group that must have been! Seventy-five years ago they probably would have been scouts for Custer at Little Big Horn. Somewhat exasperated, I went on: "As you glimpsed the car and heard the shot, your attention was drawn to the hood of the parked automobile—by the sound of the impact of the bullet, I take it?"

"Well, yes," he answered, rather indignantly. I immediately backed off.

"Was only one shot fired, Mr. Riegel?" I posed the question as politely as I could without seeming to waver in my newfound resolution.

"I can only recall hearing one," he answered, then rushed to add, "but the police told me that they'd found two bullet holes in the hood of the car. I was pretty well shaken when I realized that someone was shooting at me, and all I could think about was getting down on the ground and out of sight."

"We'll get back to the police in a moment, Mr. Riegel," I said. "Can you recall if any of the people who witnessed the incident were able to provide any type of description of the occupants of the car?"

"No," he said with the flicker of a smile. "No . . . I mean no one was able to provide the police with any useful information. The two patrolmen were quite put out with all of us by the time they'd finished questioning us on the street."

Terrific, I thought; nobody saw anything, and my client hasn't the vaguest idea who's trying to kill him. I might as well be back investigating illicit love affairs. At least then I knew who and what I was looking for. Pursuing the police line one step further, I ventured forth with another astute inquiry. "After you recounted your story to the patrolmen, did they take you downtown?"

"Downtown?" For a moment his face took on a perplexed cast and he looked genuinely confused. "Oh, you mean to a police station?" I could almost see the little light bulb illuminate above his head. "Yes," he continued, "a patrol car came around and they took me to a station house, but I'm afraid I can't tell you which one. I was still pretty upset, and I wasn't really aware of where they were taking me."

Sure, I thought, why start noticing things that late in the game? It didn't really matter, though. "That's all right," I told him, "I can check up on that pretty easily. Do you remember whom you spoke to at the precinct?"

Again there was confusion. "Uh, yes, it was a Lieutenant Harrison," he responded.

"Good; I know him," I lied. According to all the detective novels, any private eye worth his salt always knows the investigating officer, and I didn't want to destroy any of Alfred's illusions. But still, he gave me a funny look before I continued. "So what did Harrison say he was going to do about all this?"

"Absolutely nothing," he replied. "The lieutenant dismissed the events of yesterday as the product of an overactive imagination, and then he had the nerve to say that I hadn't been of much help and that there wasn't much that he could do with the little bit of information that he had at hand. That's why I've come to you." Riegel was indignant, and I didn't blame him.

"You must admit you haven't exactly been a storehouse of knowledge, Mr. Riegel, but still. . . ." I let the sentence drop, and Alfred picked it up on cue.

"Of course I realize that, Mr. Endicott, but I hardly

expected the police to send me back out on the street where I could be killed at any moment. In fact, I'm pretty sure that someone followed me here to your office."

"What?" Despite the effort, I knew that I looked as startled as I felt. "Are you sure?"

"Well, when I left the police station I saw a tall man in a gray suit, wearing a gray fedora, directly across the street. As I turned up the block, he started walking in the same direction. I didn't pay any more attention to him, but when I got off the subway down the street from your office, I saw him again. At least I think I saw him . . . it looked like the same man."

"Okay, Mr. Riegel, hold on a moment," I interrupted. "Let me take a quick look outside."

I walked to the front room, the one that serves as my bedroom and that overlooks the street, stepped to the side of one of the windows, and nudged the curtain aside. The street was fairly busy with the usual morning pedestrian traffic, but I didn't see anyone who matched the description Riegel had given me. I really hadn't expected to, but I knew that I had to look, if only to preserve the illusion.

"I didn't see anyone," I told him as I walked back to my desk. I figured that I'd gotten about all the information I was going to get from him, so I decided to make my pitch.

"All right, Mr. Riegel, I'll do whatever I can to help you, but I get twenty-five dollars a day plus expenses." Another lie; the only way I ever got that kind of money was when I hit a parlay on a couple of ball games. "Is that okay with you?"

"That's fine, Mr. Endicott," he answered. "And you can do whatever you think necessary, regardless of expense, to find out who's trying to kill me. But before you do anything, you've got to put me someplace where they can't find me."

"You mean a hideout?" I asked. It was a rhetorical question because I was way ahead of him. I'd already figured he needed safekeeping, and I knew exactly where to put him. An old professor of mine from my collegiate days had a small estate on the north shore of Long Island. He'd asked me to keep an eye on the place while he went on a year's sabbatical to Europe. I usually dropped by there once or twice a week and knew it would be ideal for Riegel for a few days while I looked into his little problem.

"Yes, that's it," he said, "a hideout. But you'll have to make sure that man's not following us also."

"Don't worry about that," I responded, with a bit more confidence than I actually felt. "I think I can take care of both of these little matters rather easily." I must have sounded like Bogart reassuring Mary Astor.

Getting rid of whoever it was who was tailing him might not prove too difficult if I timed it right. I'd spent a lot of hours staked out in front of sleazy hotels while my mark engaged in sport within, and when you have that much time on your hands you tend to daydream and fantasize quite a bit. Among the images of Lizabeth Scott, Jane Russell, and half a dozen other Hollywood stars who helped while away those long watches were occasional flights of fancy into the world of the romantic private eye. And in one of them I'd come up with what I thought was a great idea about how to dump a tail. All I wanted was an opportunity to make the dream a reality, and this was it.

If any guy in this city was on foot I could shake him in less time than it takes Robinson to steal second, so it didn't take a genius to figure that either Gray Suit or an accomplice had a car ready to take up the chase if Alfred and I hit the street on wheels. That's exactly what I intended to do, and that's where my little plan came into play. A couple of phone calls got the ball rolling. The first, to the underground garage around the corner where I kept my car in lieu of some Manhattan side street, brought Billy, the day attendant who delivers to my front door for a small compensation and a chance to be part of the detective milieu. Within five minutes he'd pulled up to the front of the building, double parking my 1950 DeSoto and darting away as though he expected to be met by a hail of bullets. While Billy performed his mission I made another call, this one to an old friend of the family, Enrico Franscotti, senior partner of Franscotti and Son, Wholesale Produce Distributors. Uncle Rico had his warehouse on the Lower West Side docks, and it was there that I intended to drop our shadow. A brief explanation to Rico, Jr. set everything in motion at his end, and with hardly a further word to enlighten Riegel, I had him in tow and we headed down the stairs.

We made a beeline for the car, and since the engine was running all I had to do was throw it in gear and we were off within fifteen seconds of reaching the street. I hadn't had time to look around when we emerged from the building, but now that we were moving I afforded myself the luxury of a quick glance in the rearview mirror before we turned down West 45th Street toward the Hudson River. My hasty quest for visual confirmation of Alfred's sinister shadow brought no results, so I turned the corner and headed for Ninth Avenue, where I swung the car southward and proceeded downtown. Riegel began to pepper me with questions, but I put him off with protestations about concentrating on locating our tail, if in fact there was one to locate.

By the time we passed West 30th Street, I thought I'd found my man. Just two cars back was a dark blue 1953 Pontiac that had taken great pains to place itself in close proximity to my car. Having weaved frantically through traffic for half a dozen blocks in order to close the gap between us, the Pontiac had now settled down to a more leisurely pace and had maintained its position for half a dozen more. Although tempted to negotiate a few turns in order to test my conclusion, I chose instead to seek confirmation from my passenger. Tilting the rearview mirror, I directed Riegel's attention to the Pontiac and asked him if he could identify either of the occupants. His reaction was almost instantaneous.

"That's him," he shouted, "the driver! He's the one I saw outside the police station and again when I got off the subway. I'm sure of it!"

"Well, that solves the problem of making sure we lead the right guy into our trap," I responded. "Now listen; I'm going to swing down toward the wharves in a minute or two, and then we'll be rid of these clowns. You just keep an eye on them, and if we have to stop at a light or something and one of them gets out of the car, you give me a holler and I'll get us the hell out of there in a hurry. Otherwise, just sit tight and watch how easy it is to lose new friends." Spoken like a true hard-boiled gumshoe, the sweaty palms and knot in the stomach notwithstanding.

I continued down Ninth to where it angles into Greenwich, while Riegel kept a watch on the Pontiac. As I went down Greenwich he advised me that we'd shed first one, then the second car that separated us from our tail. A glance in the side mirror told me that they were still keeping their distance. I couldn't have asked for more if I'd written a script. I just hoped that they wouldn't decide to close the gap and get right on my rear bumper.

We were there in a matter of minutes. Laight Street is one of those narrow byways that lead down to the docks in every port from San Francisco to New York. Loading platforms extended out into the street from warehouses that lined both sides of the road from one end to the other. As I eased the car into a turn, I readjusted the rearview mirror to ensure the proper line of sight while controlling the urge to step on the gas and pull away. About halfway down the block I could see the protruding hood and cab of a large produce wagon, with Rico, Jr., seated nonchalantly behind the wheel. The remainder of the vehicle lay hidden in the depths of the Franscotti warehouse.

I glanced in the mirror and saw the Pontiac pull into the street behind us, then speed up momentarily and slow to a near crawl to keep distance between us. He was now about a hundred feet behind, obviously trying to appear inconspicuous; just another guy out for a midmorning drive.

As I passed young Rico I had the fleeting fear that he'd pull out too soon. But he had the presence of mind to wait, and at just the right time I could see him begin moving into the street. He angled the truck across the road so that no one could get by, with the obvious intent of backing the vehicle up to the loading platform that abutted the warehouse entrance. I'd seen the Pontiac start to speed up when the truck first pulled out of the chute, and now I could hear the screech of brakes as Gray Suit realized he couldn't make it past. I gunned the DeSoto and swung in under the elevated West Side Highway, my mind's eye picturing some gunman trying to reason with an enraged Italian whose feigned broken English made less sense than Milt Stock waving Abrams home against the Phillies on the final day in the 1950 season. Everything had worked out to a T, and within minutes I had negotiated the ramp onto the elevated highway and made my way around the southern tip of the island to FDR Drive. I checked the mirror to see that no one followed, and thus assured I quickly headed for the Williamsburg Bridge. As I crossed the East River, I occupied my mind with visions of Barry Fitzgerald bringing the homicidal Garzah to justice from the girders of the bridge that rose up all around me. Alfred intruded upon the serenity of my thoughts.

"Now what do we do?" he asked, relief in his voice at the realization that he was, at least for the moment, free of his pursuers.

"We stash you, exactly as planned," I answered. "We'll be there in about two hours. But for now, suppose we go over everything just to make sure you haven't overlooked something that might be important."

I cut across Queens and then along the north shore of Long Island, all the while questioning Riegel and trying to discover that one piece of information that would give me a starting point from which to begin my inquiry. As usual, Alfred was about as helpful as a sore-armed pitcher to the Dodger brain trust. He merely regurgitated what he'd already told me about the two attempts upon his life, leaving me to pry into the periphery of his existence for the necessary clue. As it turned out, Alfred's life was as bland as a two cents plain. He had no relatives to speak of, had never been married, rarely dated, and kept pretty much to himself. He didn't smoke, and when he drank it was on a social occasion no less extraordinary than the death of a pope or president. He thought gambling the bane of the most hideously wicked and shunned all forms from the ponies to the office World Series pool. In short, he'd closed down every avenue of investigation that one would normally expect to pursue when repeated attempts had been made on someone's life. But there were no jealous husbands, no monstrous gambling debts, no seamy side to the life of the middle-aged printer from the Upper East Side.

By the time we arrived on the grounds of the estate in Glen Cove, I still hadn't found out anything. It took only a few minutes before Riegel was safely ensconced in the house, with instructions to remain where he was, answer the phone only after letting it ring an agreed-upon number of times, and to ignore anyone who might come to the door. Having told him that I'd try to stop by the next day, I headed back to the city. With no leads, I decided that my best bet was the police. Perhaps Alfred had told them something he'd forgotten to tell me, or maybe they just might be able to point me in a direction I hadn't yet considered.

As I mentioned, I didn't know a Lieutenant Harrison, but I do know some uniforms. Most of them are old high school buddies, not professional contacts, and they pound beats in Brooklyn and lower Manhattan, not the better neighborhoods uptown. One of them, Sergeant Dom Vallone, worked out of the Fourteenth Precinct near Penn Station, so it was toward midtown that I turned when I recrossed the river from Queens.

Vallone was on duty, doing the front end of a double shift, and within minutes I was seated at his desk in the personnel section. I told him everything I knew about the shooting incident and asked him to locate Harrison and try to get the details of his report for me.

"Charlie," he said, and it sounded almost like a whine, "I could get in a lot of trouble for this." There was a plea in his voice, but I knew he was going to do it.

"Come on, Dom, you owe me," I reminded him unnecessarily, thinking back to the time I'd helped cover for him when an ill-conceived night of revelry had almost gotten him thrown off the force. I never lose a marker.

Dom and I go back a long way, and I'm sure he would have helped me eventually, but I was in a hurry and figured a small nudge might speed things up. It did, and about twenty minutes later Vallone was back at his desk, a smirk on his face and sarcasm in his voice.

"Boy, has somebody ever sold you a bill of goods, Sherlock! I sure hope you got paid in advance, old buddy, 'cause it looks like your horse just pulled up lame."

"What are you talking about?" I asked, mentally kicking myself for having forgotten to get a retainer from Riegel.

Vallone allowed himself a small chuckle. "In the first place, there have been no reports of any shootings on the Upper East Side this morning; and your Lieutenant Harrison is about as real as Peter Pan. At least here in Manhattan he is; there's one works vice out of Queens, but he's been on sick leave for nearly two weeks. Tell me, though," he added sardonically, "do you do this for a living? Sleuthing, I mean. We could use a guy like you on the force." He was almost in stitches when he'd finished.

"What? What do you *mean*?" My mind was reeling, and I almost shouted the question at him.

"Just what I said," he answered, a little sympathy creeping into his voice as he registered my shock. "I checked every precinct uptown, even the ones on the West Side, and the only reported shooting was some domestic quarrel over on Tenth Avenue; and that was at 3:00 A.M., and the guy was taken to Roosevelt Hospital and his old lady's been charged. As for your Lieutenant Harrison—well, he just doesn't exist. Except for the guy in Queens, all the Harrisons on the force are uniforms, but none are in Manhattan. You've been had, Charlie old boy: hook, line, and sinker."

"But this is crazy," I protested, as if Vallone could do something to restore some semblance of order to the whole affair. "Why would anyone want to invent a story like this?"

"That I can't say," he responded. "Probably the only person who can help you out on that one is the guy who conned you in the first place. Where is he, anyhow?"

"He's . . . he's right where I can find him," I answered, stopping myself before I told Dom any more than I already had about my seeming gullibility. Rising from the chair I bid him farewell, suffered a few parting gibes at my professional competence, and hurried to my car.

I checked my watch. It was 2:15, still near the middle of the working day. I crossed town to Third Avenue, then went up a few blocks to East 32nd Street. Jacobsen and Dunlop were housed in a fifteen-story building that was dwarfed on either side by enormous skyscrapers. They occupied the top four floors, and I went directly to the corporate offices located on the eleventh. I hoped to get some personal information regarding Riegel, specifically concerning his emotional and mental stability. I was beginning to wonder if old Alfred had both oars in the water.

After making my way through two secretaries and an administrative assistant, I was granted an interview—with Alfred Riegel! But this wasn't my Alfred Riegel. This was a short, white-haired man well into his fifties, and it was clear from the start that he didn't have the vaguest idea of what I was talking about. I ended the interview as quickly as I could, then sauntered through the outer offices of Jacobsen and Dunlop, trying to leave behind an impression of cocky self-assurance. In truth, I was so confused I was lucky to find my way down to the street.

My mind whirled as I drove back across town. I couldn't make sense out of any of it, not the phony identity, the faked shooting, or the little game of hide-and-seek with the dark blue Pontiac and its two occupants. By the time I'd driven to my office, however, I'd begun to recall a few incongruities in the story of one Alfred Riegel, self-styled Jean Valjean of the twentieth century.

Why, for instance, had he come all the way downtown to find a detective if someone had tried to kill him up on East 77th Street? Surely there were plenty of reputable firms uptown that could handle something like that. Why turn to a nobody like me unless he wanted an inexperienced hand dealt into the game? And if he'd noticed the tail as soon as he'd left the police station, why hadn't he turned around and gone right back inside the station house and alerted the cops then and there? And finally, if someone really was out to kill Riegel, or whoever he was, how could you account for all the amateurish bungling? A pro wouldn't have missed once, let alone twice, and an amateur wouldn't have had the nerve to try murder on a crowded subway platform or a street filled with rush-hour pedestrians. On the other hand, he had been followed. I'd seen that for myself. None of it came together, so when I'd parked the car in the garage and come around the corner to my office, all I had on my mind was a few stiff belts.

Sometimes even the dullest of minds is permitted a ray of illuminating light, and I guess my moment had at last arrived. *The house*, my brain screamed, and suddenly it hit me. I'd let the inside man of a burglary ring into a house I'd promised to keep an eye on! Who needed to bypass alarm systems or other sophisticated apparatus when you had Charles Endicott, private eye, to just let you in the front door! I bolted up the stairs, intent on calling the Glen Cove police in the hope that they could get there before the place was picked clean. Cursing myself aloud I fumbled with the key, finally opening the door just as the phone began to ring. I picked it up in a near panic.

"Hello! Look, this is an emergency, so . . ." I began, but was cut short by a sharp command.

"Shut up, Endicott, and listen real good. That was a cute trick you pulled with the truck today, but if you want to know how cute it really was then you better turn on your radio and listen to the news. A friend of yours is the top story. We'll get back to you." The sharp click as he hung up made me wince, even though the truculent voice it replaced hadn't exactly been music to my ears.

What the hell was he talking about, I wondered? I hesitated for a moment, glancing first at the radio, then at the clock on the wall. It read 3:20, still ten minutes before any of the local stations would give the headlines and a brief news summary. Had someone followed us out to the Island and gotten to my client despite the precautions I'd taken? Or was this just a ploy to keep me hooked so I wouldn't call the police? I decided better safe than sorry and had the operator hook me up with the village police in Glen Cove. I told them who I was and that I had reason to believe that a burglary might be in progress at a local residence, then gave them the name of the realtor who held a set of keys so they could get in without any trouble. I also said I was on my way myself to conduct an inventory to see what, if anything, had been taken. Actually, I was going to wait a few minutes. I wanted to hear that news broadcast and also to be there to answer the phone should my belligerent caller ring back after I'd heard whatever it was he wanted me to hear. Besides, if someone actually had stripped the house, I wasn't overly anxious to tell the police or anyone else about my role in the affair.

I snapped on the radio and it finished warming up just as the announcer broke for the news. I listened as a nasal voice told of the pending return of American ex-POWs from Korea and the U.S. offer of $100,000 and political asylum to the first communist pilot to deliver a MIG to the free world. Before long he'd finished with the world news and gotten to the local report.

"In the top news story on the local scene," he continued, "an explosion on the Lower West Side has claimed the lives of two men and injured several others. Nearly the entire ground floor of the Franscotti and Son produce warehouse on Laight Street was reported destroyed, and police are speculating that the explosion may be linked to local labor unrest in the dockside area." The voice droned on, but I wasn't listening.

My brain was numb with the thought that two men, possibly old and dear friends, had lost their lives because of something I'd done while trying to play detective. When the phone rang, my arm moved slowly toward the receiver. I picked it up but didn't say anything.

"Okay, Endicott," said the same gravelly voice that had called earlier, "now you know that we don't play games. Where's Armstrong?"

"Who?" I asked, my voice almost choking on the word.

"Don't be cute with us," came the quick reply. "You know we ain't foolin' around."

"I'm not trying to be cute," I answered hastily. "If you mean the guy who came to my office this morning, he told me his name was Riegel."

"Riegel, Armstrong, it don't matter. Where did you take him?"

My mind raced for an answer. "I took him to Penn

Station," I lied. "He told me he was being followed and offered me a hundred bucks if I could shake his tail. I don't know where he went after I dropped him off."

"I guess you don't listen too good, do you, Endicott?" was the reply. "One more time now. We want Armstrong."

"Look," I pleaded, "don't you think if I knew where he was I'd tell you? He doesn't mean anything to me." Maybe reason would work.

"That don't wash," said the voice. "When we got onto him he made for you like you was his long-lost brother." A pause to let reason expire on fallow ground. "Now, you got until midnight tonight to have Armstrong back in your office. Otherwise, you're gonna lose a couple of fingers . . . and maybe a few other parts along with 'em. Remember, you got 'til midnight. Then you're dog meat." The phone died in my hand.

I never knew that when you were really scared your legs actually started shaking, but I was and my legs were. I knew I wouldn't look good in an Alpo can so I had to make some quick decisions. I had no doubt that these guys were serious, and the police were always my ace in the hole, but I still had over eight hours before the deadline. I decided to use the time to try and sort things out. But first I had to clear up matters in Glen Cove, and I had to do it without my new friends tagging along. It wouldn't do for them to see me talking to the police just yet, and on the off chance that my mysterious client was still at the house I certainly didn't want to lead them right to their prey.

As I look back on things now, I guess that's where

I made my biggest mistake. I should have gone straight to the cops right then, but I was angry, scared, and not thinking very clearly. In any case, hindsight is a cross all of us must bear from time to time. I just wish mine weren't so heavy.

When I'd decided on a course of action I called Billy at the garage. I asked him if he had a tenant who was out of town for a few days and whose car was thus available for loan. When he'd answered in the affirmative and identified the auto as a 1952 green Chevy sedan, I told him to bring it around and park it on West 45th, just off the corner. He was to keep the engine running and remain at the wheel until he saw me turn the corner, then leap from the car and run back to the garage via the long way around.

Having completed my instructions to Billy I hung up the phone, moved to the front room and kept watch at the window until I saw the green Chevy go by. Then I went down to the street and began a leisurely stroll toward West 45th. When I got to the corner I pretended to cross the street and saw Billy jump from the car. I immediately ran to the vehicle, got in, and gunned it down the block. As I passed Billy I saw him wave, and in the rearview mirror caught sight of an obviously distraught hood gazing menacingly after me while giving a hasty come-on sign to a motorized companion. He was wasting his time. I was out of sight within seconds, cutting around corners and darting down side streets until I was at the river.

By the time I got out to the Glen Cove house, only a single patrolman was waiting for me. Riegel/Armstrong wasn't there, of course, so I began a quick inventory of the premises. As I went from room to room it became apparent that nothing had been taken. When I'd covered the whole house I informed the cop accordingly, then listened to a ten-minute lecture on the propriety of wasting the taxpayers' assets and the limited manpower resources of the local constabulary. I staved off questions as to where I'd gotten the tip on the burglary by pleading professional sanctuary, saying only that a neighbor who requested anonymity had called and asked me to act on his behalf. After a final warning, the patrolman left and I made straight for the kitchen.

While I'd been going through the house minutes before I'd noticed a plate and glass in the sink that hadn't been there when I'd dropped my client off earlier in the day. Obviously he'd taken the time to fix himself something to eat and drink before he went on the lam. Using a dish towel I carefully lifted the items from the sink, wrapped them in some more towels, then put them in a carton I'd taken from the pantry. Having sniffed the telltale odor of scotch in the glass, I also took three open bottles of the whiskey from the bar and put them in the carton with my other trophies. Then I headed back to the city.

With a rookie on first base, the hit-and-run play on, and the ball hit to right field, an experienced shortstop will sometimes race to the second-base bag and fake receiving a throw, as though the ball hadn't gone through into the outfield. If done properly the rookie will go into a slide, thus killing any chance of making it to third even though the hit-and-run was executed perfectly. It's a real sucker play, and you have to be a bush leaguer to fall for it. Well, I had nothing on that rookie. I was only beginning to realize how badly I'd been had, how I'd helped Armstrong shake his pursuers and switch them onto myself, and how I'd gotten at least two men killed in the process. Playing at detective was a lot easier than working at it.

I must have broken every speed restriction between Glen Cove and Manhattan, because seven o'clock found me back in Dom Vallone's office. He gave me a questioning glance, raising eyebrows for emphasis, when I entered carrying the box of paraphernalia, but I beat him to the punch when I shot out my query as I laid the carton on his desk.

"Have you come up with anything on that explosion down on Laight Street yet?"

He was momentarily taken aback. "Uh, well . . . we don't have anything solid to go on, if that's what you mean, but we're pretty sure that it had something to do with a labor dispute on the docks. Of course, we haven't had anything quite this violent go down there in years. But what's all this to you?" His face reflected the confusion that must have addled his brain.

"Suppose I were to tell you that it had nothing to do with a labor dispute at all, that it was cold-blooded murder, plain and simple, and that I can deliver the killers into your hands if you'll do me one little favor?"

"Now hold it right there, Sherlock," he exclaimed. "If you know anything about a crime you're duty-bound as a citizen—"

"I'll deliver these guys to you personally, Dom," I broke in, "not to the cop on the beat and not to the boys from homicide, but to you. You'll get all the credit. But if you try and hold me, I'll deny the whole thing and you'll wind up with egg on your face instead of a likely promotion."

"Oh, come on, Charlie," he said in an exasperated

tone, but I knew that the mention of a promotion had struck a chord. I stoked the fire before the flame could die down.

"You'd be sure to get out of that uniform and into plainclothes," I continued, "but you'll have to do it my way, Dom. What do you say?"

"Just what is this little favor you want?" was his reply.

"Have your lab boys go over the stuff in this box for prints, then see if they can match them with anyone you've got in your files. If not, send them along to Washington and try the Feds. I think some of the prints they'll find on this stuff belong to a guy named Armstrong, and he's the one I'm interested in. Try that name first."

"This is crazy, Charlie," he said. "I don't see you for months on end, and then you come in here twice in one day and ask for my help. And on nothing less than murder, for God's sake! What gives? Who's this guy Armstrong? The one who gave you that cock-and-bull story about a shooting this morning? Is he the one responsible for bombing that warehouse? If you know something, Charlie, spill it now." I could tell from his voice that it was the last gasp prior to capitulation.

"He's my client," I answered, "but I don't think he had anything to do with that bombing. There are only a couple of things in the box, Dom. Surely you've got a friend down in the lab who could dust them for you. Then just tie them in to some ongoing investigation when you send them up to records."

"You've got it all worked out, haven't you?" he asked sarcastically, but I could see the wheels turning, weighing the pros and cons of my offer. After a short pause he broke the silence. "Okay, Charlie, okay," he acquiesced, "but I can get canned for this. Another thing, though: this ain't the movies. It'll take awhile to get this through to records, maybe a couple of hours. If we have to go to Washington it could be days before we get an answer."

"Try and make it hours, Dom," I answered. "Here's where you can reach me." I gave him the phone number of the house in Glen Cove, adding that I was going to my apartment to pick up a few things before going out to the Island.

"All right," he said. "I'll try to get back to you before I go off duty at midnight." I left him peering into the box, still not completely sure he was doing the right thing.

I made my way to the car and then back to the garage. The only thing I wanted from my apartment was my Colt service revolver. I should have taken it with me when I left the last time, but I'd just plain forgotten. I hadn't used it in years and was never any good with it anyway, but I wanted to be heeled, regardless. If I had to use it, fate would determine who was in more danger, me or my target.

The one thing that concerned me now was the possibility that the guys I'd shaken would be waiting for me. But I figured that I could talk my way out of that one, since they still needed me to locate Armstrong for them. I counted on conning them with the story that I'd been afraid that if I'd found their boy and they'd been too close that he'd have bolted before I could hand him over to them. They might not believe me, and I might get knocked around a bit, but I could also tell them that I'd made contact with Armstrong and laid the groundwork for a meeting later that night. All they'd have to do is keep their distance for just a little bit longer and I'd deliver him to their doorstep. I hoped that would be enough of an inducement for them to give me some operating room, and if they did I was sure I could dump them one last time on my way to Glen Cove.

When I got to the garage neither Billy nor anyone else was on duty, so I parked the car in the first empty slot I saw, left the keys in the attendant's shack, and emerged into the cool night. As I walked the short distance to my place, a brisk breeze sprang up and helped clear my head, and for the first time that day I remembered my plans for the night and the fact that the Dodgers were now under way across the river in Brooklyn. "The best-laid plans," I muttered to myself as I reached the entranceway.

When I'd climbed the stairs I cautiously opened the door and moved silently to my desk. Sliding open the top drawer, I reached in, and from among the scattered papers and cobwebs withdrew my revolver. I fumbled in the dark while trying to load it, then turned on the light and checked each room to be sure the two hoods weren't lying in wait for me. As I emerged from the front room, the phone began to ring. Too soon for Dom, I thought, so it must be my shadows. I picked up the receiver.

"You better go take a look in your car, Endicott," came the familiar gravelly voice, followed by the click that served as his signature.

My car, I thought angrily, what the hell had they done to my car! Pocketing my weapon, I ran down the stairs and quick-stepped back to the garage. There was still no attendant on duty, and the interior was dim and eerie in the pale light emanating from behind the grid-covered electric bulbs. Warily, I turned toward the slot where Billy always parked my DeSoto. Approaching the vehicle, I froze, recalling the warehouse and contemplating how easy it would be for someone with such a predilection to wire my car door with a bomb. The exterior looked untouched, and after glancing about in the shadows I chanced a peek through the window on the driver's side.

There was someone in the front seat, slumped over on the passenger side. I momentarily forgot my fear and jerked open the door. When the light came on I saw that it was Billy. What was left of his head was splattered on the passenger door and in the footrest area on the far side.

I turned away, retching. For a moment I stood there, gulping in air and trying to blot out the vision that forced itself to the forefront of my consciousness like a battering ram. My anger welled up until I thought I'd burst, and it served to quell my heaving stomach.

I ran to the attendant's shack, but as I reached for the phone the germ of an idea began to form in my mind. Instead of lifting the receiver from its cradle, I picked up the keys that I'd deposited on the desk only minutes before, got into the Chevy and started up the engine. I turned right out of the garage and, seeing a space only about thirty feet up the street from the entranceway, parked the car. Then I walked back to the shack and called the police.

As I waited for them the idea took shape in my head, and by the time the first squad car had arrived I knew exactly what I was going to do. I told the police that I'd just come down to get my car and found the boy where he lay. I ventured the opinion that it looked as though someone had tried to hold him up, that he'd offered some form of resistance, and that he'd then been taken into the bowels of the garage and silenced. They seemed to agree, and after advising me that they'd have to impound my car they let me go on my way.

I went back to the Chevy, and as I pulled out into the street I could see that I'd picked up my tail again. I made as though I was trying to shake them in the downtown evening traffic, then turned in the direction of the Lower East Side. I had to slow down a few times to keep my shadows with me. They were amateurs at the tailing game. Murder seemed to be more in their line of business.

I was heading for a bar owned by Gino Langella, a long-time acquaintance. The place was a dive and merely fronted for a policy and bookie operation that Gino ran under the protection of his father. The elder Langella was always in the news, copping the Fifth in front of one grand jury or another, capo famiglia and nobody to trifle with. Gino, on the other hand, was nothing, a punk in anybody's book. But he was family, and I knew that would outweigh all other considerations.

I hadn't much use for Gino because a long time ago he'd stepped between me and a girl I'd been going with for more than a year. It had hurt when she'd left me, but it hurt worse when I found out that after he'd finished with her he'd pushed her into one of his father's businesses. The last I'd heard, Terry was hooking somewhere on Eighth Avenue.

I'd kept up my acquaintance with Gino through casual contact, and he still regarded me as a friend. He and his family were going to be the instruments of my revenge.

I made my way down Second Avenue still seething with rage. I couldn't get the sight of Billy off my mind, and my anger went a long way toward offsetting the fear that also gripped me. I knew that I was playing with something worse than fire, that I was in way over my head and didn't belong in this league; but I couldn't just walk away, even if I was overmatched. I owed Billy and the Franscottis something . . . maybe even my own life for the ones I'd taken from them.

My whole plan was a gamble, just the stupid kind of bet that an inept gumshoe would make. But my rage fed my courage, and pretty soon I was in front of Gino's bar, aptly named The Last Stop. As I parked at the curb I tried not to think that this could be the last night of my life.

Walking to the door, my peripheral vision caught sight of the now familiar Pontiac as it pulled into a parking space at the far end of the block. When I entered the bar, Gino was holding court at a table in back, and a wave of my arm brought him out of the dim recesses, wide grin on his face and hand extended in friendship.

"Charlie," he exclaimed, "how the hell are ya? What brings you down here?"

I grasped his hand and resisted the temptation to tell him I was slumming. "How are you, Gino? I was in the neighborhood and thought I'd drop by and say hello. Haven't seen you for quite a while, you know."

"Don't I know it! And I'm glad you stopped in. Let me buy you a drink. Eddie!" he shouted to the bartender. "Set 'em up for Charlie here. He's on the house all night."

"Thanks," I said, and we walked to the bar. Within moments we were done with the amenities and engaged in animated conversation, but not so much so that I failed to notice the tall man in the gray suit enter and take a stool at the end of the bar. He ordered a beer and nursed it, feigning a lack of interest in both us and the environs.

For the next twenty or thirty minutes, Gino and I talked over old times, and he even managed to get in a wisecrack or two about Terry. There was no mistaking Gino. The stench of garbage clung to him. But I laughed indulgently, matching him drink for drink, and when I was ready to go I made my apologies and told him that I wanted to lay ten on Chuck Davey in tomorrow's fight.

"How about walking me to my car, Gino?" I asked. "I left my wallet in the glove compartment." He readily agreed, and as we stepped out I threw my arm around his shoulder and reiterated how great it had been to see him; two bosom buddies, one a little bit in his cups, stretching out a farewell.

When we got to the car I remembered I had a sawbuck in my pocket, and we laughed over my forgetfulness. It reminded me of an incident between us some years ago, and we waxed nostalgic over that final story as I caught sight of tall Gray Suit when he exited and hurried down the street to the waiting Pontiac. Sure that he was reunited with his companion, I bade Gino a final good-bye and got into my borrowed vehicle.

As I pulled out into the road I saw the lights of the Pontiac come on and Gino waving to me from the sidewalk. I soon had my boys in tow, and it took me only ten minutes to lose them in the Broadway traffic. From there I darted across town, over the Queensboro Bridge and out to the Island. I turned on the car radio in an effort to clear my mind and automatically sought out the Dodger game. They were through five innings, and Brooklyn was leading. Roe was on the mound, and he had a shutout going. At least something was right with the world.

By the time I'd gotten out to Glen Cove, the game was over. The Dodgers had won 5–1, Roe losing his shutout when Kluszewski hit a home run in the top of the ninth. I'd pushed it all the way out to the Island so it was still shy of eleven o'clock when I arrived at the house. I immediately called Dom at the precinct.

"Any luck yet?" I inquired when I'd finally been put through to him.

"Nope," he said, "but we should have something pretty soon. There was a bit of a backlog down in the lab, but we got a couple of sets of prints off the bottles and some others off the glass and plate. Records is trying to make a match right now, and if we've got them on file here we should have an answer within the hour."

"Fine," I replied, "I'll be waiting," and hung up the phone.

It was eleven by then, so I went into the living room and turned on the television for the late-night news report. I didn't have long to wait before the newscaster got to the story I knew was coming.

"Gino Langella," he intoned, "son of reputed mob boss Angelo Langella, was shot and killed tonight as he emerged from his restaurant on Bond Street on Manhattan's Lower East Side. Witnesses stated that the younger Langella had just stepped outside when shots from a passing vehicle cut him down. The car was described as a dark sedan of unknown make.

Police are treating it as a gangland-related slaying and are investigating."

I turned off the set and walked to the bar, where I poured myself a stiff shot of rye and held it aloft in mock salute. Well, Terry wasn't even, but she'd moved up a rung on the ladder of retribution. I don't know how long I stood there, thinking of her and the irony of Gino Langella breathing his last in the gutter, but the ring of the phone pulled me from my reverie.

Dom's voice came barking through the receiver. "Charlie, we got a make on those prints! They match with a guy named Harvey Armstrong. We've got one bust on him but no convictions. Seems as though he lends his talents out to the locals on an as-needed basis. And guess what his talent is: he's a chemist!"

A chemist, I thought. That explains the stained fingers I so readily assumed were evidence of printer's ink; and it also explains why he was on the run. The only place the mob had need of a chemist was in its drug operation, and if a certain chemist decided to venture out on his own with some of their cash or uncut heroin, it stood to reason that they wouldn't just let him walk away. He must have stashed whatever he'd taken, otherwise they'd have just killed him and been done with it. Instead, they were trying to scare him into returning the swag he'd stolen. The killing would come later. They don't give intentional passes to .230 hitters in the big leagues.

"How did he beat the rap?" I asked, wanting to keep the conversation going while I gathered my thoughts.

"Lack of evidence. He was in the building when we closed down a pierside narcotics factory, but we couldn't tie him in directly with the operation."

"Okay, Dom, that's what I wanted to know," I said. "I've got one or two more things to take care of before I can complete my end of the bargain." The lie came easy. The deal we'd made came before Billy. But his death had changed things, and now the only bargain I had was with the ghost of a seventeen-year-old boy whose only crime had been that he'd wanted to escape from the mundane life that trapped so many of us in the big city.

I brushed aside Vallone's protestations that I was reneging on my part of the deal, reiterating that I had to set things up before I could deliver the goods.

"How long, Charlie?" he asked, and it was obvious that he doubted that I had any intention of coming through for him.

"A couple of hours, Dom, no more," I answered. "I should have everything wrapped up by the time you come back on duty tomorrow. You on days again?"

"Yeah," he responded, annoyance creeping into his voice. I decided to cut it short before he got really rankled.

"Good, I'll call you as soon as you're on watch. I've got to run now. Don't worry about a thing." I hung up before he could answer.

Remembering that I hadn't eaten all day, I settled on a couple of cans of soup from the pantry. While they heated on the stove I stepped out onto the veranda. It was chilly now, and a mist from Long Island Sound hung low over the row of pines that separated the grounds from those of its neighbor. I thought of everything that had happened that day, and as I did my resentment and hatred of Harvey Armstrong grew. He'd been the cause of all of this, and I wished that I could have the satisfaction of making him pay for it. He hadn't been part of the plan I'd concocted after finding Billy, but thanks to Dom I now knew that he was no more innocent than the hood who had done the killing or the one who had planted the bomb at the Franscotti warehouse. He'd known who he was dealing with and how they'd react when he conned me into losing them for him. He hadn't given my life a second thought. I went back into the house.

As I sat down at the kitchen table and ate, I studied my options. By the time I'd finished, I'd made up my mind. I went to the phone and called Angelo Langella.

It took awhile to get through, his lieutenants shielding him from the reporters and media people trying to get a scoop on the gangster's reaction to his son's murder. But when I said that I had information on who had performed this civic service, they told me to call back in ten minutes. The old man knew me from the days when I'd hung around with Gino, so I was sure that he'd talk to me.

I called back and was directed to be at Pier 4 in Fulton Terminal in Brooklyn in one hour. I barely made it, and as soon as I'd stopped the car the lights from another vehicle that had been parked in the shadows flashed on and off. I got out and walked toward it, and as I did the back door sprang open. When I came abreast of the door I heard a gruff voice tell me to get in, and once I had it was evident that Angelo Langella was not in the car. The door closed automatically, and I found myself seated beside a hulk of a man whose eyes seemed to gleam in the dark. The driver was a shadow in the front seat.

"What do you know?" asked the hulk in the same hoarse voice that had commanded my presence in the vehicle.

"I can only tell Mr. Langella," I answered, and as soon as I had spoken the car was started and we pulled off the pier. It was obvious that they'd been told to take me to their boss, with no rough stuff, if I didn't immediately volunteer the promised information.

We drove into the Boro Hall section, turning onto Montague Street, where we pulled in behind a dark limousine.

"Mr. Langella's waitin'," said the voice, and the door opened. I stepped into the street and saw that the back door of the limo was also ajar. I walked directly to it, got in, and closed the door behind me myself. This was the final act in the play. Whether it came off or not, the curtain would come down.

"Hello, Charlie," he said, and I recognized both the voice and countenance of Angelo Langella. He was dressed in a dark summer suit, meticulously groomed and civil in demeanor. It was hard to associate this dapper man with prostitution, drugs, and murder. He looked more like a benign Gene Lockhart than Murder, Inc. "I haven't seen you for a long time. It's a shame we have to meet again on a night like this. But what can you know about it?"

I extended my sympathies, then gave him the whole story. I was working as a private detective, I told him, and had been doing a favor for his son. Gino had heard a rumor that the two hoods who had been commissioned to find Armstrong had located him but had been bought off by the chemist, and he'd asked me to look into it for him. He'd wanted to protect the interests of some unidentified friends, I continued, and he'd told me only that Armstrong had stolen something from them. I'd done the job and not only found out that the gunmen were now working for

Armstrong but that their boss also told them to eliminate both Gino and myself to help cover his tracks. They'd twice tried to get me, I added, killing some of my friends instead.

We were now driving aimlessly through the Fort Greene section of Brooklyn, Langella's guardians trailing about a block behind us. The old man had remained stoic while I spoke, but I'd detected an inadvertent twitch of an eye muscle when I'd said that Armstrong had ordered his son's execution.

Gino and I had agreed to meet at his bar last night, I went on, and I'd given him the details of what I'd uncovered along with a warning to be careful.

"Gino never said anything about this to me," he interjected. It came as a statement, but I knew Langella expected a response. I'd anticipated such a query and was ready for it.

"He wanted me to look into it to be sure, Mr. Langella. It was only a rumor, and Gino didn't want to say anything that might get two of his friends' employees into trouble without being sure about it. It was a pretty serious accusation."

The old man grunted an acknowledgment, then gazed at me for a long time. When he finally spoke his voice was soft, and I could detect a note of sorrow in it for the first time. "He was a good son, Charlie, but always a little headstrong, always wanting to do things on his own, as though he had to impress me; me, his own father." He paused, then added, "Thank you for your help, Charlie. This won't be forgotten."

But I wasn't finished. When I'd slowed down in the traffic on my way to The Last Stop I'd had more on my mind than keeping my shadow close. I'd wanted the license plate number of the Pontiac, and when

I'd stopped at a corner, the streetlight had enabled me to pick it up. Now I gave it to Langella, with the added information that I was sure the two killers were lurking in the neighborhood near my apartment, intent on completing the job Armstrong had given them.

He thanked me again, then advised me to stay away from the apartment for a while. Obviously he thought that I was as stupid as I'd made out his son to be.

Langella's boys took me back to my car, and I cruised the streets of Brooklyn until about three in the morning, when the news came over the radio announcing the midtown slaying of two men, one in a car and the other in a nearby doorway. The report left no doubt in my mind that it was Gray Suit and his companion. I breathed a long sigh of relief and headed home. Angelo Langella had bought my story, not bothering to have it checked out. He ordered the execution of two rogue gunmen who had, to his way of thinking, betrayed a sacred trust when they'd tried to cross the organization. He'd gotten his son's killers and at the same time performed a service for the family. It wouldn't be so quick or easy when they caught up to Armstrong, but that didn't matter. They wouldn't believe anything he had to say anyway, so I didn't care what kind of story he told them. And I knew they'd get him, sooner or later.

It was nearly three-thirty when I turned up Broadway, but the marquees and storefronts were lit up as though waiting for the arrival of the theatre crowd and the evening trade. I wondered if anyone ever bothered to turn them off.

The cool night air belied the coming of summer

and aided my contemplative mood. It had been a hard night. I'd played God with the lives of three, soon to be four, men. I comforted myself with the thought that two of them had been murderers, a third the catalyst that had set them in motion, and another a loathsome specimen of human garbage. By the time I'd parked the car I'd reconciled myself to the fact that I'd served as judge and jury for those men and set the wheels of execution into motion. When I arrived home I went straight to bed. I slept like a baby.

In the morning I made my peace with Dom Vallone. He was pretty upset when I told him that his package had already been delivered to the city morgue, and absolutely livid when I advised him that his cohorts had probably found enough evidence in the car in which one of the bodies had been discovered to tie the murdered men to the explosion on Laight Street. But he perked up a bit when I mentioned that ballistics would get a match if it compared bullets from the guns found on the dead men with the ones that had killed the garage attendant the previous afternoon. That piece of information wouldn't get him the promotion I'd hinted at, but it would earn a commendation for head work and a long look the next time the department needed a new man on the detective force.

Ten days later Vallone called and told me that a police cutter had dragged the body of Harvey Armstrong from the East River that morning. He'd been strangled with a length of piano wire, and he bore the signs of a savage beating, among other things. I found it hard to generate any remorse for having put him there.

That was the end of it, the finale of my trip to the big leagues. If I learned anything while I had my cup of coffee, it was that I needed another pitch if I intended to continue playing with the big boys. I'd been battered pretty hard in my first start, and the only thing that had saved me was Angelo Langella coming out of the bull pen. I didn't want to have to count on his type of relief ever again. But until I come up with a new pitch of my own I'll just stay down here in the minors, right where I belong.

San Diego Dilemma

MICHAEL MULDER

Michael Mulder is a twenty-six-year-old English major at North Texas State University in Denton, Texas. "San Diego Dilemma" is his first story, the result of a community service course he took in creative writing. He now teaches the course. The idea for this story came from an experience Mr. Mulder had in Southern California when he was offered an attractive sum of money to drive a vanload of illegal aliens across the border from Mexico. He turned down the offer, but his imagination was stimulated.

Martin West lit a cigarette, glanced at the clock on the small table by the door, and, settling back in his chair, blew an easy cloud of blue-gray smoke up toward the low, slanted ceiling of the loft, watching the smoke disperse and drift in the light from the single bulb overhead. It was 10:00 P.M. Although a call should have come forty-five minutes earlier—in fact, Martin's left hand now rested near the phone by his chair—his demeanor was a study in calm. The girl would call soon, or perhaps she would not. If she didn't, there were steps to be taken. Either way, his own ease was an asset.

Once, in the early days, when he and Jose Campos had run the operation alone, the old, sometimes unreliable panel van had stalled as they waited in line at the checkpoint to cross the border. Martin had not only enlisted the help of three customs officials to get the van started, but had then stopped, once the engine had finally roared to life and they were waved ahead, to back up and ask for the best route to San Diego. All the while their human cargo, valued at roughly eight to ten years in a federal penetentiary, huddled noiseless and sweltering beneath the floor panels in the back of the van.

Campos had been scared. Hell, Campos had just about shit in his new painter's pants, bought days earlier and then, with careful naiveté, splattered with paint to complete the premise begun with the logo on the side of the van, the ladders and roller brushes within. "*Por eso, tu eres el jefe*," had been all Campos could say that day, glassy eyed and breathless, when they were back on the road, "For that, you are the boss." He hadn't spoken the rest of the trip.

International painters. . . . Martin chuckled to himself. Calm. Only calm and quick thinking had gotten them through back then. These would suffice now.

On Highway 10, moving toward San Diego at a cautious fifty-five miles per hour, Patricia Zavala was concentrating with difficulty on the road ahead. Something was wrong. With her left hand she gathered and pulled back her thick, shoulder-length brown hair, blowing wildly in the breeze through the open windows, and recalled the scene at the border. The line had been long and they had waited over half an hour, but all had gone smoothly. Tate, their friend in customs, had been there—third booth from the left, just like he said—his smile beaming brighter than the badge on his chest as he pretended to check their documents before sending them on their way. No, there had been no gaffes, no unexpected obstacles. But something was not quite right. Why had Campos chosen not to wait for her with the car in Tijuana? To leave the men alone there in the lot showed poor judgment. She would have to talk to Martin about this.

Patricia glanced over at the young man beside her in the front seat and saw that he was noticing her legs again. There seemed to be no end to the amazement a woman in blue jeans could create in a Central American male straight out of the hills. His eyes, coming up, met hers, and he turned away, watching the scenery out the window. Yes . . . yes, that was it. He didn't redden with embarrassment. He just turned away. She glanced at the two in the backseat now, through the rearview mirror. They sat silently. One caught her glance and returned it evenly. The look of a man on the run—the look she saw in her own eyes before she began a transport—was absent from his gaze. Gone were the ways the men should have had about them—since everything was new to them here and they were nervous—laughing too readily at a joke or commenting too often on the unimpressive sights along the road. That was what was wrong. These men were not green. They did not smell of fear.

Maybe these are city boys, she told herself, shifting her attention back to the road just in time to see the exit for the rest stop with the pay phone. She pulled off into the parking lot and stopped about thirty feet away from the phone stand. It was not in use. Every step of the way without a hitch, she told herself, turning around to face the men, wishing her Spanish were better. "*Todo está bien*," she said to them. "*Yo regresaré* . . . just a minute." But everything was not all right. Somehow she was sure of that.

Martin answered the phone in the loft on the third ring: "West."

"Martin, where the hell are they?" It was Joey, his brother.

"I've asked you not to call like this," he told him.

"Marty, she's blown it. I know she's blown it. I told you a long time ago you couldn't depend on that girl." In truth, Martin had full confidence in that girl. It was his brother who sometimes concerned him.

"I'll call when I know something," he said.

"She's not gonna show. We've got to think. If they've got her, what are we gonna do?" His brother's voice began to rise. It would soon become . . . well, under pressure, Martin had to admit, his twenty-six-year-old younger brother became a whining child.

"Joel, sit on your hands. I will call." He set the receiver down firmly, thinking of his brother's six-foot-plus frame, his blond good looks. His baby brother fooled everybody—almost.

Martin sank back into the soft leather of the heavily padded chair, the sole luxury he allowed himself in the sparsely furnished loft, and almost immediately the phone rang again. He let it ring three times and then answered: "West."

"I'm here. We're fine." The tension was evident in the girl's voice.

"But something's up."

"I don't think these guys are Salvadoran. I don't know what else they could be . . . but their attitude . . . little things—"

157

"We have to trust Campos," he interrupted. "Maybe they're not Salvadoran. Maybe this is a special delivery."

Twisting the metal-wrapped phone cord between her fingers, she considered mentioning that Campos had run off, probably to meet some wanton TJ señorita, and left the men alone, but a detail she had noticed moments earlier in the car, when she had turned around to speak to the men, pushed itself forward in her mind. "Martin, I could be wrong, but I think one of these guys has contact lenses. At an angle I noticed—"

He cut her off again. "Take it easy. So he has contacts. Not everyone we bring out is going to be some poor *campesino*. Some people need us for other reasons."

"You're right," she said. "Nerves, I guess."

"It's all right. Take it slow."

"I'm okay. I will."

"Just get them to Joey," he told her.

"Right." He heard the professionalism coming back into her tone.

"And Patty?"

"Yes?"

"You're doing one hell of a job," he said.

"Thanks."

"And I miss you." He smiled, and he felt her answering smile some twenty miles away.

"You too."

He set the phone down, his mind suddenly flooded with images of Patricia, the sense of her. He thought of the dinner they had shared in her apartment not three nights ago. She had talked about the cause and how much their work meant to her, and he had mostly been silent because, in truth, the cause to him was only money—a lot of money. But she meant a great deal to him. So he listened. And he found within himself a certain affinity for her hopes, her ideals. Maybe she felt that too, for whatever he was . . . Smuggler? Mercenary? He smiled to himself at the improbability of it. Whatever the chemistry, it worked.

His mind drifted back to the first night they had spent together, six weeks ago, soon after she had joined the operation. They had come together so naturally. And in their lovemaking there had been something new for him: a depth of understanding that made their passion a thing very like communication—joyous, tender communication. Much, much more than his usual. That night, her head against his chest, soft hair spilling across his arm, he listened to her breathing and felt the warmth of her skin on his.

"Babe, you're really something." He was not by nature communicative of his emotions.

"Mmmm . . ." she murmured, curling closer to him.

"I really never . . ." he tried to express himself, "felt this way. . . ." He thought how banal these words sounded, but she tilted her head up, looking into his eyes.

"Me neither," she said.

"Seriously?"

"Never." She lay her head against him again. "It was really very, very special."

"Yes." Martin remained effusive. They held each other in the stillness.

"Well . . ." she began, "there was that time with the street gang in D.C." She felt him tense up next to her. Two beats of silence passed before she began to giggle against Martin's chest. Soon his laughter joined hers, and then he silenced her, turning her

159

face to him and covering her lips with a long kiss.

Yes, it was special, Martin thought to himself now, suddenly feeling a pang of concern for Patty and the risks he was allowing her to take. He picked up the phone in the loft, dialing the number for the Harbor Hotel, where Joey had waited all evening. The hotel was seedy, inhabited mainly by old winos and other assorted sad sacks, but the owner was a sympathizer, and his discreet assistance made the location ideal.

"Room 217, please."

"Yes?" Joey answered almost immediately. His voice still sounded sullen.

"They're here," Martin told him. "Do you have everything you need?"

"I'm ready. I've been ready."

"You have about thirty minutes," Martin said, pressing down the receiver button and ending the call before his brother could respond. He quickly dialed again.

"St. Andrews, Sister Dalia Margarite speaking," came the familiar greeting.

"Sister Margarite, I was wondering if the mission could accommodate three for dinner tonight?" Martin asked, lighting another Pall Mall.

"Oh, Martin, I do wish you would stop with all that secret-agent jargon already. I know this is the fourteenth, and you know I know, and the rooms are ready."

"Sister . . ." Martin began, smiling in mild exasperation, "procedure. Safety. For all you know, someone could be—"

"Well, Martin, honestly, the day somebody decides to wiretap the Mission of the Holy Order of the Sisters of the Immaculate Heart at St. Andrews of San Diego is the day I—"

"Sister," Martin cut her off, agitated, but still smiling to himself.

"I am ready, dear," Margarite replied sweetly.

"One hour," Martin said, signing off.

He sank back into the softness of the chair again, thinking about the strange diversity of the people involved in the operation.

The group he had assembled was motley, to be sure, but very dedicated. He had been smart enough to enlist the services of people who believed in the freedom fight in Salvador and the south, rather than those merely out for big cash—like himself, he thought with irony. The believers hung on through the worst because the men mattered to them. Some even worked for free. Since the old days of the panel van, when the partnership with Campos had first begun, their unofficial payroll had grown to include only three other people, and Patricia had been added just two months earlier. Yet the actual operation involved more than twenty people somewhere along the route from San Salvador to San Diego. Some, such as Tate at the border, performed tasks as simple as allowing a thirty-second lapse in job efficacy once a week. Others provided information. Some, a quick rest-stop along the way. A few, like the Sisters of St. Andrews, took the great risk of harboring fugitives for longer periods of time while situations were found for them. All these volunteers acted on moral convictions that may have seemed frivolous but were undeniably useful to Martin West.

Such was Martin's confidence in his subordinates that he actually fell asleep in the chair by the phone as he waited for Joey's report that the next step in the run had been completed. He was awakened, however, not by the phone but by pounding at the street-side entrance to the loft. Puzzled and immediately cautious, Martin rose from the chair and moved toward the door. His crew usually used the back door at the top of the stairs from the alleyway, and he could think of no one else who would come to the loft at this hour. He opened the door a little and then fully, as he saw Patricia standing ashen-faced in the doorway. She stepped into the room silently, closed the door behind her, and turned to him. Tears sprang into her eyes and rolled down onto her face.

"Pat, what's wrong?" Martin asked.

"I left them with Joey. I started back here," her voice was mechanical. She forced the words out with an obvious effort of control. "I stopped to put the traveling papers in the box in the trunk. . . ." Her voice choked off with hard sobs. She made a move forward as if to step into his arms.

He raised his hands to her shoulders, holding her at arm's length. "Talk to me, babe."

"Campos is in the trunk."

They were both silent for a moment, the shock weighing more heavily than the implications of the discovery.

Suddenly, Patricia stopped crying and raised her eyes to Martin.

"Joey," was her terse realization. Martin was already reaching for the phone, dialing quickly. There was no answer.

"Okay, we've got to move now." Martin stared hard at her, keeping his voice free of the emotion making his throat tighten with fear for his brother's safety. "I don't know what's happening here, but we've got to move. I'll go to Joey at the hotel and on to the mission, if he's already gone there. You," he watched her closely now, looking for signs of the strength he needed to see in her face, "take the car back to TJ. Get Campos's body to his family. Whatever is coming down here, a murder in Tijuana is much less messy than a murder in Southern California." He paused now, thinking quickly, "The wound?"

"Gunshot." Strength was there now in her voice, in the resolve in her glistening eyes. "High caliber, I think." She stopped, looking downward, the fingers of one hand clenching those of the other. "Most of the back of his head is gone. Not much blood."

"He was killed and then put into the trunk?"

"Yes." She was ready now, he could see.

He stepped toward her, suddenly feeling an impulse, himself, to take her into his arms. He thought better of it.

"Let's go," he told her. "Call me here at one o'clock."

The time to comfort would come later. If they all survived.

The distance from the loft above "C" Street to the hotel on Harbor Drive took less than five minutes by car. Martin drove fast, his mind raging. Thoughts of revenge. Whoever had killed Jose Campos would pay. He was not a killer. But he was a man.

And please, God, please, let Joey be all right. He thought of his brother now, saw his easy smile. The doubts he had struggled with before allowing Joey into the game in the first place came back to him. Those very possibilities now real, now here, facts in motion. But Joey was his brother . . . and he hadn't been doing really well at anything else. He had dropped out of college and married, and soon his young marriage was on the skids. For once, Martin cursed the logic, the reasonable, level-headed decisiveness that had convinced him the work might help Joey. Why hadn't he listened to his emotions, for Christ's sake?

He pulled the car up quickly but silently in front of the dilapidated frame building that sported HARBOR HOTEL in aging neon tubing. Stepping inside, he passed the desk clerk and did the fifteen green-carpeted steps to the second floor in three quick bounds. Room 217 was halfway down the hall to the left. He kicked the flimsy door open easily. The lights were low in the room, but he saw he was too late.

He knew it was Joey on the floor by the bed, but he stepped first in one continuous motion to the bath, pushing the door open, finding it empty, and then to the closet in the corner. Then he saw the body on the far side of the bed, near the cheap, oak-look dresser, the man's left side pressed to the closet door as if thrown against it by the force of the bullet that killed him. He grasped the man's shoulder, turning him over, and saw the dark Latin death-mask.

Martin turned and walked to the other side of the bed, bending down to Joey now. He was breathing. Maybe he had a chance. But then Martin saw the gaping wound in Joey's chest and realized he probably didn't. He pressed his hands against the sides of his brother's face.

"Kid, can you hear me?"

Joey groaned, and hearing the agony in his brother's voice, Martin felt a horrible, sickened clench in his gut.

"Joe, it's Marty. Can you hear me, brother?"

The eyes opened slowly. Filmy, unfocused. Dying eyes. His voice was barely audible. "I gotta tell you . . . what I did. . . ."

Martin could only listen in silence. He was crying.

"Campos and me . . . we were running coke . . . sometimes . . . on the men."

"God. . . . Joey . . ."

"When they couldn't pay, Campos would tell 'em . . . 'You take this . . . in your bag, you go for free.' Martin, somebody's on to us. . . ." A trickle of blood appeared at the corner of Joey's mouth.

Martin's mind was reeling. "But, baby, why'd they shoot you? They shot Campos. What's happening here?"

"Tonight . . . I told 'em, 'Where's the stuff? Hand it over.' They played dumb . . . like they didn't know. I locked the door. I got out my gun. I said . . . 'You guys are going exactly nowhere till I get the stuff.' One of them pulled a pistol. We both fired . . . Marty, am I gonna die?"

Joey died then.

Martin went out of the room, his vision blurred with tears, down the stairs and out to the street. He walked slowly to the car, wiping his eyes clear, telling himself it was necessary to act now. But once he had firmly pulled open the car door and sat down inside, he allowed himself to break just for a moment—the car door still open, fists clenched, head down, almost touching the steering wheel. He sobbed hard and without reserve for several minutes. Control returned slowly, and he finally did rest his head against the wheel, trying to picture a blank, white screen in his mind.

But another image flashed, dissipating the attempt to calm himself. It was a glint of silver. His spine tightened slowly, and he stopped an involuntary sound rising in his throat. Silver flashing for just a moment in the light of the streetlamp as he climbed into the car. Now his head was fifty pounds of pressure against the wheel. He was sure. The door lock in the back-seat on the driver's side . . . it had been locked. It wasn't now. That glint off the streetlight . . . through the window. Now it was raised.

As will happen when entirely too much comes down far too quickly, Martin, for this moment, became completely reactive. A survival machine. He turned his head very slightly to the left, forehead still against the steering wheel. His right hand moved toward his belt, where the small pistol rested, while his left arm, car keys gripped in his fist, moved outward through the open car door, letting the keys fall with a quick metallic jingle onto the concrete.

"Shit," he muttered softly, deliberately, under his breath, and bending down and out now to retrieve the keys, glanced quickly into the space between the side of the seat and the car wall. He saw enough. A half inch of blue trouser leg. The tip of a brown hard-sole shoe. As he began to raise himself up and back into the car, his right arm with gun in hand, as if a separate animal from the rest of his body, traveled up in a stiff-armed arc across the seat and then curled downward into the backseat floorboard. He fired once, moved his arm eight inches farther up, and fired again. There was silence in the backseat. Martin stepped out of the car and walked slowly into a nearby alleyway. Several minutes later, he began to run.

Patricia was nearing the border crossing now, going back the way she had come only a short time earlier. It had not occurred to her to worry yet about getting back into Mexico without Tate's blind smiling as-sistance, without even a decent cover story. She would make this crossing alone, with nothing but her perfectly legal and current driver's license—and the body in the trunk. No, for now she was busy replaying the drop-off scene in front of the Harbor Hotel when she had stopped with the men before sending them up to Joey. She had been trying to explain in her clumsy Spanish where they were and why. Reassured by the talk with Martin, she had been up—even smiling a little—as she turned again, in front of the hotel, to speak to the men once more.

"*Aquí espera un amigo*," she had said. This was her favorite part of the trip. Time to say, "Guys, from here you're basically home free." But in her lousy Spanish it continued more or less like this: "This friend is a good man. Perhaps you will not have problems now . . . he . . . with him. . . ." She had stopped, perplexed, half-giggling to herself as she tried to remember how to say "you will go." She had only partly noticed the communication between the man in the front seat and one of the two in the back.

Had the one in front said, "*Cuando*?" When?

She had heard the answer clearly: "*Nunca*." The eyes of the man in back had smoldered. "*No me pagan bastante*," Never, they don't pay me enough.

At the time, she had taken the half-heard and unconsidered remark to be a reference perhaps to his country. He'd never return, because the money for his work there in that sad economy just wasn't enough. She had completed her botched "Welcome to California" tour-guide speech without improvement and had told them to go on up. "Room number *dos-cientos-diez-y-siete*," she had managed. Good God, was she green. They had hesitated just a moment, sitting in the car, looking at her, looking at each other, and finally getting out. They had been deciding whether to kill her.

Martin had run nonstop, with fierce determination, for almost fifteen minutes through blind alleys and deserted streets. He had made one detour, running a few blocks over on a slightly busier street, to reach St. Andrew's. Down the steps at the side of the old building to the basement parlor where Sister Margarite would be waiting, he had pounded on the door, and when she answered, he spoke quickly, his breath rushing, "Dinner's off!" and started up the stairs at a run.

"Martin!" she had called, wanting an explanation.

He had turned back quickly. "Don't open that door for anyone, not even Pat or me, until I call you and tell you it's safe."

Now, slowing to a walk, covering the last three blocks to the "C" Street loft by cutting through the downtown red-light district overrun with sailors and noisy bars and garish porn shops, he thought to himself, God, keep her safe. He realized none of them were. Yet he felt strangely secure here now. Music and laughter poured out of the bars. The hustlers on the curbs hawked whatever they had to sell, and a few things they didn't have. The bright light from the neon on nearly every storefront and establishment almost constituted warmth. Life continued as usual here, and for a few minutes he let his mind stop ticking off each instant and floated along in the illusion that everything was okay.

But nearer the dark end of the street the music faded, there was no more neon, and the reality he faced thudded like a hammer in his chest. He cut into an alley and ran the last block, crossing an empty lot to come out on the street directly across from the loft. The little grocery below was dark and uninhabited at this hour. The front window of the loft above was also dark. Good or bad? Who could know at this point?

Martin moved back through the empty lot and into the alley again, running easily to the first cross-street, over to the alley on the other side of "C" Street, and down to the back side of the loft. He had the beginnings of a plan now. Calm. Level-headed decision making. Contingency planning, he told himself.

A few months earlier, Mr. Davilla, the shopkeep who had the grocery and allowed them to use the loft, had told Martin of a car parked down the street from the store several hours each day for three days prior to a run. Martin knew that Davilla was a very old man who was also, perhaps, a bit intoxicated with vicarious excitement. He was involved, he surely thought to himself, with a "covert refugee transport operation." Martin had not been concerned with this report. Perhaps Davilla was right. But the car was, at worst, vice squad, there to watch any number of residences and businesses on this block. Many were far from reputable. Martin had discussed with the group what they would in fact do if immigration somehow caught their scent. Many ideas had been tossed about. Most of them seemed ridiculous after much in-depth consideration. Busted is busted, and if *la Migra* got on to them, well, they would just have to shut down. The meeting had degenerated into a general bull session.

One idea, however, had seemed reasonable and possibly useful. Martin had accepted it for this reason, but also because it had been Joey's idea. Joey was not exactly ideaphoric, and when the thought had occurred to him he had stared at them, dumbfounded, like a man who has just gotten an inspiration from God, and said, "Call-forwarding on the loft phone." Even Pat had praised Joey for the ingeniousness of the idea, and those two were very sparing with compliments regarding each other. Joey had gone on to suggest that maybe each week they could change the communications-base location by forwarding all the incoming calls to a different room at the Harbor Hotel, or perhaps even St. Andrew's itself, and really keep *la Migra* on the run.

Now Martin was immensely grateful for this technological convenience. He crept slowly up the alley stairs to the loft, thinking how simple it would be. He would just forward all calls to the pay phone at the corner. He could wait for Patty's call there and still have a decent view of the loft if the remaining ill-mannered transport felt an urge to reach out and touch someone. God love Ma Bell, he repeated to himself softly as he pushed open the door to the loft.

He crouched low now to avoid being an easy target against the moonlit night outside, but some automatic, animal sense gave him the certainty that the loft was empty. All the same, he did not turn on a light or move around the room but crept quickly, noiselessly, by feel to the phone by the chair. He punched numbers rapidly and had crept back out onto the landing in possibly no more than sixty seconds. He would have whistled. Easy. They were going to make it. God love and bless good old Ma Bell. Coming down the stairs, though, he heard Joey's excited voice in his mind, "That'll keep *la Migra* on the run," and a wave of sadness and rage enveloped him. In truth, part of the rage was at Joey, as well as his killers. Dumb kid. Coke on the transports . . . so dangerous. Stupid, sweet kid.

As he rounded the corner from the alley, the phone booth in sight now, he considered: Could the men have been from Narcotics? Were they up on Campos and Joey's game? Surely narcs wouldn't kill so easily. Still, Joey said he had threatened them. But Campos? Why had they killed him?

With a quick look around, Martin stepped into the phone booth. He closed the door behind him, noticing how visible the light and the glass doors made him. He turned and was immediately startled into disappointment. The receiver was gone. Ripped from the base of the phone. He slammed the door open and started back toward the alley. "Damn Ma Bell to hell," he muttered, shaking his head.

Patricia had not imagined she might find herself sitting at a musty bar in a Tijuana tavern called *El Gallito Loco*, the Crazy Little Chicken, but they had told her Nico might be there. He was.

"*No sé nada*," he repeated, for perhaps the fifth time.

Pat refused to believe he knew nothing at all about what had happened to Jose Campos and the three real transports she had begun to speculate must exist somewhere. But she had gotten no information from the Campos family either.

The scene at Jose's house had been worse than she had allowed herself to imagine. An inexplicable number of older women had been there, six or seven at least, and when she told them they had all begun to wail and cry as if on cue. Had they known? Had the family gathered because there was a death among their number? Many children also; they were crying too. And the men, she had seen five, the youngest perhaps seventeen, the oldest ageless and gray. They had stood about silently with dark, dry eyes as the women wailed and the children cried. She had thought how the men's hands seemed strong and expressive and masculine, yet right now so very impotent at their sides.

She had wanted to get this over and done with and get away, but with a sickening lurch in her belly she realized that Jose's body was still in the trunk of the car. She couldn't move him herself. For a wild instant she thought how she might tell them: "Just excuse me and I'll go and get his body now," and then maybe she could drive and pay someone to move him to the backseat. But there was nothing she could do now. She was sickened at how it would seem to these old women, and she tried, at least, to make it better, bringing two of the men aside and asking them to help her. They went out to the car, and Patty opened the trunk. The horror that had accompanied this act the first time was gone now. This was her friend Jose. She was bringing him home. She helped them lift his body out.

The women had come out on the wide front porch now, and they saw what she had hoped to spare them. But it seemed to be okay. Their cries, their tears as they rushed out into the yard were all for him. There was no room and no need for sorrow at how he had come. They were filled with love for Jose, as she was, she thought. But they had known. Gut level, she was certain, they had known he was dead.

Now she studied Nico beside her at the bar.

"*No sé nada, chica,*" he said again. He stared straight ahead at the rows of cheap tequila and bourbon bottles behind the bar. His dark hair looked dank and dirty, and his complexion was bad. He pulled at the Corona before him and set it down again, watching the tiny bubbles in his beer rise up through the clear glass bottle, with eyes that always seemed wary to Patricia. His ignorance, she knew, was feigned. Why was nobody talking to her? Nico knew. That was why they paid him, because Nico knew just about anything worth a few bucks to anyone. He was a listener. And a drunk, she thought. But he always had his ear to some secret rail line somewhere, picking up vibrations. He seemed to know what was going on everywhere. Now he said he didn't know who killed Campos, his own friend. Patricia had never liked Nico. She looked at him in frustration once more.

He was a small man, thin and angular. Small enough to make Patty consider her chances of success at physically forcing the information out of him. She was only five-six herself, but in her growing anger and frustration she thought of the small pistol in her bag. Could she get him outside somehow? But this was not realistic, she knew. She stood, turned away, and left *El Gallito Loco*. She would have to get the information elsewhere.

On the street, she walked dejected among the tawdry, ramshackle buildings and shops that were Tijuana, thinking, as always, how hard life must be here. Or maybe not: Human beings are adaptable and easily habituated to worse, she knew. There were few people on the streets, even for a TJ midnight.

Then a young man stepped out into the darkness from a tavern thirty feet ahead. He looked around, glanced in her direction, and began walking toward her. She was frightened at first, but as he approached she recognized him as one of the younger men from the gathering at Jose Campos's house.

"*Te busco*," he said, turning, and falling into step beside her. He had been looking for her.

"*Por que*?" she asked him, looking up into his face.

"Jose Campos," he continued in Spanish, while she struggled to understand the words, "he gave us our lives. My brothers, Gustavo, Mario, and myself, we were with him. Three men came. They talked to him. They argued. Jose turned and said to us, '*Corre*! Run!' and we did. They shot him. He gave us our lives."

"You were the men I was supposed to bring out!" she said to him in English. "*Ustedes son del Salvador*?"

He nodded silently.

"Who were the men?" she asked, hoping she had at last found someone willing to talk.

"Nico says they killed a man in Mexico City." His expression was grave.

Patricia turned, not even thanking the boy, and strode rapidly, purposefully, back toward *El Gallito Loco*. She was white-hot, livid. She pushed the door to the bar open hard and saw Nico still seated at the counter. She walked up beside him. He turned, saw her, and quickly raised his open hands in a gesture of good-natured exasperation.

"*Chica*, I told you," he said, "*no sé nada—*"

Her hand was in the bag at her side. She removed

174

the pistol, the butt clinched in her hand, the barrel out like a hammer, and brought it down hard across the side of Nico's face. Entirely unprepared for an attack like this, he was caught off-balance, and the force of the blow knocked him to the floor.

"Talk," she said, staring down at him, her eyes fierce.

"They were *asesinos*," he said, his eyes on the gun still in her hand, not meeting her steady gaze.

"Who did they kill in Mexico City?" she grilled him.

"Ortega," he replied without hesitation.

Her mind whirled with this new information. Manuel Ortega led a rebel group that opposed Mexican President Miguel de la Madrid.

"Who were they working for?"

"*No sé*," Nico's eyes flashed on the gun again now.

Patricia stepped on the fingers of his right hand, which lay passively at his side.

"*No sé! No sé! En serio, no sé, chica!*"

Patricia turned, left him, and walked again from the bar. On the street, she glanced at her watch. It was 12:50. She rushed ahead, searching for a phone. She would call Martin now. He needed to know.

Martin moved once again up the alley stairway to the loft. He knew that one o'clock was nearing, and he could not afford to miss the call from Patty. She needed to know she must lay low. She had no idea how far out of hand this thing had gotten. He slowly opened the back door, again crouching, and remained that way as he moved across the carpeted floor to the phone by the chair in which he had slept comfortably only hours before. He canceled the call forward to the booth at the corner just in time for the phone to ring.

"Patty, are you okay?"

"I'm fine, listen, Martin—"

"No. Wait. I've got to tell you some things," he interrupted. "Joey and Campos were sending out drugs in the transports' bags. Joey is dead. Two of the transports are dead. I'm certain the third must be looking for me. I think someone found out about the drugs, and maybe they infiltrated the line to try and—"

"No, Martin. Listen. I talked with one of the real Salvadorans I was supposed to meet here. I also had a chat with Nico. They were on the run from Mexico City. Someone killed Manuel Ortega. Martin, these guys were paid assassins."

"Good God. . . ." Martin was silent, taking it all in.

"We'll never prove it, but I think Nico set us up." Her anger was still evident. "What do we do?"

"I suspect we have only one option." Martin, still crouched low on the floor, leaned his weight against the back of the heavy, padded chair. "I want you to stay where you are for twenty-four hours."

"I'm coming back now." There was no mistaking the determination in her voice. "You may need me there."

"All right." Martin tried to think of a safe place to meet her. He made a quick decision. "Langley pier. Two o'clock," he told her.

"All right."

"Lose the car."

"Okay."

"And be careful, kid." He placed the receiver softly down and tilted his head back against the leather of the chair.

A voice came from somewhere in the darkness of the loft.

"She's an attractive girl. How is she in bed?"

Martin's right hand went to his belt, finding the pistol. Now, in the corner of the loft, he could see the form of a man seated in a chair, a faceless silhouette in the dim moonlight from the open door. Martin let perhaps fifteen seconds tick away. He knew the man would be armed. He brought his own gun up but left it hidden in his hand beneath his jacket.

"What do you want?" Martin knew the answer. He stalled for time.

The voice spoke again, and Martin saw a slight glimmer of light reflected, perhaps off a contact lens.

"Mr. West, I need an oath of silence. For your country . . ."

"For *my* country?" Martin was incredulous. Some seconds passed, and he asked, "Who are you?"

"What would you believe?" The question was spoken evenly, without inflection.

Martin heard the rustle of cloth, and he sensed the movement of the man's arm coming up before he could actually see it in the faint light. He raised his own arm quickly, reflexively, pulling himself halfway behind the protection of the chair, and fired a shot at the form in the corner. The man fell heavily to the floor.

Martin stood cautiously to turn on the overhead light in the room. The heavyset Latin man was dead, sprawled on his side. He checked the man's pockets and found he carried no identification. He turned the man's head slightly, closing the eyes with the fingers of his left hand. He looked into that now impassive face and spoke the truth he and his adversary had both known: "Only dead men keep an oath of silence."

177

He waited for her at the water's edge, on the sand in the shadows of Langley pier. As he sat, watching the small waves wash up onto the beach, he was lost in his grief, his thoughts of all that had been destroyed that night. He hardly felt her hand on his shoulder as she lowered herself beside him to sit on the soft, shadowed beach.

"I'm so sorry. . . ." she said. He did not answer, but continued staring out into the ocean while the moon set slowly. As dawn approached, they talked.

"What do we do?" she asked.

"We wait," he told her.

Gulls began to call out, circling over the small bay. Light was growing in the east.

"Do you think there are more of them?" she asked.

"Maybe." They stood, he put his arm around her, and they walked together up the slight incline of the beach, toward the road that marked the edge of the quiet city in the dawn.

At the corner of the first city block they approached coming up from the bay was a public phone. He picked up the receiver, dropped a coin in the slot, and dialed, pulling her to him again as he listened to the phone ring at the other end. Please, God, please let something still be sacred.

"Yes?" came the familiar voice.

"Sister Margarite—" he began.

"Martin, for the love of Christ! Why haven't you called? Are you okay? I've been up all—"

"Sister Margarite, could the mission accommodate two for dinner?"

We've Been Invited to a Party

J. AQUINO

J. Aquino, a Washington, D.C., based writer and
magazine editor, is the author of an unpublished
novel and several stories featuring the heroines
of "We've Been Invited to a Party." Concerning
the genesis of the story, the author states, "I was
weaned on Hitchcock movies in which danger
suddenly appeared in unlikely settings and situations. A firefight at a Christmas party was in
keeping with this approach. Most of all, I've been
interested in and have tried to develop this relationship—both professional and personal—between Jenny and Lynn. I mean, there's Holmes
and Watson and McGee and Meyer, but not as
much of the high level of professional skill, the
playing off each other, the symbiotic relationship,
the camaraderie and friendship that exists between Jenny and Lynn. That's what's important
to me in the story."

Snowfall does various things to Washington, D.C. If
it starts after midnight, school officials cancel classes
in anticipation of icy hills on suburban streets. If it
falls around noon, government officials take pity on
their workers from suburbia and grant them leave,
whereupon they rush to their cars, clog the streets,
and paralyze traffic. Immigrants from the Northwest

have difficulty understanding this phenomenon. Whenever Washington National Airport is closed because of snow, the local news always interviews someone from Butte who shouts incredulously that if they closed Montana every time it snowed ten lousy inches the state would never open. More objective observers point out that Washington, D.C., which is near the moisture of the Chesapeake Bay and neither north nor south, is visited by a wet and slick snow rather than the powdered Montana variety.

It was in this atmosphere, at eight o'clock in the evening on December 23, with four inches already on the ground, that Lynn was pacing in the slush on "O" Street off 21st, waiting for Jenny. The pace of the flakes had slackened to a gentle, numbing falling. "O" Street was lined with stone town houses dating from the 1930s; the dwellings seemed to huddle together in the cold. Suddenly, the trim and agile figure of her companion, dressed all in black and seen starkly against the white of winter, appeared. Jenny walked by with her head down, but when Lynn caught her arm she whirled around, laughing with uncharacteristic girlishness, showing that she had only been fooling.

"Where you been, silly?" Lynn asked as she kissed her.

"I've been silly all over the place," Jenny said loudly but not happily.

"Yes, I can see that. You went to Jaimie's party?"

Jenny nodded, her head bobbing without the hold of muscles, like that of a rag doll. Jenny's drinking was usually confined to a fashionable glass of white wine. "Traffic stank. And then the party went on and on. You know how I hate these things. All you do is eat and drink eggnog and get hit on and drink eggnog. And now you're going to take me to another stupid party!"

"It won't be stupid. Terri's an old friend. And I want my friends to meet you. I'm proud of you. Come on, it's down the block here."

"Then can we go home?"

"Then we can go home. You didn't bring anything, did you?" Jenny started walking and didn't answer. "Oh, come on, Jenny, you promised. Did you bring any weapons?"

"Lynn," Jenny whispered. "I have a secret to tell you. We're spies. We're supposed to carry weapons."

"Why? You see a supermarket robbery, what are you going to do? Pull your piece and blow apart all the customers? You're going to be at this party with lots of people with a Detective Special sticking from your pocket or sitting in your purse? Come on, what did you bring?" Lynn saw that they had reached the end of the block and took Jenny by the arm to the wall of the town-house row.

"Come on and search me," Jenny laughed as she leaned against the wall.

"Don't think I won't," said Lynn as she ran her hand between Jenny's thighs.

"I love it when you do that."

Finding nothing, Lynn pushed herself close to Jenny and looked her directly in the eye. "What . . . did . . . you . . . bring?"

Jenny cast her eyes heavenward in childish frustration. "A knife in my boot! That's all. I'm not going around without any help. But no one is going to steal my gun at your dumb party. And if anyone robs a supermarket, we'll stand and watch, okay?"

"Okay," Lynn said softly. Jenny's eyes were half

closed; Lynn smiled and brushed the hair away from them. "You're so beautiful. But most especially, I don't feel that one of us is strong and the other weak, like the stereotypes. We pull off each other as needed." Passersby saw the two women so close against the wall and muttered, but Lynn ignored them.

Jenny opened her eyes and grinned. "Do we have to go to the party?"

"Yes," said Lynn sternly, suddenly like a mother. "Come on."

Terri's town house on the corner was like the others, gray stone block, picture window behind two square azaleas, two stories, entrance up cement steps with a black iron railing, a sloping yellow hill for a front lawn, and a slate roof sloping from the second-floor windows. They rang and rang, and the door was finally answered by a lady, not Terri, whose name they didn't catch because of the noise from the party, but they followed her in. Someone handed them eggnogs; Lynn went to find Terri. The front hallway led to the polished oak stairs on the right and a living room on the left where a small group was decorating the tree that stood in front of the picture window. Jenny's eyes drifted up to the paneled oak ceiling, evidence that the house had originally been owned by someone very wealthy. Terri, when Lynn brought her over, was tall and slim, auburn haired and hollow cheeked; she muttered something about tennis and health clubs and how the oak ceiling had been black until her Uncle Dominic had bought the house with her four years ago and scrubbed away until he found oak. Jenny didn't hear them say something about going to see someone else, but she figured that they must have, since they walked away.

Left on her own, Jenny wandered into the living room, declined an offer to help decorate, and sat on a green-velvet-cushioned chair as soon as one became vacant. It was directly across from the stairs to her left and in front of a fireplace happily blazing.

I hate eggnog, she told herself, and placed the glass she had been given on a side table. She had a gnawing feeling in the pit of her stomach and knew she should eat something. In the room behind her, seemingly meant for dining, people were helping themselves to food, but what they emerged with seemed to be soft stuff, deviled eggs and vegetables coated with dip. Jenny leaned back and hoped that Lynn would come to get her before she either got sick or fell asleep.

"Hellllo there." Jenny looked up wearily and saw that he was tall and muscled and lean; his hair was tousled as if he were in an April wind, his skin browned. "My name's Rick. You a friend of Cary's?"

"Terri's," she corrected him. "A friend of a friend. And I'm gay. No, really. I am. Have I ever lied to you before?" She closed her eyes and assumed that he would walk away, but she could hear he stayed for a while, maybe glaring. Was there ever a time, she asked herself, when she got all excited over the likes of him? That was unfair. She wasn't feeling well. He was probably a very nice individual, deep and profound, gentle and caring. But she was happy as she was. For the first time in her life she had the three things that she felt mattered in life: a career she enjoyed, someone she loved, and that same person in love with her.

A deep, mellow voice caused her to open her eyes. "Are you all right, signorina?" The bang of hair that went from left to right on his forehead was white, and it highlighted his generally beet-red face; the color suggested high blood pressure or at least the result of his obesity, the wide belly that pushed the limits of his white turtleneck and snugly belted gray pants. His use of "signorina" and his general pronunciation identified him as being from southern Italy or Sicily. "*Bene, grazie.*"

"Ah," he beamed with satisfaction. "*Mi chiamo Dominic Bonsignor.*"

"Jenny Gwynn. Are you Uncle Dominic? I mean, Terri's uncle?"

"*Si,*" he beamed. "Has she told you about the ceilings?" he asked above the noise.

"About how they were black? Yes! That must have been a lot of work." She felt she had to talk to him to be polite. But he seemed friendly enough and wasn't hitting on her.

"*Si, si.* I am seventy now. I could not do it now."

"Where are you from?"

"Siciliano," he said proudly.

"You speak English very well," she said.

"I should. I was a translator for the OSS during the war."

"Oh," she nodded impressed. The OSS! That was in the beginning, when Americans had just started opening up other people's mail and listening in on conversations and agents began accepting the possibility of being thought a traitor by their families or of being shot in the back of the head and shoved in an unmarked grave, their tales untold. OSS agents had been pioneers in what Jenny and Lynn did.

It was as if he read her thoughts. "And you are a spy too." He was not asking a question. It was a statement of fact.

184

"What are you talking about?" she said evenly. "Lynn and I work for the government, but—"

"Agents nowadays are very easy to spot. Terri said you worked in information processing with Lynn. Not you. You are not the clerical type. The way you walk and see things. I know your kind very well." He leaned closer and whispered, which made it all the more difficult to hear him in what seemed to be an ever-growing din. "I was active for a while. And that is why I need to talk to you. Something has happened—" People began to come into the room, laughing. Jenny strained to hear. "Long ago . . . dead . . . must help."

"Uncle Dominic!" Terri shouted, and gently pulled him away from Jenny. "It's time to place the last ornament on the tree and say your Italian prayer." Her tone was overly loud and patronizing. "I know the rest of you will indulge us. It's a family tradition." Uncle Dominic blended into the crowd, looking back anxiously at Jenny. It wasn't fear so much as an indication that he had begun something that he needed to finish.

Jenny got up and found Lynn. "I've got to talk to you."

"What's wrong? Are you okay?"

"Something has happened," she said, unconsciously echoing Uncle Dominic's words.

"Okay, Uncle," chortled Terri as he gingerly climbed a metal step-stool. "Take it easy." The group of twenty-five or so smiled as the weighty Sicilian shoved his ample behind toward them in an effort to achieve balance. He righted himself, then leaned forward, aiming a tattered but still gleaming cloth angel toward the tree's tip. All eyes were on him, relaxed, leaning with him into the party mood. And so all

185

ears and eyes experienced it at once as the old man's head snapped to the crowd, the tree and he fell forward, and the window glass flew out into the air with a burst of gunfire.

"Down!" Jenny screamed, throwing herself at people, bringing them to the floor. She'd been quick; most of the group had been far enough back, so it looked as if only the uncle had been hit, although many were bleeding from the broken glass. The gunfire stopped, but Jenny rolled over toward the stair, bobbed up, and saw a shadow in the glass window of the door. In an easy motion, her previous lethargy banished, she pulled the knife from her boot. The door was kicked open; she saw the muzzle of a semi-automatic and threw her knife just over it. The form pushed in, round face, featureless, the blade in his chest, his gun falling. Lynn was now next to Jenny, saw the opportunity, and slid across the carpet, banging her shoulder into the door. The man's hands twisted, caught in the jam, and the Uzi dropped free. Jenny jumped to catch it, then pulled back as Lynn did, just before the glass and wood shattered from the fire of the dead man's partner. Aiming at the door's center then moving up, Jenny fired back a short burst, there being only one clip. She didn't know whether she'd hit him, but she did know they'd be surprised at the response, that there were more of them, and that she and Lynn would have to act quickly.

At once, she tossed the gun to Lynn, seized the fireplace poker, and gestured to the stairs. Lynn nodded and crouched, positioning herself to cover both the window and the door. Running to the stairs, flicking out the lights, Jenny passed the young man called Rick. There was a bar by the stairs; the eggnog had been splattered by the disruption, but some brandy bottles were still intact. Jenny swiped at one with the poker, knocking off the head. "Use your tie, big shot, make a bomb." As she disappeared to the second level, Rick pulled at his Pierre Cardin and loosened his collar.

Standing on the roof, dressed only in boots, sweater, and pants in the freezing night, Jenny could see them: two sprawled on the steps, one trying to push those bodies out of the way, two to the left just away from the window, and one on the sidewalk. Neighbors were coming out of their doors, and in the distance there was the shrill, promising whine of sirens. Still, Jenny could see cars sliding in the street. Help might take awhile.

To the left, clear of the roof, she saw an open place. The snow would not cushion her much from a height of twenty feet, so she would need the room to roll. She grasped each end of the poker and dived off, used the poker and her arms as a crux when she hit the ground, somersaulted, sprang up, and buried the poker in the stomach of the man who had just turned around. He fell, she freed the poker with a twist, took both ends and leapt upon the second man before he could pull his gun up. They landed together, the poker deep underneath his chin. She pushed it up until his knees stiffened and his arms lost their solidity.

Inside, Lynn saw a shadow disappear, which meant one of them was leaving the door. The bodies, she thought, were probably blocking it. He would either go around the back or come through the picture window, now open, without glass or pane. She realized she didn't know how many there were; even now, a handful could be coming around the back. But she couldn't worry about that now. It was only her and Jenny. Or was it? Out of the corner of her eye she saw one of the guests holding a bottle of brandy in one hand, a red tie floridly sticking out of the jagged mouth, and a match ready for striking in the other. "Wait for me to tell you," she hissed, then saw a muzzle visible through the shattered window. It moved fast like a snake into view; she fired at the arms and head attached to it, and the strange beast collapsed. She'd hit it. But now her gun was empty.

Suddenly it lurched up, visibly bleeding from the head, staggered back, gun at the waist being waved around but still pointed at the roomful of people who were trapped within the window's frame.

"Now!" Lynn shouted. The flare of the match roared in her ear, the light from the flame spread over her shoulder, and she felt the whisk over her head of the fiery missle that struck the gun's barrel and instantly consumed the man in flames, fire that spread to the bushes around him and then to the edges of the picture-window rectangle.

Jenny crawled on her belly to a fallen Uzi. Bullets blowing up snow whizzed past her, creasing her arm. She rolled and spun up into a crouched position, only to see him running around the back. A blast knocked her over, and snow pressed against her bare back and middle, since her sweater had ridden up. Shaking her head to gather her senses, she saw a human figure melt within a single flame as if he had been made of ice. The flames spread across the front, making the entrance impassable. "Lynn!" she screamed through the wall of fire. "Lynn! He's coming from the back."

The back was the only way out now for all of them, and they had started to move toward it, but Lynn stopped them at Jenny's shout. She grouped them to either side of the wall, then ran into the darkened dining room, long and deep; dips, relishes, and pastries, no longer festive, covered a table. She almost made it to the kitchen, where she at least might find knives, but held back at the sound of the door opening. She grabbed at something tall on the table and came back with a pepper shaker, wooden and heavy. Standing to the right of the door, she waited as it was pushed open, the door itself shielding her from his view, then leapt on him, crashing the pepper shaker down on his head. He staggered forward but then turned, the gun still tight in his hands. She swung again at his open face. The wood cracked, and pepper shot from both sides, filling the air and blinding them both. The man fell back onto the table, sliding over eggs and vegetables, grabbing at the tablecloth, pulling it up to rub into his eyes, to clear them. Lynn fell on the floor, eyes shut tight and burning, and crawled on all fours straight ahead into the living room. She heard him behind her, picking something off the floor—his gun, *his gun*—as she crawled faster. The sound of shots ate into the air behind her, but they seemed muffled, blocked, and were followed by that of a body falling. "Lynn!" shouted Jenny.

"Over here! I can't see!" She felt Jenny haul her up. "Everybody out this way!" Jenny shouted. Lynn felt herself being passed to other people and carried outside where the air was sharp and wet. She was laid down on her back and someone dabbed at her face with snow. Lynn opened her eyes slowly, and the wetness of the snow seemed to clear them. The burning eased. And the first thing she saw was Jenny.

Twelve thirty-eight, and the city was asleep, imprisoned in an icy white glaze. The storm had passed, and the temperature had consequently dipped. The fuzzy white coverlet that had once yielded to the formidable edges of snowplows now took the plows' blows in stride.

Jenny leaned against the headboard, similarly covered and imprisoned in white, only this was a gown that was bare in the back. The hospital census was down due to the weather, and so the bed next to her in this second-floor room was empty. She listened to the irregular drip of the IV. A thirteen-inch, black-and-white television set was attached to the wall to her left by an expandable black rod, but it hung neglected.

Lynn rushed in anxiously. "I just found out. Are you all right?"

"Oh, okay. How about you?"

"Some cuts and smoke inhalation. And they pulled about a quarter of a pound of pepper out of my eyes. But they released me, and I was waiting for you when they told me—"

"Oh, well," she said with a yawn. "They didn't worry about the bullet crease so much as the fact that I had that *and* a fever and chills." With a wave of her hand, she anticipated and dismissed a response. "I know, I know, I shouldn't have gone into the snow without my coat."

"As I recall, you didn't have much choice."

"True," she yawned.

"Hey, are you all right? You seem to be taking it all rather calmly."

"It's my own fault. At the party, I wished and wished that I could go to bed and get some sleep. My wish came true. It's the antibiotic that's knocking me out. But the doctor said I'll probably be released tomorrow."

"Christmas Eve," Lynn observed tenderly and stooped to kiss her.

"Don't," Jenny said, closing her eyes coyly. "I probably have strep."

"I'll risk it," Lynn whispered, kissing her lips. "Now scoot over." Sitting next to her tightly she reached into her purse and showed Jenny a portable cassette player the size of her hand. "Here. I bought you this for Christmas, but maybe it's better I give it to you now. It'll help pass the time." She placed it on the table near the window and pushed the volume to a barely audible level, whereupon the machine produced the sweet and mellow sounds of Glenn Miller's "Sunrise Serenade," a song Jenny particularly liked.

"That's nice. Thanks." The music gave the room a gentle, loving aura. "So!" Jenny said abruptly, as if keeping herself awake. "They save the house?"

"Most of it. The firemen did a good job. Neighbors are pretty upset, though."

"And not particularly grateful, I bet. Well, they're just not used to firefights on their block. Boy! I'm tired. Police know why they shot Uncle Dominic?"

"No," Lynn said simply.

"Terri give you any idea?"

"No, because—"

"Because she's not really his niece."

"Hey! How'd you know that?"

Jenny kept her eyes closed and answered as if she were a wise man making a pronouncement. "Terri didn't look like she had any Sicilian blood in her to me. And that 'Italian prayer' crack! There is a difference between Sicilians and Italians, you know. It sounded like she was a stranger to him. Were they related at all?"

"That's what he said when he suddenly appeared four years ago. Told her he was her mother's uncle's cousin. Terri didn't really believe it, but she believed his money. Anderson ran a check on his name. No Dominic Bonsignor ever worked as a translator for the OSS. In fact, according to the computers, no such person ever existed."

This made Jenny open her eyes. "So, the name's a fake. Dominic Bonsignor. In English that translates as Dominic the Good Man. An interesting choice of names! I wonder who he was. What did the police say?"

Lynn had been holding something back and now eased into it. "That computers are not infallible. That it didn't necessarily mean anything that there was no record of him. What did interest them were *our* records. The police say that the men were after us and Uncle Dominic got in the way."

"Any chance of that? The killers look familiar to you?"

"No friends of mine. The whole idea's a crock, but the neighbors and the police are giving Anderson a lot of grief, so guess what he's ordered us to do?"

"Clear it up for him. Well, babe, I don't think I'm going to be of much use to you from here. I think you're on your own."

Safely at Jenny's house on Dexter off Foxhall, Lynn sat on her legs on one of the couches, sipped some of Jenny's Martell from a snifter, and started to make some notes before she called Anderson again. The oaken grandfather's clock in the corner with Tempus Fugit scripted under the face had just chimed three. Lynn had waited until Jenny was asleep and then piloted her white Fiat down the steep incline of Foxhall Road that seemed steeper and bottomless because of the ice. Her eyes felt heavy, but Lynn knew she couldn't sleep. Not without Jenny. Also, this was something Lynn had developed from their being together, a restlessness, an energy that would not die.

Jenny's head shot up from the pillow. She was gasping and wet with sweat. Running her hand over her face, she shook her head, trying to decide whether she had remembered something or dreamed it. Her hands fumbling, uncertain from sleep and sedative, she pushed the clock on the side table near the phone and tape recorder so that she could read the numbers: 3:37 in red-orange digitals. Stretching, she grabbed the phone slowly and deliberately punched the push buttons to call her own number.

"Lynn?"

"Jenny? What's wrong?"

"Just . . . hold on," she slurred, haltingly. "Let me . . . get it out. I remembered something. Something about this Rick . . . that wasn't right. When he came up to me, he asked if I was a friend of *Cary's*. I figured he thought one thing and said another, it happens. But the more I think about it, it was like he was a stranger there, like he didn't know Terri—"

"Well, neither did you. He could have been—"

"I know, I know, he could have been a friend of a friend, but that's not all. I know I told him to make a bomb with the brandy, but what amateur throws a Molotov cocktail thirty feet and makes a direct hit on a man with a gun? He wasn't an amateur! Hell, when everyone else was on the floor, I passed him in the hall. He was standing, he was out of the line of fire! He knew the killers were coming."

"Okay, Jenny, slow down. I think you're on to something. Anderson just called. He ran a check on Uncle Dominic's description. His real name was Pasquale Gabrielli. He was a translator for the OSS who was sent back to Sicily in 1944 to get information on Nazi troop movements. He moved in with a Mafia chieftain who was playing both ends against the middle; he learned what he had to learn; and he passed it on to the Allies. The Nazis thought that the chieftain was leaking it and killed him and his family. Gabrielli was called a traitor by his own people."

"That's why he named himself Dominic the good man, to justify his actions."

"The U.S. gives him money; he assumes a new identity, years pass, he moves in with Terri as still another way of covering his tracks. But then he sees you at a party and tells you that something has happened, he needs help."

"They'd spotted him! So that's it! It was an old-fashioned hit for the oldest motive around—revenge. Rick was the inside man. They could have done it in the street with a knife, but instead they wanted to even the score by killing Uncle Dominic with his family and friends. Yet they wanted to divert suspicion from the Mafia, and that's where we come in. We're there, everyone gets killed, and the police think we're the target 'cause we're spies."

"How'd they know we would be there? How'd they know we were—"

"They followed you when you left Terri's one day,

194

then they tapped the phones, maybe. I don't know how! But Rick wasn't hitting on me. He was sizing me up, seeing exactly what he'd brought into his plan."

"It works. But why did he throw the bomb? Why did he kill his own men?"

"Because we were too good, damn it! We killed two of them right off. Dominic was dead, the main part of the plan was completed, but if anyone got caught they might implicate Rick. So he helped us kill them all."

"Jenny, call Anderson. I'll be right there."

"What?"

"Unless he's dumb, and he's not, he knows you can finger him. He was sizing you up; maybe he's smart enough to know that you'll put it together exactly like you just did. Call Anderson, now!"

Lynn dressed quickly in sweater and jeans, pulled her .38 Detective Special from her purse, but then thought twice about it and took Jenny's .357 Magnum from the lingerie cabinet. As she ran out to the driveway, her boots slid to the left, and she landed heavily on her side. Looking up, she saw that the sidewalk and street were literally shining from the reflection of the streetlights against their mirrorlike coat of ice. "Damn it," she hissed, as she crawled on her elbows and knees to Jenny's Fiat. She started the car, and it floated into the center of the street, but then waddled there, its wheels spinning silently since the ice was so smooth the tires found no traction. Slowly, the Fiat started to slide backward down Dexter. Lynn took control and hit the gas, accelerating the backward motion. Like a wayward missile, the Fiat shot down Dexter, but Lynn played with its curves and the pull from the ice, yanking the wheel from left to right. The front spun too far to the right and bounced against a placid, yellow Volvo, but by then Lynn was at the bottom of the hill, which was still icy but at least level and a straight shot to the main avenue where the salt trucks go first because it's a bus route.

Jenny rested her head on her outstretched arm, the receiver in her hand, the dial tone buzzing, summoning up the strength to call Anderson. The light from the window to her right was fitful and weak, which matched how she felt. Slowly, she pointed her finger at the buttons, but then the buzzing stopped. What was it? Did they turn off the phones at a certain hour? If so, they didn't wait until three o'clock in the morning, that much she knew. Someone had shut off her phone.

She grabbed the buzzer from the side table to call the nurse, but when she pressed it she could sense that there was nothing electrical about it anymore, that it was connected to air.

Without thinking about the pain, she plucked the IV from her arm, then pushed her back up to the headboard. But even that tired her. She looked across at the door. The space between it and her was dark and seemed to grow in length as she stared at it. But if someone had cut off her phone and nurse buzzer, she'd be better off in the light of the hallway.

The door opened. Maybe her buzzer had been connected after all. But the figure just stood there, tall, too tall for a nurse, dressed in white, an orderly perhaps; but then why did he shut the door behind him, why stand in the darkness?

"Rick?" she whispered.

"I knew you were good, that you'd guess it. That's why I'm here."

There was no way she could find the light switch in time. She heard him moving toward her. With every ounce of strength she had, Jenny stood up. "Don't—don't come close," she said. "I have strep."

He was coming around the bed. She could see something glistening in the darkness, the way in the movies of her youth a floating object would indicate the presence of an invisible man. He had a knife, which was reflecting the few rays of light in the room, and she was too weak to fight him. "It was supposed to look like you and your friend were being eliminated," he was saying. "And that's how this will look."

Jenny's only real hope was to raise help. Remembering that Lynn's gift, the cassette player, was on the side table, she reached down and flipped the volume to maximum. The room was filled with the mellow melodies of Glenn Miller.

At the sound of the music, he lurched toward her. Then she felt it against her bare back, the television set that was attached to the wall by an expandable metal arm. Jenny moved a step to her left, reached behind her and found the back of the set, and just as the knife came down shoved the set at him as hard as she could. As it shot forward into his face, she heard the glass screen shatter. He fell backward screaming, and the glistening knife disappeared from view as if it had been dropped and lost.

Jenny's confidence was renewed. He was down, the knife was gone, and she had a chance to make it to the door, the hallway, and its light. He was blocking her way, and the only path was over the bed. Instinctively, she placed both hands on the sheets and started a sommersault, kicking her feet high in the air. But her arms were suddenly weak and numb and caved in under her. She fell across the bed, her feet thumping against the floor, the center of her back hitting the metal bed frame. Jenny screamed out, both in pain and because she felt that she had now been rendered immobile.

Rick, bleeding from the forehead, clumsily wiped the blood from his eyes and savagely struck out at the tape player. It crashed against the wall, lost its tape, and stopped its music. Turning, he saw her sprawled across the bed, grabbed her pillow, and leapt upon her.

Her chin was up, her mouth open. The pillow covered her face completely, forcing her breath out and sealing her mouth with cloth. Jenny struck at him with both hands but could not see and almost immediately felt the energy of her mind ebbing with the loss of breath.

The hallway's light cut through the darkness as the door opened and an orderly rushed in. "What's the matter with you, playing music at—" Then he saw them in the focus of the light, a man suffocating a woman.

Caught, with the only open exit blocked, Rick let go of the pillow, picked up the side table and threw it through the window. The orderly pulled the pillow off Jenny's face. Her head jerked up, snapping at the air around her.

The white Fiat wheeled into the hospital parking lot just as the side table came through the second-floor window. Lynn approached the hospital building to her left, barely avoiding the snow-covered parked cars to her right. The broken window meant that Jenny was in trouble, but if Lynn hit the brakes on that ice she'd spin out of control. Lynn turned the ignition key off. The car slowed down, swerving slightly to the left. Lynn grabbed the .357 Magnum from the seat, opened the door, and jumped out. She hit the ice on her belly and slid swiftly forward toward the building.

Rick stepped out, his feet on the sill. It was a short jump, and there was a mound of snow directly beneath him from an abortive attempt to clear the parking lot before the temperature dropped. And then he saw Lynn.

She swung her feet in front of her, then pulled herself into a sitting position, still sliding on the ice. Digging her heels in, she stopped just twenty feet from the building, with Rick standing above her. She grabbed her left wrist with her right hand and fired. The impact threw her back onto the ice, her head feeling the asphalt beneath it. But she heard the ploppish sound of his lifeless form falling into the snow bank.

While snowfall affects Washington, D.C., in various ways, the aftereffects are usually the same. Unless it's a major storm, the rays of the clearing, morning sun swiftly melt the ice and snow. The streets stay damp for a while, but soon, except for the mounds in the parking lots that become hard and crusty and difficult to get rid of, there's no indication that anything ever happened.

At four o'clock in the afternoon on December 24, Lynn came into Jenny's new room on the third floor. This one had a window that was intact.

"How are you?" Lynn asked, pointing to the back brace visible through the neck of Jenny's gown.

"Another week, but no real damage," she said resignedly. "How 'bout you?"

Lynn touched the bandages around her head. "A little spongy yet. But they're releasing me. Anderson's happy. The FBI is happy. The neighbors aren't quite as angry. And the hospital would like us out as soon as your legendary recuperative powers allow. But they too have a heart. The census is still down, so they said I could stay in the next bed tonight."

"Ah, yes," Jenny sighed, reaching for Lynn's hand. "Merry Christmas."

Funeral for a Friend

PETER HEYRMAN

"Funeral for a Friend" is one of a series of stories
Peter Heyrman has written about the relationship
between an artist and his work. Most of these
pieces are works of fantasy or science fiction; this
is the only one about crime and the only one
about a writer. Mr. Heyrman has completed a
science-fiction novel that is awaiting publication.
The author has dedicated this story to his brother,
Jack Heyrman.

They wanted me to stick the spade into the dirt and
scrape away nearly half a century. A thousand people
had asked the questions. For some reason I was supposed to get the answers. Maybe it would work. The
questions were so dusty now that they might be a
surprise. Or so I thought, as my plane landed in L.A.

The next morning I found myself in a car, driving
over a freeway that hadn't even been imagined in
that last year of peace, forty-six years earlier. A million cars swarmed through the sunlight, and rock 'n'
roll blared from the tape deck. It should've been
Tommy Dorsey on a radio with bad reception. For
that matter, the road should've been two lanes, and
the car deserved a running board. It was that kind
of project.

From the freeway I turned onto a boulevard. That
made more sense. A few of the structures on it
might've even dated back to the time I was looking

for. Finally, I got to the driveway. My car rolled through the entrance, and I found myself in the shadows of a row of overgrown palms. The lawn was shaggy, and the shrubs hadn't been touched for years. The mansion sat at the top of the hill, paint peeling from its stucco walls. Chintz curtains covered the french doors. Canvas blocked the oriels.

The house hadn't been breathed on since 1939. Grant Marshall, the greatest mystery writer of the '30s, had lived there then, along with the actress Glenda Townsend. Glenda had fled the lights of Broadway and run to Hollywood for Grant—and, some said, for money. I'd heard that she hadn't set foot from the mansion in forty-six years. She hadn't given an interview either.

An hour earlier I'd spoken to her on the phone. I'd asked her if I could speak to her in person.

"Yes, and you'll want to talk about the party we had here all that time ago," she'd croaked. I could hear the empty mansion around her.

"That's right," I admitted.

"Perhaps it's time." Her voice was tired. "I suppose you may come out." That was more than she'd ever said to any writer.

"Today at noon?" I'd asked.

"Yes . . . all right." Then the phone had clicked, leaving a hollow sound for me to listen to.

I parked and climbed the steps. I could smell the mustiness of the house from outside. I knocked. Nothing. I knocked again. I heard footsteps. The door opened, spilling out the house's ancient breath. A maid stared at me.

"I'm from *Suspense* magazine," I started. "I'm here to see Miss Townsend."

"I'm sorry," the maid said. "Miss Townsend has changed her mind."

"What?"

"Miss Townsend is indisposed."

"But she said she would talk to me."

"She is sorry to have caused you undue trouble." The maid began to close the door.

"Just a minute. Couldn't she tell me herself?"

"I'm sorry." The door shut, forcing out another musty breath.

I banged on it, then stopped. I could hear the echo of my fists bouncing off barren walls. No one was listening.

The party Glenda Townsend had spoken of had taken place in 1939. Grant Marshall had given it in late summer. The cream of Hollywood and New York had been there to see the end of a character. It was the end of an era too: August 31, 1939. Grant Marshall was never seen after that night. Nor was the world that had spawned him.

There were only two people left who'd remember the party. One was Glenda Townsend. Even when she'd been a movie star she hadn't been the gregarious type, so I shouldn't have been surprised when her maid turned me away. As I drove back down the hill I could feel Glenda Townsend's ageless eyes watching me from behind the chintz curtains. Her chicken neck would be contracting as her lips formed words she might have said to me.

The second person was Mike Carmell. He'd been thirty when it happened, the same age I am now. Carmell was a minor mystery writer who'd turned out some good short stories for the hard-boiled pulps.

Eventually he'd written a good novel. Grant Marshall had brought him to Hollywood and put him to work polishing scripts. After Marshall's final party, Carmell never published another word. He turned to directing, and worked on several cheap gangster films, but he never made a name. He was a private man and liked it that way. Carmell hadn't said any more about Marshall's final party than any of the other guests. He'd confirmed accounts of arriving, and he'd told the names of the other guests, but he never spoke of what had happened after midnight. No one did. At the time, reporters had referred to it as "The Pumpkin Act." It took them thirty years to stop asking about it. Now here I was with the same old question.

When I called Carmell he said he'd talk to me. As I drove to his house I wondered if he'd turn out like Glenda Townsend, but I shouldn't have worried: He let me in.

He lived in a small split-level in the San Fernando Valley. It was high enough to escape most of the smog. Carmell met me at the door and led me into a dark-paneled living room. Thick curtains allowed only one lonely shaft of light through the picture window.

"Every Californian likes light but me," he rasped. His voice was raw from years of cigarettes. He lit one as he sat down. I sat across from him in an armchair. Light glinted in his eyes, making them the only bright spots in a faded, wrinkled face. He had no hair.

"You want to talk to me about Grant, don't you," he said.

"Yes."

"You're the first one in fifteen years. I suppose you'll want to ask me about the party."

"That's right."

"And you want to know how it ended." A tiny smile bent his lips.

"That's the big question."

"And I'll say, 'I turned into a pumpkin at midnight.' "

"Are you sure you'll say that?" I asked.

He leaned back and exhaled smoke. "No." He stared at the ceiling. "Did you ever suppose I might not know? Maybe none of us knew. Perhaps Grant left us in a trance and disappeared into Mexico like Ambrose Bierce."

"Bierce was his favorite author," I said.

"You've read the old clippings, haven't you? They all cite that. I don't know if it was true, though."

"Marshall said it."

"Yes, he told interviewers that at least a dozen times in that last year. He never said it to me, though. Did you try to talk to Glenda?"

"Yes. She invited me to come out, but when I got there she'd changed her mind."

"Glenda told you to come out there?"

"Yes. Then the maid slammed the door in my face."

His eyes grew distant. "But she started out saying you could. She'd never really be able to talk."

"Will you talk?" I asked.

"If I did, what would you do?"

"Write about it."

"Who'd you say you write for?"

"*Suspense* magazine. I've written fiction for them. Last week the editor called and asked if I'd try this."

"One last attempt, huh?" Carmell coughed. "Soon Glenda and I will be gone, and the story will die with us. It's supposed to work that way . . . but Glenda wanted to see you."

"At first."

"She must've wanted to tell. I always thought she might." He said it dreamily. For a moment his eyes got lost in reverie, then his eyes sharpened. "Let's start where we always start. I'll tell you about the invitation, arriving, and all that, then we'll see what develops."

"I'm listening."

He closed his eyes. "Grant always told me to begin at the beginning." Carmell proceeded to do that.

Marshall had called Carmell a week beforehand, the same day he called Faulkner, Hammett, Bogart, Parker, and the rest of them.

"I'm calling to invite you to a funeral," he said. His tone was frivolous.

"A funeral?"

"Well, maybe it's more like a wake. It's certainly an ending."

"What the hell are you talking about, Grant?"

He laughed. "Now, don't be worried, old sport. I'm simply celebrating the demise of my detective, Robert Emmet. He's no longer with us." Emmet was Marshall's best creation. Some thought he was the best fictional detective ever.

"You're not using him anymore?" Carmell asked.

"That's right. He's my character, and I say he's finished. I'm burying him. His dark hour has come." *Dark Hour* was the title of Marshall's latest book.

"Are you killing him off?" Carmell asked.

"I guess you could put it that way."

"Why?"

Marshall's voice grew weary. "He's turned into a burden, Mike. I think this is the best way to get rid of him. Will you come?"

Carmell hesitated. "What night is it?"

"The thirty-first. How about it, old sport? There'll be people to meet, liquor to drink, and a good time will be had by all. I'm inviting Bill Faulkner, Mae West, Dash Hammett . . . you'll have the time of your life."

Carmell glanced at his calendar. He had no excuse handy. "I'll be there."

"Fine. Glenda's been asking about you. She wants to see you."

They hung up, and the following week Carmell found himself in a limousine, being chauffered to Marshall's mansion. Grant was at the door to greet him. His smile was so wide it looked as if it hurt his face.

"You haven't been around here since we added the new wing," Marshall said. "Let me show you around."

He guided Carmell through house and people. Harpo Marx stood in a corner making faces at guests. Bill Faulkner hovered over a table laden with food. He munched on something and amused a bejeweled starlet between bites. Retired police chief Jack Turlock, who'd helped Grant with research from time to time, danced with Glenda as a band played swing music.

"They'll all be here tonight," Grant said. "I think people are mystified."

"I'm mystified myself," Carmell said. "Throwing

a party for the death of someone who isn't even real."

Grant whirled and stared at him. "Mike, every person we put on paper is real. Robert Emmet is as much flesh and blood as you or me. How could I write about him otherwise?"

"I know he's real in a sense."

"In every sense," Marshall insisted. "The only difference is we can't quite touch him. Or you can't."

"You're really never going to write about him again?"

"That's right. He's truly dead."

"He couldn't just be in limbo?"

"No. I've brought him through the morgue, pumped embalming fluid into his veins, and dressed him for burial. He won't rise again."

Carmell saw that he meant it. The subject changed, and Marshall regained some of his humor. More guests arrived, and soon the floor sparkled with people. Liquor flowed. Conversation flapped on threescore tongues. An hour later Carmell found himself talking to Glenda.

"Has he talked to you about Emmet's dying?" he asked.

She smiled a sad, beautiful smile. "He promised me it would happen. He's got everything set for it. God knows, I hope it's true."

"But it's his finest creation."

She poured him a drink, then took him into a corner. Carmell gazed at her, wondering what it took to keep a woman like that. She said: "You only see the creation in a book you can't put down. You admire Robert Emmet's mind as he finds the truth in characters you never have to say hello to. What you don't see is when Robert Emmet looks at us." She looked across the floor at her husband. "I live with two men. I love one, and I hate the other."

"You hate Emmet?"

"I detest him. He's almost driven me away from here. Maybe that's why he's dying."

"Is it that bad?" Carmell said, taking her hand.

"He knows every secret."

"And Grant doesn't?"

"No." Her eyes softened. "Grant wears blinders. That's why he can love me. That's why anyone can love anyone."

"Did Grant do this for you?"

"I hope so." She looked desperately into the crowd. "Excuse me, Mike." She escaped onto the dance floor with Dashiell Hammett. Carmell watched them for a moment, then walked away.

Carmell told me a lot of what I already knew. He talked of Glenda most of all and told tales about the other guests. He described the huge swimming pool behind the mansion; he spoke of couples slipping down into the dell, then coming back rumpled and laughing. Now and then I'd stop him to ask when a certain event had taken place. "Nine-thirty," he'd say, or, "That was at ten-fifteen."

Finally the clock of our conversation struck midnight. Marshall had just served each person a glass of champagne. I'd read Faulkner's account, which attested to that. I'd heard Dorothy Parker describe the same scene in an interview. When the interviewer asked her what had happened after that her voice had caught. She hadn't said anything more.

Carmell's voice stopped. I heard his breath wheeze from his lungs. I felt as if we were teetering on the edge of a chasm. Carmell relaxed. He laid his head back and gazed at the ceiling.

"I might as well tell you," he said softly. "Someone ought to tell, even if it is me, the one who wasn't famous, or beautiful, or anything else."

"Tell me," I said.

Suddenly the words gushed from him.

Marshall told his guests: "Don't drink yet, boys and girls. We're going on a little trip. We need a breath of night air." He led them out by the swimming pool. The servants waited there with half a dozen lanterns. Marshall distributed the lanterns, then dismissed the servants.

"You might wonder where we're going now," he said. "At a funeral there has to be a burial. It's a short walk to the grave site. Come along."

He led them through the dell, onto a wooded path. People stepped delicately, doing their best not to spill their champagne. Moonlight seeped through the trees. Marshall walked in front with ex-chief Turlock.

"You love a mystery, don't you, Jack?" Marshall said to him.

"I haven't minded helping you with a few," the old cop admitted.

"You must love yourself then, because you are a mystery."

"I don't get you."

Marshall whispered: "You don't get yourself either. You wonder why you get those urges in the middle of the night. You don't know why you look at that little girl across the street before the lights go off. I've walked by your house in the dark and seen you up there, your eyes aching for her."

"You—"

"That's right. What would your daughters think, Jack?"

Turlock's voice trembled. "G-Grant."

Marshall shook his head. "She can't be more than ten years old, Jack. You really ought to get help."

Turlock slowed, then fell back with the rest of them. Only Carmell had overheard the exchange. He hung behind his friend.

A few minutes later they arrived in a wide clearing. In its center, a casket rested on straps that stretched across a grave. Marshall set his lantern by the hole and faced his guests. "We must drink a toast to the dearly departed," he said. "At midnight, Robert Emmet officially expired. The manuscripts that were his flesh are in this coffin. We'll bury it, and tomorrow a construction crew will cover this hole with a thousand tons of earth. They're making a hill here, and then they're putting a house on top. That should be a good enough grave marker. And none of us shall ever tell."

He paused. "But back to Robert Emmet. Can he really be dead? He's pulled through novels and stories for a decade. We've seen him in movies, heard him on the radio." Marshall looked at Hammett. "A few critics thought Sam Spade paled in comparison. I never agreed. But he's joining Spade and the Op. They're dead too, aren't they, Dash?"

Hammett stood silent.

"I'm surprised you never gave them a fitting funeral," Marshall said. "Or maybe they weren't available, having drowned in a sea of booze." Hammett's eyes flared, but he didn't budge. Marshall turned to Faulkner. "Bill, did you cry when you murdered Joe Christmas?"

"Now, Grant . . ." Faulkner drawled.

"I'd like to know. I've killed thugs and innocents, and I've cried sometimes. Now I'm murdering my greatest creation, and I haven't a tear to shed." He glanced at Bogart. "Why, Bogie, you've died in half your pictures. And you're young. I'd think you'll die a thousand deaths with that face. Do you mourn the men you were?"

"When it's done I still get up in the morning," Bogart said, flames flickering light across his face. "When do we get to drink this stuff?"

"In a moment. First let me tell you what killed Emmet. He died of truth. In each chapter he became more real, and while I was writing the last novel I half-expected him to step off the page and join me. It wasn't a prospect I enjoyed."

"It's fratricide," Faulkner muttered. Eyes turned to him. "You're killing your own brother."

Marshall smiled. "Don't take it so hard, Bill. He's not your brother."

"No, but to you . . . it's like murdering your son, too."

Carmell looked at Glenda Townsend. She stood closest to the grave. "Let's get this over with," she breathed.

"This isn't a ceremony to be hurried," Marshall said. He raised his glass to the crowd. "I've saved this champagne for a toast to the dead. Robert Emmet's life amused us and fattened many of our bank accounts." Marshall paused for a moment. A grimace crossed his face. "I suppose he filled someone's empty hours, so he's owed something." He forced a smile. "But that's the problem with these damn people on pages: We can never pay them for their trouble. And when you can't pay someone a debt it festers like an open wound. We call it resentment. It can lead to murder." A chuckle escaped him. "To the late Robert Emmet."

Other hands lifted glasses in the lantern light. A few lips echoed the words. Marshall tossed his drink down his throat. Everyone else followed.

Marshall eyed the crowd. "Have I any volunteers to put this in the ground?" Three came forward, including Carmell. They lowered the coffin into the ground and shoveled dirt on it. The work went quickly. "It doesn't have to be perfect," Marshall said. "The bulldozers will do the rest."

They slipped back through the woods to the house. Once they were inside Marshall called for the band. "Let's have some music!" Notes from the piano rippled through the room.

Carmell lost himself in the crowd. He danced with Mary DeWitt, a rising starlet, then talked with Jim Granger, another Hollywood comer. Granger's first role had been that of a young gunman in the Robert Emmet film *The Round Room*.

"What did you think of the toast?" Granger asked.

"I think he's a little drunk," Carmell said.

"I haven't noticed him drinking much."

"Then maybe he's giddy. That might come from killing your meal ticket."

Granger said: "You're a writer. Can you get dependent on a character?"

"Ask me when I've taken one through six novels."

"I think he's going nuts," Granger said bitterly.

"Possibly."

Marshall came over to them. He was somber, almost withdrawn. "I hope you're having a good time," he said quietly.

"Fine," Granger said.

Marshall eyed the actor. "Yes, a fine time picking my behavior apart. You think I'm a little off, don't you, Jim?"

Granger stepped back. "I never said—"

"Oh, I may be, a little. We all have three-in-the-morning thoughts, don't we, Jim? I know what it's like for you, waking from another drunk, looking into the dark. I know what you see in those shadows. That's when you must be glad the woman lying beside you doesn't stir. If she ever did and saw what was in your eyes—"

Granger backed away. "Shut up."

"If she saw that would you let her live?"

Granger fled through the crowd.

"What the hell are you doing?" Carmell asked Marshall.

"I can see inside people tonight. It's as if they're all my own characters."

"What you need is a drink."

"I have one," Marshall said, plucking a glass from the table. "Does it ever happen to you, Mike?"

"What?"

"You look at someone and see straight through him. You see the stuff he's made of, what his secrets are. You know how fragile he is and what he can stand. Tonight I can do it with anyone." He gulped his drink. "You're right. I need another."

The two men went to the bar. Carmell noticed guests slinking away from Marshall's path. A moment later the men were sipping scotch-and-sodas. Mary DeWitt approached them. She eyed Marshall curiously.

"How are you, Mary?" he asked. His voice was

low, as it had been with Granger. "Would you dance with me?"

"Well—"

"Come now, a dance with the host."

She looked as if she'd like to be somewhere else.

"Just a short one," Marshall said.

"All right."

Marshall took the blonde woman's hand and led her onto the floor. Carmell watched them. Marshall danced gracefully, and Mary lost her reluctance as she followed his fluid steps. Marshall never took his eyes from her. He smiled, he talked. She barely said a word.

Faulkner and Hammett came within earshot. They saw Marshall dancing with the starlet. "He's giving it to her now," Faulkner said sadly.

"He doesn't know the goddamn danger," Hammett added.

Their steps were still smooth, but Mary stopped smiling. Marshall's lips moved, but Carmell couldn't hear the words. Couples stepped away from them. Mary turned her head away from her partner. It was as if he'd stripped her naked. Her steps grew clumsy. She stumbled. The music ended mercifully. She almost fell from his arms and walked away unsteadily. There was a flat, hard look in his eye. It faded as he returned to the side of the room. Marshall picked up his drink and downed it.

"What the hell is wrong with you?" Carmell demanded.

Marshall glared at him, then let the glare die. He chuckled sadly. "No, no," he muttered, "not to you."

"What are you talking about?"

"It's like I told you. I saw through that girl. I saw every nasty little thought."

"I still don't get it."

"Don't you? I'm the ultimate psychoanalyst tonight, Mike. Freud can't hold a candle to me. I don't know why, but it's true."

"Like the man you killed," Carmell said.

"What?"

"Like Robert Emmet. I remember you wrote that he could read motives the way most people read traffic signs."

Marshall looked hard at Carmell. "I could tell you a few things about yourself. I've read your work. That tells all."

Carmell's stomach tightened. He struggled to keep his voice from shaking. "I know you see it. Say it if you want. I can't stop you. But if I were you I'd go up and sleep it off, Grant."

"One night you told me something about your father, something you'd seen. You were drunk. Maybe you don't recall now—"

"I remember," Carmell hissed. "I had to tell someone, so—"

"You said more than you thought. It was in the words you chose, your tone of voice. You thought you were speaking of him, but you were really talking about yourself."

"Grant, please. I'm asking you as a friend." Carmell struggled to keep his hands by his sides. He tried to wipe the fear from his face. "You're saying too much—to me, to everyone. You'll be happier in the morning if you go to bed now."

The knifelike look left Marshall's face. "You're lucky, Mike. You're not bad with words, but you don't have to feel the world you put on paper. Maybe Bill and Dash do. Maybe that's why Dash hasn't written a damn thing except plot outlines for silly movies in five years. We've learned to hate our characters as much as we love them." He finished his scotch and put down his glass. "Thank God you aren't like me, Mike. I didn't do what I meant to do tonight, but thanks for helping me try."

With that the party's host thrust his hands into his pockets and walked to the stairs. Carmell watched him climb them. Glenda came and took Carmell by the arm. He liked the feel of her fingers.

"He's done some damage," she whispered.

"People are angry, aren't they?"

"They're livid. He's never gotten like that with anyone but me. I wanted to kill him, but I learned to take it. Now he's seen them all that way."

Marshall took the final stair. He was the weariest soul Carmell had ever seen. "I think Robert Emmet is dead," he breathed.

"No," Glenda replied. "He's just going to sleep."

Carmell glanced at his watch. It was two-thirty. He watched Glenda drift into the crowd, smiling, glittering like a diamond.

Without Marshall the party took a freer air. Mary DeWitt did a fan dance while people cheered. Hammett and Faulkner argued briefly but then were calmed by other guests. It was no longer a night for quarrels. People seemed to share the common bond of the injured, and now they tried desperately to heal.

At three o'clock, Carmell wondered when the party would wind down. He told Glenda he'd be glad to stay and help clear away the excess guests. People started leaving in twos and threes. Mae West took her entourage, and the gathering dwindled to fewer than a dozen. At three-thirty Carmell was watching Hammett pour a nightcap when the scream came. Everyone looked up the stairs to the shadowed hall. Carmell bolted up the steps two at a time. The others stood mute, then slowly followed.

Carmell rushed down the hall and found Glenda standing in a doorway. Her hand was to her mouth. She barely breathed. Beyond her, Grant Marshall sat behind his desk, his head toppled at an improbable angle. His lips were bent in a crazy smile. His eyes saw nothing.

"Goddamn," Carmell breathed. He turned to Glenda and touched her cheek. She came out of her trance.

"Is he dead?" she said levelly.

Carmell stepped forward and felt for a pulse that wasn't there. "Yes," he told her.

A half-dozen guests crowded around the door. They stood behind Glenda and stared at the corpse.

"What happened?" someone asked.

Glenda cleared her throat. "He killed himself," she said softly.

"Are you sure?" Jim Granger asked. He didn't take his eyes off the body.

"He told me once that he kept poison in that desk. I never looked to see if it was true. I didn't want to."

Carmell looked down at the floor and spotted the tiny glass bottle. It was where it ought to be.

"Why would he do it, Glenda?" Hammett asked quietly.

She glared at him. "Because he knew he was already dead."

"I don't see it," Hammett said.

"It was the thing inside him, it ate him up."

Hammett looked at the dead man and nodded. The rest of them kept looking at Marshall to avoid each other.

"It's not the way Grant should've gone," Faulkner said.

"It's not the way he went," Glenda said. "Grant withered and faded from the world some time ago. I hoped he'd come back to life tonight, but the death was real."

Mary DeWitt whispered, "Mightn't someone've . . . ?" No one finished the question for her.

Glenda touched the dead man's cheek. "The world mustn't think Grant died this way." She faced the others. "Lately he's talked a lot about Ambrose Bierce, and how he disappeared and was never seen again. That's what happened to Grant. The world must believe that."

Mike Carmell glanced from her to the body. "What do we do with him?" he asked, holding back a sob. He wondered if he was crying for the dead man or himself.

Carmell sat in the gloom, his old eyes squeezed shut.

"What did you do?" I asked.

The eyes opened. "We took him to the grave. I don't even remember how we did it, but we buried him. I remember praying. We all prayed."

I thought of the legends, the articles, and the interviews. There was the Grant Marshall who'd gone into Mexico to find Bierce, or the one who joined the army under an assumed name and was killed in some distant battle. Some said he still roamed the world and sometimes slipped back into Hollywood to see his reclusive wife.

"Did you plant the crazy lies about him?" I asked.

"We didn't have to. We just kept our mouths shut, and the stories created themselves."

"But sixty people . . ."

"That night he'd talked to every one of us and seen what was inside. If anyone had told, they would've had to tell their own little secrets. The rest of us would've made them tell. Among ourselves we called it suicide."

"What about the police?"

"Turlock helped us there. Grant's affairs were in order, almost as if he'd planned it all along. We told all questioners that we'd last seen him at midnight. No one quite believed it, but what could they say?"

"Who killed him?" I asked.

"You said that, not me," the old man said coolly.

"Someone did kill him," I said.

Carmell eyed me. "You're a young man looking for mysteries to solve. I grew old that night. When I saw him dead I'd had my share of mysteries. Some things aren't meant to be discovered. They're only meant to be concluded."

"What if I publish what you've said?"

"I'll deny it."

"Then you don't want me to write the story?"

"You say that you write fiction. Are you good at it?"

"I think so," I told him.

"Then stay with that. It's a rare talent. Don't bother with the facts."

I stared at him, but he wouldn't meet my eyes. "You never wrote again, did you, Carmell?"

"Not a word," he rasped. "He took my stories with him. I don't know how, but he did."

"Did you try?"

"Every day."

"Did you kill him?"

"No," he stammered.

"You had reason to. You wanted Glenda."

"I never said that."

"Your whole story said it."

He sucked what air he could into his worn lungs. "I watched him die."

"You went up and saw him, didn't you?"

Carmell glared at me. "Yes. I found him with the poison in his hand. He was calm. He asked me if I thought he should take it, but I think he'd already made up his mind. I said he should."

"You let him do it so you could get his woman, but you never got her, did you?"

"You've got it wrong," the old man croaked. "I did it because he wasn't Grant anymore."

"You're hiding."

"No more than any man hides. I did what any person there would've done, what anyone on Earth would've done. He'd seen too much. It made him a monster. I told him to take his secrets with him."

"Then you watched him die."

"Yes, and he watched me." The old man coughed, then wiped his lips. "I saw everything in those eyes."

I looked into Carmell's face and saw the decades of barren pages, a thousand stories he could never tell.

"He took you with him, Carmell. Why'd you let him do it?"

"Damn you," he hissed.

"How could you let him take that one piece—"

"Get out!" he cried. A sob welled up from his stomach and left him like a last gasp.

For a moment I stood mute, then said, "I'm sorry." He didn't hear me. He sat staring into the darkness of memory.

I walked out into the bright sun of the Valley. Behind me an ancient pair of eyes peered into nothingness, measuring the distance to his grave. Every few seconds he would draw in a shallow breath, then let it go. It sounded like a death rattle.

A Perfect Gentleman

JOSEPH KOENIG

Joseph Koenig's *Floater*, published by the Mysterious Press, was nominated for an Edgar Award as the best first novel of 1986 by the Mystery Writers of America, and for a Macavity Award by the Mystery Readers of America. His second book, *Little Odessa*, is due out early next year from Viking. Mr. Koenig, who has written some 900 true-crime stories for pulp magazines, made his fiction debut with "The Scoop" in *New Black Mask #4*. Currently, he is at work on a novel with the working title *Smugglers Notch*.

We got another legal eagle down at the public defender's office that handles shopliftings and spittin' on the sidewalks, but you're the first private mouthpiece we've seen since R. J. had to haul in his shingle. You was his gal in law school, that right? I hope you won't take it personal if he don't look happy to see you, as you might say he's down on the fair sex in general. Oh, he's still all man, that's what you're thinkin'. I just wouldn't stand too close, I was you.

Of course, when you two was an item, R. J. was the perfect gentleman. Lord knows he always had plenty of gals to practice on. Charged it off to public relations and got his dollar's worth for sure, 'cause it was his way with the ladies that brung him Dove Parker durin' the big hubbub over her husband.

Old Buster Parker, of which Dove was his better

half, was the 180-degrees opposite of R. J. A real jokester is what you'd call him, and he saved all his best gags for the femmes. A funny thing he liked to do, he'd wet a twenty-dollar bill in battery acid and quick hurry down to the five-and-dime and change it for a mess of cheap stuff he didn't hardly want. Couple of hours later, the twenty was all ate away and the clerk'd be wonderin' how come the register was runnin' short. He pulled that one on Tess Finch and it cost her to the tune of forty scoots till she caught on. But that was just Buster's way of sayin' hi. Ain't no secret he had the hots for Tess ever since she come back to Lincoln Falls. Only Tess wouldn't of give him the time of day even if Dove wasn't her best friend when they was at school together. She'd claw his eyes out is more like it. After samplin' Buster's sense of humor, Tess run out of patience with men who liked games.

How a randy old goat like Buster come to hitch up with a genteel lady half his age is another gag, only it got played on Dove. Dove come from one of the best families in Lincoln Falls and loaded, too, till her pa lost everythin' in the market. Dove couldn't abide Buster comin' around to see her, but as he held the note on the house, her pa had give him the pick of the litter. When Dove disappeared from Main Street after the nuptials, we figured she'd had a change of heart and the honeymoon wouldn't never end. Wasn't till the trial we learned Buster was usin' her for a speed bag and she was ashamed to show the results in public.

This went on a good two, three years till Dove wouldn't take no more. One night Buster come home and duked her around like always, tore off her undies, and told her exactly what he was fixin' to do to her. Dove didn't say nothin' as she was savin' up a surprise for Buster. While he was tuggin' his shirt over his head she grabbed under the bed where she'd stashed his pump gun and painted the walls with his brains. Then she rung up the sheriff's office so cool it could of been a pizza she was orderin' with anchovies and mushrooms, the works. When the deputies dropped by, Dove was on the horn with R. J. beggin' him to get on her defense.

They ain't nothin' rankled R. J. more'n to see a lady took advantage of, so it didn't require a lot of persuadin' to put him in her corner. By split decision, Dove was the best-lookin' woman in Lincoln Falls if you care for 'em shapely and well-bred all wrapped up in one. The other contender was Tess Finch, who's a brassy sort of redhead, and there's somethin' to say for that, too. Hands down Dove had the most dough, least she was gonna if she got her hooks on what her late husband had left her. What with all the rough stuff she'd been fieldin' from Buster, R. J. guaranteed he'd get any jury in the county to let her off scot free. When Dove wanted to show her thanks in addition to the usual fee, that didn't strike him as cruel and unusual punishment. He just tipped the guards a sawbuck to turn their backs and bring a champagne breakfast in the A.M. Those two got so lovey-dovey they was even talk of weddin' bells and the patter of little feet. But as R. J.'s dance card was already filled, he had to burn the candle at several ends so's not to let down his steady dates too hard.

Now, as he generally made her skin crawl, Dove had never got nearer to her late husband than the bare minimum. That don't mean she wasn't tryin' to make up for lost opportunity with R. J. By the time Dove's day in court rolled around, R. J.'d spread himself so thin he was lookin' like somethin' the cat had in the alley. He still had his wits about him, though. Since Buster was not what you would call a favorite with the femmes, R. J. packed an even dozen of 'em on the jury. Instead of their sunny dispositions, he picked 'em mainly for looks. They's a school of thought it was somethin' of a mistake, considerin' that if you don't count Tess Finch at number twelve, all them gals had it in for Dove startin' when she won out for queen at the junior high prom three years runnin'.

Pretty quick R. J.'d got another problem with the jury. Which was that he couldn't take his eyes off of that red hair of Tess or get too comfy with her either, as this is a violation of the judicial canons right there and Dove Parker'd go to pieces if she had an idea his affections was up for grabs. The way Tess was starin' back at him, it was every gal for herself soon as Dove was off the hook. But what with R. J.'s mind on other matters, District Attorney Riley was makin' points each time he asked a witness was he still beatin' his wife. Dove could see her best chance for keepin' out of the slammer was to tell her story like it was. If that didn't pan out, a no-decision was her only prayer.

As R. J.'d been offerin' equal time to all his gals, he hadn't took his beauty nap several nights runnin', the result bein' that he didn't want to stand around questionin' Dove no longer than he had to. So he just asked her was Buster roughin' her up and then drug himself back to the defense table and lay his head in his arms. He was so whipped, he didn't hear the DA take his turn with her. First thing Riley had to know was what it was Buster had said that made her want to part his hair with a shotgun.

Dove looked like she'd been poleaxed. She tells Riley, "This was the worst thing I heard in my life. I can't say those words, so please don't even ask."

Riley is not a fella to take a no for an answer when yes can get you twenty years, and he let Dove know she didn't have no choice. Dove bit her tongue and kept on waggin' her head. This wasn't gettin' nobody nowhere till Judge Walker butted in and asked Dove did she have any objection to writin' down what was Buster's partin' remarks. Dove went as red as a Rome Beauty apple, but she got busy with a pen. Soon Judge Walker's puss was like hers, 'cause what Dove had wrote was, "I want to screw your eyes out, baby."

The judge got ahold of himself and give the note to Riley, who flushed a little around the gills and started it movin' around the jury box. One by one them gals went various shades of pink, if you don't count Tess Finch whose kisser matched her hair. Tess was starin' at the paper like they was germs all over it when Walker said it was only fair the defense got an eyeful and since she's closest why don't she play the mailman.

R. J.'d just got back from the gents, where he'd gone to splash cold water on his mug, when Tess trotted over and give him a nudge in the short rib and slipped him the note. When he saw what was on it, he like to pinch Tess to make sure he ain't dreamin'. A funny kind of grin come over his pan and it didn't wipe off till Walker banged his gavel and says, "Young man, I'd like that note back, you don't mind."

Now R. J., I don't have to tell you, ain't a one to

227

compromise a lady, and not havin' a clue the note was evidence he figured maybe he could stonewall Walker and save Tess a bunch of embarrassment. "What note, your honor?" he asks.

"Why, the one juror twelve just give you," Walker tells him.

"You must mean some other fella. I didn't get no note."

Walker took off his spectacles and shined 'em on his robes to improve the view. "If you don't fork it over, I'm gonna have to call a mistrial and you will be held in contempt and fined and that's just the start of the trouble I'm gonna make."

"I'm sorry, your honor," R. J. says, "but I didn't get nothin' at all from juror twelve."

Walker tells the bailiff, "Officer, I want you to yank the evidence out of defense counsel's hand, forcibly if you got to."

R. J. turned to Tess like he didn't know what to do, but when he saw her kisser all lit up his choice was already made. As the bailiff was comin' up on him, R. J. popped the note in his mouth and gulped it down without a sip of water for the chaser. And then Walker . . . but, hey, here's R. J. now. You're the first gal he's seen in ninety days. If he gives you any trouble, just holler for the guards. He don't know you're here to spring him.

Walter Ego

MICHAEL AVALLONE

In a field where it is common to describe writers as prolific, Michael Avallone stands out. He has written some 210 novels and over 1,000 stories. Mr. Avallone describes "Walter Ego" as "an unusual little yarn that seems to illustrate all of Ed Noon's virtues and faults."

They let me talk to my client just before the fatal windup. It was the screwiest, saddest case of them all. Only a week ago, the client had walked into my office, babbling all about a man called Walter Box who was persecuting him. A day and a headline later, Walter Box was dead—not the *real* Walter Box, that is.

Confused, are you? Well, so was I, until my last interview with my client. I sneaked a tape recorder into his cell and got it all down in his own insane words. Poor bastard. Bellevue Psychiatric ended him.

I'll let him tell the story in his own twisted words. It isn't pretty, but insanity never is. People who go off the wall somehow find a private world all their own, and there is never room in that territory for anyone other than themselves. And their own upside-down look at things. 'Twas ever thus, as the poet said, but it sure can scare the hell out of you. And make you wonder about Poe, Lovecraft, and Bierce.

Insanity is a stranger who stalks the corridors of

the mind seeking entrance at one of the many tiny little doors. . . . Mark Dane, the mystery writer, said that in one of his books on mental illness. I think he would have had a field day with the Walter Box case. I don't think even the Great Dane had ever run across a condition like my client had.

But who knows? I don't know everything. Nobody does. All I can tell you is that what you are about to read is gospel. The truth according to Ed Noon. Once the pride of his Bible-reading class.

And my poor, bedeviled client . . . here's his story:

"You're going to ask me about Walter Box again, aren't you? You still want to know why I killed him, don't you? I'll tell you, though I must have said it a thousand times. What's the matter with all of you? I thought I had made it pretty clear.

"He was smart, Walter Box was. Very smart. He was proud that he was so smart. Very proud. That's one of the reasons I killed him. Because he was so smart and so very proud of it. I thought everyone would understand that, but I guess they didn't.

"Is it wrong for a man to get rid of a rival? A strong opponent? Wasn't that the original law of survival? Survival of the fittest? If I'm wrong about that, please correct me. It doesn't do to think a thing is right when all the while it is wrong.

"I haven't been well lately. Since Walter Box's funeral, I've lost weight steadily. Food doesn't interest me these days. Memory of his dead face sickens me.

"No, it was not wrong to kill him. I'm sure about that. I found out I didn't need him anymore. He'd grown fat and contemptuous of me. He deserved a bullet at my hands. It was justifiable homicide. The law can't touch me.

"Murder it was, certainly, and crime should never be condoned. But my crime, if it must be called that, was different.

"Had I shot a skulking thief at the wall safe in my home or had I fired at a crazed lion in defense of my life, it would have added up to the same thing.

"Walter Box was a skulking thief and a crazed lion. How else can you explain his avarice, his greed, the ruthless methods he used to drive his way to the top of the business world? He deserved the complete annihilation I gave him. The widows of all those suicides should send me flowers and candies.

"The electric chair? No. The hangman's pleasure? Certainly not. This futile life imprisonment they gave me? Ridiculous! I deserve a medal or a statue in Union Square, cast in deathless bronze.

"I killed Walter Box. The world ought to know—the schoolboys, too—about my magnificent sacrifice. I have reduced a national menace, erased the darkest blot on our civilization. Walter Box is dead.

"His pride defeated him. You see, he was afraid of no man. He should have been afraid of me. For I meant him harm—all the harm in the world. How he trembled and turned white with fear when he saw the gun in my hand!

"His servants, bodyguards, the high walls of his estate, and all his money could not save him. He had wronged me. That was his first mistake. I wasn't like that fool Wareham who committed suicide because Walter Box had ruined him. I wasn't like him at all. Walter Box should never have bothered with me.

"Look: It's against the rules, I know, but would you bring me a copy of the *Times* if they let you come again? Just the financial pages. Thank you. I like to keep up with the money-mad men of the universe.

"You don't think I'm crazy, do you?

"Of course not; you're not Walter Box.

"You see, he called me crazy. I didn't like that, so I shot him. What right had he to say that to me?

"What's that? Who am I?

"Why, I'm Ego. You know. The Inner Man.

"Walter Box called me crazy and tried to kill me. That wouldn't work. So I had to get rid of him. Self must always be a lot stronger than the flesh. You see that, don't you? If you can't, please remember this: I am Walter Box's soul. This is his body you see before you.

"Ugly thing, isn't it?"

Well, that's it.

The client, of course, was Walter Box himself.

The man he killed was a policeman who approached him on a sunny afternoon in Bryant Park because he was talking to himself and frightening the passersby and loiterers in that once pretty place now infested with the dregs of the crooked city. Box pulled a Saturday Night Special out of his side pocket and shot to death Patrolman Clarence Tilney, black.

Box himself?

Maybe you guessed it.

A wifeless, childless, unemployed college professor with a degree in physics who could not find a job. A man who had lost all contact with the reality we have stuck ourselves with. Have you taken a good look around lately?

The case had the usual, sorry windup.

Walter Box hung himself in his cell four hours after I left him. Even in death, he baffled the experts, the interrogators, the jailers. Smart he was, indeed.

He looped his shirt-sleeves around one of the bars of his cell and garroted himself as effectively as any thug in old India strangling a victim for Kali.

He stood on the old box they brought his clothes and possessions in to do it, too.

Of course, he was a black.

What else?

Haven't you been paying attention to the tape?

On The Prod

L. J. WASHBURN

L. J. Washburn is the pseudonym of Livia Washburn Reasoner, who lives in Azle, Texas, with
her husband, James, and their two children. The
Reasoners are both writers, and they have col-
laborated on several stories and novels, including
Mike Shayne stories in *Mike Shayne Mystery
Magazine*. The Hallam stories are the work of
L. J. Washburn alone. The first Hallam novel is
scheduled for publication by Tor in November
1987. The character reflects Mrs. Washburn's
hobby of collecting tapes of old Western films.

The kid was on the prod. Hallam could see that as
soon as the boy stepped through the door of the
Waterhole.

About nineteen or twenty, Hallam guessed, with
sandy hair, broad shoulders, and a tight-jawed look
on his face. His clothes were cheap and rumpled,
probably from a long bus or train ride, and he clutched
a cloth cap tightly in his left fist. He couldn't have
been more than a few days off the farm back in Iowa
or Nebraska or some such place.

The boy paused just inside the door of the speakeasy and let his eyes adjust to the dimness. When
his gaze hit Hallam, a fresh determination came over
him and he strode across the room. Hallam watched
him come and wondered what the hell *this* was all
about.

"You're Lucas Hallam?"

The words came out flat and hard as the boy stopped beside the table. He paid no attention to the other three men seated there.

They were a formidable-looking bunch. Hallam had been sharing a drink with Jack Montgomery, Neal Hart, and the youngster known only as Sonora. All four of them were still in costume from that day's shooting, and they would have looked more at home in a saloon in Dodge or Abilene or Tombstone forty years earlier, rather than in a speakeasy in downtown Hollywood. All the boys from Gower Gulch came to the Waterhole, though, when the day's riding jobs were done. It was the closest thing to the life they had once known, the closest thing to home.

Hallam wore boots and buckskins, and his battered old hat was on the table in front of him. The big Colt holstered at his right hip was loaded with blanks at the moment, but it was no prop. Neither was the bowie knife that rode his left hip. But the kid didn't look dangerous, just mad and a little uncertain of himself, so Hallam sat easy.

"Happen I am," he answered after a long moment. "What business is it of yours, boy?"

"My name is Jamie Brinke. I'm looking for my brother, and I'm told you know him."

Hallam picked up the rest of his drink, tossed it off.

If this had to do with Joe Brinke, chances were there would be trouble after all. There usually was.

"I know him," he said. "Don't reckon I could tell you where to find him tonight, though."

For the first time, the boy looked at Hallam's companions, then said, "Could we talk in private?"

"These here are my friends. Anything you got to say to me, you can say in front of 'em."

Jamie Brinke's expression grew more sullen. "Joe made you sound like a real lobo wolf. Don't look like much to me."

The young man to Hallam's right started to rise, his hot blood showing. Hallam put a big hand on his arm to stop him. "Hold on there, Sonora," he said softly. "Boy's got a right to his opinions."

"And I got a right not to like 'em," Sonora growled.

Hallam stood up and jerked his head at a vacant table in another corner of the big room. "Maybe we'd best go over there and talk after all." He turned away and stalked across the room without looking back to see if Jamie Brinke was following.

He was. As Hallam dropped into a chair, automatically taking the one that would put his back against the wall, Jamie sat down across the table from him.

"I've gotta find Joe," he said. "It's real important. Sorry if I hurt your feelings over there. It's just that you don't look like a famous gunfighter."

Hallam shook his head. "Don't go pinnin' that name on me, boy. All the famous gunfighters are dead."

"Don't look like a private eye, either," Jamie objected.

Hallam sighed. "Got any more statements you want to make, or do we get on with this business 'bout your brother?"

Jamie ducked his head, chewed his lip for a moment, then blurted, "Dammit! I always say the wrong thing. I guess I'm just a stupid farm boy, Mr. Hallam—"

"No call for that," Hallam quietly told him. "Los Angeles is a mighty big town. I got a mite rattled

236

myself, first time I rode in. Now you just settle down and tell me why it's so important you get in touch with your brother."

Jamie nodded, took a deep breath. "Well . . . it's our pa. He's sick, and he wants to see Joe again before he . . . before he . . ." His face twisting with emotion, Jamie broke off for a moment, then went on hurriedly. "Ma's been gone a couple years now. I thought Joe would come back home then, but he didn't. And now with Pa sick, I just thought I'd come out here and find Joe. I know he'll go back with me now."

Hallam didn't say anything. He sat and tried to find the words to tell this boy not to get his hopes up.

But how do you tell a kid that his big brother is a cold, no-good, half-crazy bastard?

It had been about three years since Hallam had started hearing stories about Joe Brinke. At first, Brinke had been on the wrong side of the law, running liquor in from Mexico. Word had it that he was for hire, too, for any kind of illegal job as long as the money was right. He had done some work for a bail bondsman and had eventually gotten his PI ticket, though Hallam figured he had had to grease a few palms along the way. There were several unsolved killings that seemed to have Joe Brinke's name on them. Supposedly, the things Brinke had endured over in Europe during the war had hardened him to death and suffering and left him little better than a vicious animal. He and Hallam had crossed paths uneventfully a few times, being in the same line of work, but Hallam had always watched his back around Brinke, just from instinct.

He didn't believe for a minute that Brinke would

pay any attention to his brother's plea to come home. Hallam didn't think there was that much human feeling left in the man. But he might be wrong, and he sensed that there was a mighty upset boy beneath the tough show Jamie tried to put on.

"You got an address for your brother?" he asked.

Jamie nodded. "Joe don't live there anymore, though. Landlady said he moved out about six months ago. She didn't have no idea where he is now."

"Who put you on my trail?"

"Mr. Messner, the fella Joe used to work for. He said you might know how to get hold of him."

Hallam nodded. He had done a few jobs for the same bondsman who had employed Brinke, Kenneth Messner. It had been a while, though, since he had talked to either Messner or Joe Brinke.

Seeing Hallam's hesitation, Jamie dug inside his coat and started to say, "If it's money, I guess I can hire you—"

"Put it away, boy," Hallam snapped, letting his annoyance show through for the first time. "I'll do what I can to help you, and you don't need to be payin' me."

"It wouldn't have been much," Jamie said as he took his hand back out, "but it'd'a been worth it to find Joe."

"Well . . ." Hallam stood up, settled the big hat on his head, lifted a hand in farewell to his friends across the room. He wasn't sure he was doing the right thing by going along with what Jamie Brinke wanted, but he had been a kid once too. A long time ago, to be sure, but Hallam remembered.

They left the Waterhole together.

———

Hallam knew where most of the speaks in town were, even though the Waterhole was about the only place where he did any drinking. He and Jamie spent over an hour going from one to the next. The bartenders didn't mind telling Hallam that they hadn't seen Joe Brinke lately and didn't know where to find him now.

"Don't get discouraged, boy," Hallam said as they drove away from their eighth stop in Hallam's flivver. "Lots of places to drink in this town. Somebody's bound to have seen your brother."

Jamie was clearly torn between concern over finding his brother and awe and excitement at being surrounded by the lights and bustle of the big city. Their route took them within a couple of blocks of a mob behind police barricades. A maze of spotlight beams crosshatched the night sky. Jamie pointed at the uproar and exclaimed, "What's that?"

"Movie première," Hallam told him. "DeMille's got a new picture openin' up. Lots of folks show up to see and be seen."

"Cecil B. DeMille?"

"Yep."

"He's a real famous picture-man, ain't he?"

" 'Spose so. Some folks think so."

Jamie glanced over at Hallam. "Sounds like you don't."

Hallam spat out the open window beside him. "He don't know sic 'em about cowboys, I'll tell you that much. Man ought to respect the folks he works with. DeMille's goin' to get some good men killed some day. Already killed some good horses makin' 'em do damn fool stunts."

Jamie was silent for a moment, then said, "How'd

you wind up in the movies anyway, Mr. Hallam? A man who's done the things you have, I mean."

Hallam grinned. "Hell, boy, the money's good. And I get to work with fellers like the ones back there at the Waterhole. You don't find them ol' boys just everywhere. It's better than workin' in some broke-down Bill show, that's for sure."

"What about being a detective, though?"

"Guess being in the Pinkertons got that in my blood. But I take the cases I want to, and I do picture work when I want to, and if I feel like taking a drive out to the desert and rememberin' old times, I do that. Not a bad life for an old feller like me."

The car was quiet again after that, but Jamie seemed a little more impressed with Hallam now.

Another half-hour went by, and they had stopped at three more speakeasies before their luck changed. The bartender in a red-lighted dive called Lucifer's Lagoon had talked to Brinke earlier in the evening.

"Couldn't tell you where he's staying now, though," the man said. "He just comes in here for a drink now and then. He wouldn't be home tonight anyway."

"Why's that?" Hallam prodded. He had bought a drink for himself and left his change on the bar. Now he casually nudged a dollar bill a little closer to the bartender.

The bill disappeared as the man swiped his bar rag across the mahogany. "He was working. Said something about going on a job up in the hills."

"He say whereabouts in the hills?"

The bartender shrugged. "Wouldn't know for sure. You might try up behind the Hollywoodland sign."

Hallam knew the area. The hills up there were

pretty sparsely settled. The main feature was the big sign that a land speculator had put up to advertise a housing development below. Some shady dealings went on around there, and Hallam wasn't surprised that one of Joe Brinke's cases might take him up into the hills.

Hallam left his drink unfinished, thanked the bartender, and took Jamie in tow. When they were back in the flivver, Jamie asked, "Do you think we'll find Joe now, Mr. Hallam?"

"Got a chance, anyway. Time'll tell, boy."

He pointed the nose of the car toward Hollywoodland.

Traffic was still heavy, but then it never slowed down much until well after midnight. For a town where the main industry was moviemaking with its early-morning calls, folks sure didn't sleep much.

Hallam had little to say on the drive. The wide, palm-lined boulevards turned into narrower blacktop roads that snaked through the canyons and led onto the heights. There were a few houses up here, but they were well off the road and far apart. Lights were spread out in a broad blanket below, but darkness had closed in on the car. The weak beams of the headlights only made the blackness more intense.

"Do you have any idea where to look?" Jamie asked. Now that they were away from the bright lights, his worry about his brother had resurfaced again.

"Not for sure," Hallam said. "Only so many roads up here, though, and I know most of 'em. We'll just drive around for a spell, see what we see."

For a while, all they saw was the road, the scrubby bushes pressing in from the side, and an occasional rabbit darting through the lights. Hallam's route twisted and turned until Jamie was hopelessly confused. Hallam knew where he was, though, knew how to get back out.

Then the headlight beams bounced back off the chrome of a parked car.

Hallam hit the brakes gently and eased the flivver to a stop. The parked car was a nondescript roadster, but he thought it was familiar. Seemed like he had seen Joe Brinke driving a car like it.

"Is that Joe's car, Mr. Hallam?" Jamie asked. He was sitting forward in the seat, young face intense.

"I think it might be," Hallam said. "You just stay put. I'll take a look around."

Hallam eased out of the car and walked toward the other one. He had left his headlights on, and the glow from them threw a long shadow at his feet. As far as he could tell, the parked car was empty. Something about the situation sent a tickle of warning along his spine, and he wished he had slipped live cartridges into his Colt, rather than the blanks from the movie set. If trouble came, he'd just have to make do with the bowie.

He stopped beside the roadster and bent his big frame to peer in through the window. As he had thought, the vehicle was deserted. Carefully, Hallam opened the driver's door and reached inside to check something. Yep, this was Brinke's car, all right; Hallam's fingers found the specially made pocket under the seat where Brinke usually kept a pistol. The gun was gone now, and Hallam wondered what that meant.

Feeling Jamie's eyes on him, Hallam went back to the flivver. He stooped and spoke through the open window. "It's your brother's car, all right. But there's no sign of—"

A woman's scream shattered the stillness of the night.

Hallam jerked upright, his hand flashing to his gun. Then he grunted, yanked open the car door, and snapped, "Box o' shells in the car pocket. Get 'em, boy!"

Jamie looked stunned, but Hallam's harsh command spurred him to action. He grabbed the shells from the glove compartment and passed them to Hallam.

The scream wasn't repeated, but Hallam had picked up the general direction during the few seconds it had lasted. He swung in that direction and called back over his shoulder, "Stay in the car!"

He didn't wait to see whether or not Jamie did as he was told.

Hallam ran through the night, his stiff right leg slowing him down some. As he felt the aches and pain, memories of the gunfights and brawls that had caused them flashed through his mind. Souvenirs of wild times. . . .

And it looked like tonight might be added to the list.

Without thinking about it, he dumped the blanks and jammed fresh shells into the Colt's cylinder. He suddenly heard running footsteps off to his right and veered in that direction, pushing his way through the thick brush, thankful that he was wearing the tough buckskins. The ground was sloping up now under his feet. He kept climbing the hill, the Colt ready in his hand.

He broke out into a clearing. There was enough moonlight for him to see another man burst into the open across from him. The man turned, reached behind him, and pulled a girl out of the brush. Neither of them noticed Hallam until the big man roared, "Hold it, you two!"

They froze and stared across the clearing at Hallam, seeing a tall, broad-shouldered man in boots, buckskins, and hat who was pointing a heavy Dragoon Colt at them.

They must have thought they had lost their minds.

The scene lasted only a moment. Then another man popped out of the brush, to Hallam's left this time. Hallam turned that way and saw the dim flicker of moonlight on steel.

He dived forward as gun blasts boomed and muzzle flashes split the darkness.

As he landed on the hard ground, slugs zipping over his head, Hallam's finger was tightening on the trigger. The Colt roared and bucked in his hand, and he saw the second man throw himself to the side to dodge the fire. Hallam rolled, trying to get to cover himself, and caught a glimpse of the fleeing couple disappearing back into the undergrowth.

Hallam found a little clump of rocks and settled himself behind them as best he could. The other man had faded back into the brush, too, so all Hallam could do was wait. It would be a fool play to try to move now. He would just have to wait out the other fella. Wasn't the first time he'd been in a spot like this, but it could still get powerful hard on the nerves.

A ways off, probably on the other side of the hill, car doors slammed and an engine kicked over. Hallam grimaced in the darkness. Probably the first man and the girl making their getaway in a car they had stashed. He wondered if the man had been Joe Brinke—the light in the clearing hadn't been good enough to determine identities—then decided it probably wasn't. Brinke's car was parked on this side of the hill.

Other than that, Hallam didn't have one damn idea what was going on here.

He decided to take a chance. "Brinke!" he called. "That you out there, Joe Brinke? This's Lucas Hallam! No call for us to be shootin' at each other!"

A pebble rolled, close at hand, just to his left.

Hallam whirled, saw a shadow coming at him, kicked out just in time. His boot heel sank into the man's stomach and sent him spinning away. Hallam was up and after him in a second, cracking the Colt across the man's wrist and making him drop his pistol. Hallam brought his left around, felt the satisfying jar up his arm as fist met jaw, and knocked the man sprawling.

Then Hallam was standing over him, the Colt lined on his forehead, the click of the hammer being drawn back unnaturally loud in the sudden stillness.

"Just take it easy, Brinke," Hallam said, a little out of breath. "You know what this horse pistol'll do to your head if I pull the trigger."

Brinke looked up at him with a killing glare and said, "You goddamn idiot cowboy! You know what you did, Hallam? You just let a kidnapper get away, you stupid bastard!"

Hallam's eyes narrowed in surprise at Brinke's bitter words. He had walked into something bigger than he had thought here, but he still didn't intend to let Brinke take any more shots at him. He stepped back a pace and gestured with the muzzle of the Colt. "Get up," he grated. "We can hash that out later.

Right now we're goin' back down to your car. Your brother's probably worried sick about you after all that shootin'."

"Jamie's here?" Brinke sounded only vaguely interested as he climbed to his feet under Hallam's watchful eye. "What the hell does he want?"

"Wants to see you. I'll let him tell you the rest of it."

Hallam collected the gun he had knocked out of Brinke's hand, then the two of them walked down the hill, Hallam ready and perfectly willing to put a slug in Brinke's leg if he tried anything. Brinke cooperated, though, and in a few minutes they emerged from the brush onto the road. Jamie was waiting in Hallam's car, but when he saw them coming he leaped out and ran toward them.

"Joe!" he cried. "Are you all right, Joe? I heard the shooting—"

"What do you want, kid?" Brinke cut in. His voice was icy.

"I came out to find you, Joe. It's Pa. He's real sick, and he wants to see you. Can you come back home with me, Joe?"

"Too busy. I've got a case . . . if your cowboy friend here hasn't totally ruined it."

Jamie glanced at Hallam, saw the gun in his hand. Anger and confusion played over his face. "What are you doing, Mr. Hallam?" he demanded.

"Just keepin' your brother from killin' me," Hallam answered. He holstered the Colt, though, feeling that the violence was over . . . at least for the moment.

In the harsh yellow glare of the headlights, Joe Brinke's taut, flat-planed face was set in emotionless lines as he growled, "Go home, kid. I've got no time for you or Pa."

Jamie stared at his brother, unable to believe the heartless words he had just heard. Looking at him, Hallam felt like knocking Brinke down again. He was sure it would feel mighty good. . . .

Brinke turned away from Jamie, dismissing the boy. He said to Hallam, "I've got to go explain to my client how this job got botched. I want you along so I can show him who's to blame."

"Suits me just fine," Hallam told him. "Like to know more about this business, anyway."

Brinke held out his hand. "My gun."

Hallam had stuck the pistol behind his belt. He took it out now, unloaded it, and handed back gun and cartridges separately. He ignored the sneer on Brinke's face.

Jamie caught at his brother's arm. "What about me?" he asked. "What do I do now?"

"First thing, get your damn hands off me! Then go home, like I told you."

Hallam said, "Come along with me, boy. After we go see your brother's client, I'll take you to the train station."

"All right," Jamie said numbly. He stood there and watched while Brinke got into the roadster and started the engine. Then Hallam touched his shoulder.

"Let's go," Hallam said.

As they drove down out of the hills, Hallam right behind Brinke, Hallam thought about skipping the meeting with Brinke's client and taking Jamie directly to the station. But he kept coming back to Brinke's angry accusation. If he was responsible for a kidnapper getting away, he wanted to know the details of it. This whole thing didn't sit well with him.

Something was wrong, damn wrong.

There was a lot of money and power in this room, indicated by the thick carpet, plush chairs, and massive mahogany desk. The three men who glowered at Hallam and Brinke were used to wielding that power. Hallam knew all three and didn't particularly like any of them.

Arthur Norton was one of the studio's top executives and occupied the chair behind the big desk. His hair, what was left of it, was iron gray. He held a pencil in blunt fingers and tapped it annoyingly on the desktop, but no one complained. Leaning against the desk, one hip perched on the corner, was Kurt Prescott, a tall man with dark, curly hair. He was wearing a tuxedo, which told Hallam that he had been called to this meeting from the party following DeMille's première. As an up-and-coming director, Prescott couldn't afford to miss such a party. Hallam had worked for him on some two-reelers, before Prescott graduated to features, and thought he was a competent picture-maker.

The third man, Leonard Yates, stood in the background and watched while the other two did most of the talking. He was the mildest looking of the three, with sandy hair and watery blue eyes behind rimless glasses, but Hallam knew that many people in town were afraid to cross him. They had good reason to be. He was the most influential agent in Hollywood, and his word could help make a career . . . or break one.

"I hope you know what you've done, Hallam,"

Norton snapped. "Elysse Millay is going to be one of our biggest stars. At least she will be if that maniac doesn't hurt her!"

"Said I was sorry," Hallam rumbled. "I'll help get her back, if that's what you want."

"The hell you will!" Brinke snarled. "The studio hired *me* to handle the ransom payoff and bring the girl back."

"Perhaps that was a mistake," Prescott put in.

Brinke took a step forward, his face contorting in rage, then stopped himself with a visible effort. Prescott hadn't moved from his casual pose, but Hallam thought he saw a flicker of fear in the director's eyes.

"There's no need for violence, gentlemen," Leonard Yates said. "The harm has already been done."

Brinke reached inside his shirt and pulled out a paper-wrapped packet. "At least you've still got your fifty grand," he said as he tossed it on Norton's desk. "Too bad you probably won't get another chance to spend it."

"We don't know that," Norton said. "The kidnapper may call again."

"And if he does," Prescott added, "I think we should let Mr. Hallam handle the transaction." Afraid or not, the director seemed determined to speak his mind.

"I don't mind helpin'," Hallam said. "But it wasn't Brinke's fault. He might've caught up with them two if I hadn't come along."

"The kidnapper had already panicked and started running, taking Elysse with him." Norton picked up the pace of the tapping pencil. "No doubt because of something Brinke did to scare him."

"I didn't do anything!" Brinke objected hotly. "I

followed orders. The guy just spooked, that's all."

Hallam could accept that. He had been filled in on the background and had seen the ransom note and had come to the conclusion that Elysse Millay's kidnapper was an extremely lucky amateur. The man had walked into Miss Millay's Hollywood apartment in broad daylight and taken her out through a lobbyful of people. The actress had evidently been too frightened to make any kind of outcry. Then he had called the studio and told Norton to expect a ransom note with the directions for the payoff. The note had demanded fifty thousand dollars and had given specific instructions about delivery. Brinke had been hired to handle that delivery, but then the kidnapper had run for some reason.

And that was when Hallam came in.

"What happened up there doesn't really matter," Leonard Yates said quietly. "The only thing we're concerned with is Elysse's safe return. I'm sure the poor girl is terrified."

"We have a lot of plans for her. She's going to be a big, big star when *Passion Flower* comes out." Norton rubbed a weary hand over his eyes.

"It's my best picture yet," Prescott said. "Elysse is marvelous in it. She's going to outshine Swanson and Pickford and all the rest. Mark my words."

Hallam said, "Sounds like quite an epic. But gettin' the gal back safe is more important, ain't it?"

"Of course," Yates replied. "Consider yourself hired, Mr. Hallam."

Brinke tensed and was about to explode again in protest.

The shrill ring of the phone on Norton's desk made everyone in the room freeze.

Then Norton snatched up the phone and barked, "Yes?" His drawn face became even more tense as he waited and listened.

"Yes," he finally said. "We've been waiting to hear from you. Listen, I don't know what happened, but I assure you all we want is Miss Millay's safe return. . . . Yes . . . yes, I understand. No tricks. Of course. You have my word on it."

There were beads of sweat on the movie executive's brow.

"All right," he said, then cradled the phone. He looked up at the anxious circle of faces around the desk. "We've been very lucky, gentlemen. The kidnapper still wants to deal."

"He tell you why he spooked earlier?" Hallam asked.

"No, he said nothing about that. He just told me that the site for the payoff has been changed. He wants the money brought out to the ranch house on our location lot." Norton glanced at Hallam. "I'm sure you're familiar with the place."

A grin tugged at Hallam's wide mouth. "Made a few pictures there."

"Anything else, Arthur?" Prescott asked.

"Yes. The price has gone up." Norton grimaced. "He wants seventy-five thousand now."

Yates took a deep breath, then said slowly, "We can put our hands on an extra twenty-five. Elysse is worth it."

The other two nodded in agreement. "Well, Mr. Hallam," Norton said, "will you be ready to go as soon as we have the money for you?"

"I'll be ready," Hallam said.

"Wait just a goddamned minute!" Brinke objected. "This is my case. I'm not being cut out of it!"

"You *are* out of it," Norton said coldly. "Now leave the studio, or I'll call the police."

Hallam saw the fires in Brinke's eyes, the way the man stood, and knew they were real close to trouble—blood trouble. He let his hand fall on the butt of the Colt and said softly, "Don't do it, Brinke."

Brinke's eyes flashed from Hallam to the three movie men, then back again. Abruptly, his lip curled and he spat a couple of vile names at them, but then he turned on his heel and stalked out of the room.

Hallam went to the door as Brinke stormed out through the anteroom where they had left Jamie to wait for them. Jamie watched his brother's disappearing back but didn't try to go after him. Instead, he turned and said, "What now, Mr. Hallam?"

"Don't have time to take you to the station after all," Hallam told him. "Got a chore I've got to do. We'll get you a cab, though."

"Couldn't I come with you?"

Hallam smiled. "Don't reckon that'd be a good idea. You go on back home, son. Your pa needs you now."

"What about Joe?"

"Was I you . . . I'd say I never found him. . . . "

Norton brushed past him in the doorway. "Come along, Hallam," he snapped. "We'll get the rest of that money for you."

Hesitantly, Jamie said, " 'Scuse me, sir, but while I was waitin' I noticed a bunch of men outside. Some of 'em had cameras, and they were all yellin'."

"Dammit!" Prescott and Yates had followed Norton out of the meeting room, and the exclamation

252

came from the director. "Reporters! If the press has gotten hold of this kidnapping, they'll turn it into a three-ring circus! We'd better get Hallam out the back way."

"I agree," Yates said. "We can't take any chances, not now. Not with Elysse's life at stake."

Hallam had to go along with that.

Besides, he would have rather faced the Wild Bunch again than a bunch of story-hungry reporters.

Hallam had lost track of the times he had been out to the ranch. He had worked for all of the studios at one time or another, from Poverty Row to the big boys, and knew all the location shooting areas. This one was about fifteen miles from town and had a lot of rugged country on it. Just the kind of nice, isolated place a kidnapper might choose for an exchange.

He had bid a quick good-bye to Jamie Brinke after arranging to have the boy picked up at the studio and taken to the train station. Jamie had gripped his hand hard, and then Hallam was gone, hustled away by Norton, Prescott, and Yates. They had handed him the package of money, fatter now that the extra twenty-five thousand had been added. Hallam hadn't asked where they had been able to lay their hands on that much money after ten o'clock at night. With their business being so scandal-prone, some of the studios had taken to keeping emergency funds on hand.

Now, as he drove through the warm night, Hallam's thoughts were divided between Jamie Brinke and this kidnapping business. Joe Brinke's callous treatment of his brother was just one more black mark on the man's record. Wasn't really any of his affair, though, Hallam decided. It didn't pay a man to mix into any kind of family troubles.

The kidnapping was something else; that was more in his line of work. But he had still been surprised at being handed the job. Much as he hated to agree with Brinke about anything, he was partly to blame for the first exchange attempt going wrong.

He had a chance to make up for that now, though. If he could only shake the feeling that he had been lied to somewhere along the way. . . .

Hallam left his headlights on and didn't try to be the least bit unobtrusive as he drove onto the ranch. He headed straight for the old homestead that was used for ranch-house scenes. Instinct told him that he was being watched. He hoped so.

He came to a stop in front of the house, killed the flivver's engine, and climbed out. The money was tucked inside his fringed buckskin shirt. He reached up and patted the bulge, and again he had the sensation of being watched.

He stood still for a long moment, listening, letting his senses work. A faint creak came to his ears, and he knew it was a floorboard. He was ready when the screen door of the house flew open and a lantern threw a harsh yellow glare in his eyes.

Hallam stood stock-still and let the man with the lantern study him. He had picked up a rifle, too, since the skirmish in the hills. Hallam could see the barrel of it poking into the light.

"Who the hell are you, old-timer?"

The voice was nervous. Hallam was careful to stay still as he answered, "Lucas Hallam. I've got the money from the studio."

A quick intake of breath from the porch. "Let me see it."

Hallam slowly reached inside his shirt and pulled out the packet.

"Toss it up here."

Hallam shook his head. "Not till I see the girl."

"I could just shoot you and take it."

Hallam grinned. "Then shoot straight, son. Happen you don't put me down right off, I'll have time to throw a little lead myself."

The man was silent for a moment. Hallam was aware of movement just inside the door of the house, and then the kidnapper growled, "All right, get out here."

The girl came out of the house and into the circle of light. Her expensive frock was now torn and dirty, and her blond hair, once carefully styled, was in disarray. She looked more exhausted than frightened.

Hallam studied her for a few seconds, then rumbled, "You all right, girl?"

She nodded wearily. "I'm fine. I just want to go home."

Hallam weighed the money packet in his big hand, then lightly tossed it toward the porch. The thought of going for his gun while the kidnapper's eyes followed the money had occurred to him, but he didn't do it. He was willing to play it straight as long as the other fella did.

The lantern shifted; the barrel of the rifle dipped. The man was going for the money—

The crack of a shot and the crash of the lantern shattering sounded together.

Closest cover was the porch. Hallam went for it as another shot boomed in the night. The man on the porch gasped. The rifle clattered to the ground.

"Hank!" the girl screamed.

Then Hallam wrapped an arm around each of them

and dove on through the open door as more slugs thudded into the walls of the house. All three of them sprawled on the bare floor in the darkness.

The girl was struggling; the man was limp and his shirt was wet, sticky. Hallam got a hand on the girl's shoulder and put some weight on her.

"Damnit, settle down! I'm on your side. I'm not with whoever's doin' that shootin'!"

The girl stopped fighting, but only because a bubbling moan from the man made her stiffen and start crying. "Hank . . . " she whispered.

Hallam let go of her and came up in a crouch. In the dim moonlight that filtered in from outside, he saw her scuttle across the floor and throw herself on the man. That brought another groan of pain. Hallam felt sorry for him, but there was nothing he could do, not as long as they were pinned down like this. Bullets were still hitting the walls, screaming through the open door and windows.

Hallam spotted a table shoved into one corner of the room. He went to it, hauled it closer to the two figures on the floor, turned it on its side. It was better than nothing.

He hunkered down behind the table and said harshly, "All right, Miss Millay, tell it quick."

She turned to look at him, her face a pale splotch in the shadows. "He's hurt!"

"And he'll likely die happen we don't get out of here right quick. The truth now: This was no kidnappin', was it?"

"Of course not!" Elysse Millay sobbed. "Hank and I are . . . friends. He agreed to help me out when this came up."

"You needed money, that it? Way your bosses

talked about you, you could've just asked for it."

"No! No, it wasn't the money. He's going to bleed to death—"

"Publicity, then," Hallam cut in.

"Yes, yes! What else do you want out of me? It was all Kurt Prescott's idea. My name would be in all the papers, he said. He said everybody would want to come see *Passion Flower*, to see the beautiful, brave girl who got kidnapped. The bastard!"

Hallam put his hand on Hank's chest. The man was still bleeding heavily, and his breathing was irregular. Hallam had heard that sound before. He didn't like it, not one little bit.

"What happened earlier tonight?"

"That man, the one who was supposed to deliver the money, he was crazy! He tried to kill Hank. I think he would have killed me, too. Surely Prescott let him in on it. He had to know the whole thing was a gag! Why would he try to kill us?"

"Maybe he wanted the money for himself. Maybe he just felt like it," Hallam said softly. "But whatever the reason, I figure that's him out there takin' pot shots at us."

"Oh, Lord, what are we going to do?"

Hallam knew the answer to that one, but he didn't like it.

"Reckon I've got to go out there," he said.

Suddenly, he became aware that the shots had stopped. He thought he heard something else, though.

There was another car coming.

Colt in hand, Hallam went to the window and looked cautiously out. He saw the headlights of the approaching vehicle on the trail that ran through the trees. It came to a stop behind Hallam's old flivver, and he could tell that it was a low-slung roadster. The driver left the motor running and got out.

"Brinke?" The call was low-pitched, barely carrying to the house. But Hallam recognized the voice anyway, just he as recognized the tall, lean figure.

It was the director of *Passion Flower*, Kurt Prescott.

A grin creased Hallam's leathery face. Looked like there was some double-crossin' going on tonight.

"Get out of here, you damn fool!" Joe Brinke called from the trees. He was too late.

Hallam's Colt roared and bucked, and the slug kicked up dirt between Prescott's feet.

"Hold it right there, Prescott!" Hallam called. "Be still or I'll drop you."

Prescott didn't move except to start sweating. "Hallam? Is that you, Hallam? My God, man, what are you doing?"

"Call off your dog, Prescott," Hallam said. "Game's over. You and Brinke lost. Miss Millay and the money are both safe with me, and they're goin' back to the studio."

Frightened though he was, Prescott couldn't keep anger from seeping into his voice. "I don't know what the hell you're talking about—"

"Nice show you and Brinke put on back there," Hallam said. "I reckon you were both tryin' to cover yourselves after the first murder attempt went sour."

"Murder!" Elysse Millay gasped from behind him.

"Yes, ma'am," Hallam said to her, his words loud enough that Prescott and Brinke could still hear. "That phony kidnappin' might've been good publicity, but it was even better as an excuse to get back at you and your friend. That Mr. Prescott likes being known as a ladies' man. Guess he didn't take kindly to bein' turned down."

Hallam was guessing on that part, but the way Prescott's face contorted told him that he had hit close to home.

And if a picture with a kidnapped star would do good business, one with a dead one might do even better. Hallam remembered seeing the stuffed corpse of a famous gunfighter and bounty hunter on exhibition in a traveling medicine show. Nope, you couldn't go wrong banking on the morbidity of the paying customers.

"You're crazy, Hallam!" Prescott shouted. "Elysse, if you're in there, come on out, darling. I promise no one will hurt you."

"Hank's hurt!" she cried in reply. "You've got to help us, Kurt!"

Hallam saw the brief, furtive smile on Prescott's face. "Of course I'll help you—"

"Don't listen to him, girl," Hallam warned.

"Come on out, darling," Prescott urged.

Now he was ready to play the hero, Hallam saw. Had to give the man credit for trying to seize the opportunity. He still thought he had a chance with Elysse Millay.

"No!" Brinke's voice came from the woods. "I'm doing the job I was paid to do. Get out of here, Prescott! Now!"

Prescott half-turned, and his hand went furtively under his coat. "Forget it, Brinke. Our deal's off—"

And then he was snatching a pistol out, turning, raising the gun. He fired twice toward the trees, then tried to duck to one side as Brinke fired back.

He staggered, grunted, folded up in the middle.

He sat down clutching his stomach and then swayed over onto his side.

Hallam was out the window in a rolling dive as soon as he saw Brinke's muzzle flashes. He lit down shooting. Slugs chewed the ground around him as he rolled toward the cars. He came up, ducked between them, and froze, sights lined on the shadowy figure that was Joe Brinke.

There was a click. Brinke's hammer fell on an empty shell . . . just as Hallam, after counting the shots, had gambled his life that it would.

"Got a couple left, Joe," Hallam said. "Wouldn't mind usin' 'em, either."

A mirthless chuckle came from the gloom. Carefully, Brinke emerged into the glow cast by the lights from Prescott's roadster. His gun was in his hand. He dropped it to the dirt, a cold smile on his face.

"You wouldn't shoot an unarmed man," he said.

"You're not a man," Hallam said. "You're a mad dog, let run loose too long."

"What the hell are you talking about? What did I do?"

"Killed a couple of men, for starters."

"A kidnapper and a would-be killer." Brinke gestured at Prescott's body. "There's your villain. He planned the whole thing. He wanted the girl and her boyfriend dead right from the start. I could have handled it, too, but he got nervous after you stuck your nose in. Thought it would look better if he fired me and hired you. That way I could work behind the scenes. He was afraid Norton and Yates would eventually figure out how he manipulated them. Hell, he even got them to pay my salary for doing his dirty work. That ransom money's mine."

"You're admittin' your part in it, though."

"Admitting, hell." He nodded toward the house, where loud, racking sobs told Hallam that Hank had died. Brinke went on, "The girl's too broken up to know what's happening. As for the rest, this conversation never took place. As far as the cops are concerned, I just did a public service by knocking off a kidnapper and the guy who hired him. If you say different, then it's your word against mine. No proof, Hallam, not a bit. It'll just look like I pulled your fat out of the fire and you got jealous."

"I really ought to shoot you," Hallam breathed.

"You won't. Your stupid cowboy code of honor won't let you."

Hallam stood for a long moment looking at the sneer of contempt on Brinke's face. Then he sighed heavily and let down the hammer of the Colt. "You're right," he said as he slid the big pistol back in its holster.

"Damn fool."

Brinke's hand was a blur as he went for the hideout gun Hallam knew he carried at the small of his back.

A flicker of steel, a thump—

Brinke stepped back, his draw unfinished, and looked down in surprise at the bone handle of the bowie knife that protruded from his chest. He stared at it for at least five seconds, then pitched forward on his face.

"That's a chore been needin' doin' for a long time," Hallam said to the night. Too bad the man named Hank had had to die, too, just for going along with what he thought was a publicity stunt to help the girl.

A lot of people would be asking questions about tonight, Hallam knew, from the cops on down to

Jamie Brinke. He'd tell them the only thing he knew to tell them—the truth. What happened from then on out wasn't up to him.

Hallam reached through the open window of Prescott's car and killed the engine that had been purring all along.

Then he went into the house to collect the girl.

Just a Poor Working Girl

HAROLD D. KAISER

Harold D. Kaiser is a retired scientist at IBM, where he developed semiconductor packaging. He first began writing crime fiction some thirty-five years ago, but quit because he was dissatisfied with his work. Since retirement, he has begun writing again. "Just a Poor Working Girl" is the result of Mr. Kaiser wondering what would happen if a crime figure got a taste of his own medicine.

Gino's Bar was crowded, smoky, and noisy. A typical Saturday night. The two men sat at a corner table in the rear, where they could watch the entrance and the door to the men's room. They sat with their backs to the wall, not because there was any special reason for doing that tonight, but because both Rocco Manelli and "Knees" Cardone had learned early in life not to leave their backs exposed.

They were both relaxed, but Cardone's eyes automatically kept scanning the activity around them. It was his job to keep Manelli in one piece, and he took his job seriously. Manelli's eyes also kept scanning the room, but for a different purpose. He was out for a good time tonight. He stretched expansively.

"It sure feels good not to have that crumb Vitelli in our hair any more. That was a nice funeral they gave him. More than the scum deserved, trying to cut in on our numbers like that."

"Yeh, sure, Rocco." Knees sounded a little uncertain.

"What's the matter?"

"Nothing, Rocco. I'm just not sure you shoulda had him hit like that. If his brother Vinnie finds out, he might get ideas."

"How's he gonna find out? Nobody knew we was wise to what Vitelli was up to. Besides, we brought in that greaseball from Houston who didn't even know who put out the contract. By now he's back in the barrio eating tamales."

"Yeh, I suppose so. Even so, you shoulda let me do it. That way we woulda kept it in the family."

"Not a chance, Knees. My way, we're both looking clean. Forget it. You worry too much."

A three-piece combo started to commit assault on "Body and Soul," and an overweight blonde picked up a mike and began to screech into it in the belief she was singing.

"Jesus, I've heard better catfights. Gino oughta know better."

Manelli grunted.

"So who's here for the music? Besides, she's his sister-in-law, and Rosa said give her a break. You know Rosa."

"Yeh, if I was Gino I'd give Rosa a break."

"Count your blessings."

His roving eyes suddenly stopped at a table on the far side of the bandstand.

"Hey. Get a load of that."

"Where?"

"There. At that table next to Fannelli and his bimbo. And all by herself."

"Yeh. Hey, that's okay. But I ain't seen her around before. Wonder who she is."

"That's easy." Manelli nodded to a passing waiter.

"Gus, who's the hot-looking broad in the black dress at that table next to Fannelli?"

The waiter slid his eyes in that direction.

"Oh, that's Mrs. Bondino. Angie. She's new around here. I hear from Chicago."

Cardone straightened up in his chair.

"Bondino. Bondino. I wonder. Rocco, remember that Harry Bondino, the enforcer who got hisself taken out a couple of months ago? He was iced by a couple of Dutch Lachner's boys for trying to do his thing on Dutch. They said that Moozie Sanchez was behind it cause he wanted to take over Dutch's coke trade. Right afterward, Moozie went back to Mexico. Inna box."

Gus nodded. "That fits. I hear she's a widow."

Manelli licked his lips. "A widow, eh. That's the best kind. But what the hell she's doing here?"

Cardone shrugged. "They say Dutch was pretty pissed off and threatened to wipe out everyone who even knew Bondino. Maybe she figured a little distance was healthier."

Manelli grinned. "She looks pretty healthy to me. Gus, why don't you go over there and see what the little lady is drinking. Compliments of Rocco Manelli."

"I'll ask, Mr. Manelli. But she's already turned down a couple of guys."

"Be persuasive. And if she goes for it, ask her to join us. Tell her this is a much better table."

They watched as Gus threaded his way through the crowded club and bent close to the girl to make himself heard. Suddenly, she swiveled her head, her soft, auburn hair flaring out, and peered through the murk in their direction. Manelli raised his glass. She smiled and nodded. Gus gestured as if to accompany her, but she rose lithely, laid a hand on his arm and said a few words to him. He nodded and she started across the floor.

Manelli muttered to Cardone. "Get up, you ape, and help her to a chair."

Knees grinned. "The whole bit, eh?"

"Good evening, Mrs. Bondino. You looked sort of lonely over there all by yourself, so I thought you might like to join us for a drink and a little . . . conversation."

She slid into the proffered chair and crossed her legs with a flash of trim thigh, then decorously arranged her skirt over her knees.

"I was feeling a little bored. And being so close to that . . . singer was getting to be a little annoying. I appreciate it, Mr. . . . . Manelli?"

"Yeh, Rocco Manelli. And this is my associate, Knees Cardone."

At the girl's raised eyebrows, Cardone laughed.

"From when I was a collector. I used to speed up collections by breaking kneecaps. But no more."

"Yeh, he's just a pussycat now."

Gus brought another round of drinks, grinned as Cardone slipped him a twenty, and left. Manelli eyed the glass of slightly bluish fluid Gus had set before the girl.

"What's that stuff? Water and lime juice?"

He did not like his women too sober.

She smiled at him. "Are you kidding? Gin and tonic. Love the stuff."

Manelli grimaced. He had tried that only once. He thought it tasted like some of his old man's home-made vino that had gone bad.

"Yeh, sure. Great stuff."

He tried to look sympathetic.

"Gee, Mrs. Bondino, I was real sorry to hear about Harry. I hear he was a great guy."

A shadow crossed her face.

"He was good to me. I sure miss him." She sighed. "But like they say, life must go on. So here I am."

"What are you doing here? I mean, how come you left Chi?"

"Well, the climate there can be real nasty at times. Besides, a working girl has to go where the jobs are. But if it's okay with you I'd just as soon not talk about it. It makes me kinda sad, and I'm out for a good time tonight."

So was Rocco, and he figured this was it.

"Sure, sure, Mrs. Bondino—Angie. I know just how you feel. Nobody likes unpleasant memories." He looked at the well-filled black dress. "But at least you show respect."

They talked for a few minutes, and then Knees said he had spotted somebody who owed him some money and he wanted to discuss it with him. He headed for the bar.

Manelli chuckled. "That Knees is a great guy. Knows when to bug off."

"Has he been with you a long time?"

"Yeh, we go way back. I even offered him a piece of the action for hisself but he said he was happy. He'd lay it on the line for me. I would for him. But I don't tell him that."

Angie looked thoughtful. "You don't find too many like that these days."

The combo slouched back on the stage and began playing "Time on My Hands." They did not go for rock at Gino's, by request of the more influential patrons.

Rocco looked at Angie's well-developed curves and asked her to dance. Sort of a test drive.

She did not squash her body into him but got just close enough to rub against him occasionally and let her perfume flow around him. By the time the number ended, Rocco's armpits were soaked, and not from the heat in the place.

The band started into what they thought was a tango, so they went back to the table, where Rocco tossed down the rest of his bourbon and even ate the ice in the glass. He caught Knee's watchful eye and nodded. He was ready to go. Knees strolled back to the table, a grin on his face.

"Got my business settled."

After the tango, the blonde came out and began to caterwaul again. Manelli winced.

"God, I can't stand that screeching. Gino better get rid of her or she'll empty the place."

He smiled at Angie.

"What say we get out of here to someplace quiet. Like my place. We can have a couple of drinks and . . . talk."

Angie moved her shoulders. "And where is your place?"

"Not in this crummy neighborhood. No more. I got a nice place in Fairview. Hot tub and everything."

"Sounds nice. Only thing, that's pretty far out and I've got an early appointment tomorrow." She hesitated. "But my hotel is only a couple of blocks from here. It doesn't have a hot tub, but it has other attractions. Why don't we go there and . . . talk for a while. Except . . ."

She glanced at Knees, who was studiously watching the dance floor.

"Don't worry about him. He needs his beauty sleep."

They got up to go. Gus came over with a small paper bag in his hand.

"Here you are, Mrs. Bondino. That'll be eight bucks."

Cardone eyed the bag. "What's that?"

Angie looked at him coolly.

"A pint of gin and some tonic water. I like a nightcap, and my hotel doesn't have a bar."

She started to open her purse, but Cardone gave Gus ten dollars and said, "Beat it."

When they got to the hotel, Rocco glanced around the lobby. Angie noticed the slight curl to his lips.

"The rooms are a lot better than the lobby. Besides, when you're a working girl, you have to take what you can afford."

"A looker like you, you play your cards right, you could afford a lot more."

"I'll keep that in mind."

When they got to the room, Angie unlocked the door and was about to go in when Knees said, "Hold it." He moved Angie aside, pulled a gun from his hip and put his hand on the knob.

Angie raised her eyebrows to Rocco. "What's with him?"

"Don't mind him. He's the nervous type."

"Be my guest."

They stood in the corridor while Knees searched the room. When he came out and nodded, Rocco said to him, "See you later, Knees. Go home and get some sleep."

"But Rocco—"

Rocco's face flushed.

"What you want to do? Hold my hand? I'm a big boy now. Beat it."

Knees muttered something but turned and wandered down the corridor to the elevator.

The room was shabby, but clean and very neat, almost like no one was staying there. Rocco put the bag on the dresser, took off his coat and tossed it on a chair.

"Oh, damn."

"What's the matter, Angie?"

"No ice. Look, Rocco, there's an ice machine down at the end of the corridor. Near the elevator. Be a dear and get us a bucket of ice. I'm dying for a cold drink."

"Sure, baby."

Rocco stomped down the corridor to the ice machine. The ancient machine groaned and did not want to give up its ice. It was only after Rocco had given it three quarters and a hard kick that it decided to cooperate.

When Rocco got back to the room, the door was locked. Rocco knocked softly at first and then louder.

Finally he heard a muffled "Who is it?" from within.

"Me. Rocco. Who you think?"

The door swung open.

"I was—powdering my nose. Why didn't you just come in?"

"The damn door was locked."

"Oh. Yeah. It locks by itself unless you push in the little dingus on the knob. Sorry 'bout that."

"No harm done."

Angie had taken off her coat and had put two glasses next to the gin and tonic water.

"What took you so long?"

"Ah, that damn ice machine wanted to play games. But I got some finally."

"Great. Fix us a couple of drinks, huh?"

Manelli looked at the bottles with faint disgust. Then he looked at Angie, her full breasts pushing taut the black dress.

"What the hell," he thought, "a lousy gin and tonic is a cheap price for a crack at that."

Rocco threw some ice in the glasses, cracked the plastic seal on the gin bottle, poured two healthy portions of gin, and topped them off with some tonic water.

"Here's to . . . getting acquainted."

He took a deep breath and knocked back half of his drink. It was even more bitter than he remembered it.

Angie walked over to the bed. Rocco tensed when she put her hand under the pillow but relaxed when it came out holding a filmy nightgown.

"Make yourself at home, honey. I'm going in the bathroom and getting into something more comfortable." And carrying her drink and the gown, she swayed into the bathroom and closed the door.

Rocco gulped down the rest of his drink and grinned

to himself. It looked like this was going to be a fun night.

He took off his suit coat and laid it on the chair. Then he took his revolver out of his hip pocket, and laid it on the bedside table. He stared at it for a moment, then picked it up, flipped open the cylinder, and dumped the cartridges into his hand. He put the gun back on the table and the cartridges in his pants pocket.

The bathroom door opened and Angie came out. She was still in the black dress.

"Rocco, honey, I can't get this zipper to work. Will you see if you can open it for me?" She rattled the ice in her empty glass and set the glass on the dresser. "And I need another one of these."

She walked over and stood with her back to him. Rocco was surprised to find that his hands were trembling slightly. He gave the zipper a tug and it slid downward, releasing warmth and a subtle body scent. Rocco began to feel warm.

Angie delicately shrugged her shoulders and the dress slid down around her feet, revealing a lacy slip that reached only halfway down her rounded thighs. She stepped out of the dress and walked over to the dresser, picked up her glass, and rattled it at him.

"Come on, honey, let's have a nightcap."

Rocco made up two more with plenty of gin and a little tonic. He was ogling Angie out of the corner of his eye and spilled some of the tonic water on his hand. He did not notice.

"Here's mud in your eye."

"God," he thought, "what piss. Like sucking lemons."

Angie waved her glass at him and sauntered back

into the bathroom. Rocco watched her intently. He began to sweat.

Rocco took off his tie and shirt. He had trouble getting his pants off. He could hear Angie moving around in the bathroom. "Christ," he muttered, "how long does it take her to get ready for a little action?"

He was looking down at his paunch and wondering if he should take off his underwear now or wait until the lights were out when the bathroom door opened and Angie posed there. The light behind her made the gown almost invisible. Rocco took a deep breath as he felt a hot flush spread over his body.

Angie smiled at him. "You sure don't waste any time." She raised her glass. "Here's to a great . . . friendship."

Rocco downed the rest of his drink. He was beginning to feel really woozy and had just decided that he had better cut it off before he was too drunk to have any fun when he realized that Angie had barely touched the glass to her lips.

"Whatsa matter, honey? You're not drinking." He was having trouble forming his words, and his face felt numb.

"A working girl has to watch herself, Rocco."

"What's this working girl stuff you keep yakking about? What kinda work do you do?"

"You remember the line my Harry was in? I decided to take over his business."

Rocco snickered.

"No offense, baby, but Harry didn't do so good in his work."

"Yeah, poor Harry. He always was a little careless and it cost him. But I learned from his mistakes, see?"

"Like how?"

"Like making damn sure I have my mark alone before I hit him."

A warning bell went off in Rocco's head. His eyes swiveled to the gun on the night table. He started to move toward it but he felt like he was walking through jelly. Angie easily beat him to it. She picked it up, glanced at the empty cylinder and threw it on a chair at the other side of the room.

"Just so you don't strain yourself, Rocco."

She walked over and stood in front of him.

"Vinnie Vitelli sends his regards."

He tried to grab her, but his arms were on a coffee break. The numbness was spreading to his chest, and her voice sounded like she was in an echo chamber. She gave him a light shove and he sat down heavily on the bed.

With an effort, he shaped the words.

"Vinnie—how did he—"

"Hell, Rocco, I don't know. I don't ask for reasons. I just ask who and how much."

He began to sway and she deftly caught him under the legs, spun him around, and laid him out flat on the bed.

"There, Rocco, you finally got in my bed. You'll look real nice when they find you in the morning."

"Wha— What did you—"

"Smack, Rocco, high-grade horse in the gin. None of that stepped-on street shit. I even bought it from one of your own boys. You're OD'ing on your own stuff, baby. Ain't that a laugh."

"Plastic—sealed."

"Right. But when you were getting the ice, I lifted up the tax seal on the top, punched a little hole in the cap, and used this." She rummaged in her purse and pulled out a syringe that looked like it should be used on horses. "Looked like it was never opened. And the tonic hid the taste. Neat, huh? It's my own little idea."

But by then Rocco really did not care about details. He could sense his brain starting to say the hell with it and telling his lungs to close up shop. He heard a humming in his ears, but it took him a while to figure out what it was. Angie was humming "Saint James Infirmary." With an agonizing effort, he swiveled his eyes from the spotted ceiling. Angie had pulled out a battered suitcase and was packing. She stripped off her nightgown and was folding it when she noticed his eyes on her. She smiled and wiggled her rounded hips at him.

"How did you like your fun night, baby?"

He tried to swear at her but could not move his lips.

Angie dressed slowly and carefully, then took another look at Rocco Manelli. He did not look back. She snapped out the light, picked up her suitcase, and opened the door.

Knees Cardone was in the corridor, leaning against the opposite wall. He put a finger to his lips.

"Jeeze, Angie, don't let Rocco know I'm here. There was a couple of weirdos prowling the lobby and I thought I'd come back up here and keep—"

Then he saw the suitcase. His hand went to his hip pocket.

Kansas

JAMES S. GAMBLE

James Gamble is a free-lance writer from Penfield, New York. For ten years he taught in several public schools, most recently for the Williamson (New York) Central Schools, where he served as district language-arts coordinator. He has been engaged in public relations and copywriting, and he has written, produced, and broadcast radio news and drama. He currently teaches writing at Writers and Books, a nonprofit literary arts center, in Rochester, New York. Mr. Gamble writes about "Kansas": When I was a public-school band director, I used to remind my students to bring as many family members as they could to our concerts. I emphasized the importance of bringing Uncle Harry, on the assumption that *everyone* has an Uncle Harry. A while ago I hit on the idea of writing a story about a boy who is walking to Kansas. I was faced with the obvious problems of *why* a boy would be walking to Kansas. The solution was just as obvious: The boy was going to see *his* Uncle Harry.

Bobby Benjamin shivered with his face pressed against the steamy window of Lucky's Diner in the deepening November twilight. Inside, a lanky, balding man in a frayed T-shirt and soiled apron set a plate of spaghetti in front of a brown-coated man who sat hunched over the counter. The brown-coated man began to eat, reaching from time to time into a yellow plastic basket for a thick chunk of bread. After he finished the spaghetti, he took another chunk of bread and mopped up the rest of the sauce from his plate.

"Looks good, doesn't it?"

Bobby looked up. The biggest policeman he had ever seen towered over him.

"Lucky makes the best spaghetti in town," the policeman said. "Let's go in and have some. Whaddya say?"

Bobby hesitated. He didn't have much money and he wanted to save it. It was over a thousand miles to Kansas. But the peanut-butter-and-jelly sandwiches and the package of Oreos he had thrust into his knapsack the day before were long gone.

"I'll buy," the policeman said, and opened the door.

Bobby went in.

The policeman ushered Bobby over to the gleaming counter where they each took a red-leatherette-covered stool. Bobby took off his knapsack, glad to rest his sore shoulders. His blue Kansas Jayhawks sweatshirt had been poor protection against the chafing straps and the cold. The policeman waved at the lanky, balding man who wiped the far end of the counter.

"Hey, Lucky. The usual for me and my partner here. Lotsa sauce."

"You got it, Tony," Lucky said.

The spaghetti was wonderful. Bobby's mother used to make spaghetti this good. She hadn't made spaghetti in a long time. Bobby wondered if she would make spaghetti again now that she and Bobby's father were with Uncle Harry and Aunt Melissa in Kansas.

When Bobby had finished, the policeman smiled and nodded at Lucky, who brought another steaming plate of spaghetti.

It was when Bobby was mopping up the last of the sauce with a chunk of bread that the policeman started to ask questions.

"My name's Tony DiPaolo," the policeman said. "Call me Tony. What do I call you?"

"Bobby."

"You packed away that spaghetti pretty good. Been a while since you had a square meal, huh?"

Bobby's mouth was full of bread. He nodded and swallowed.

The policeman pointed to the knapsack at Bobby's feet.

"Where you goin'?"

"To meet my parents. They're with my dad's Uncle Harry and Aunt Melissa."

"Where's that?"

"Kansas."

"Is that right? That's pretty far. You live around here?"

"Near the river."

"Who with?"

"My parents."

"I thought they were in Kansas."

"They went out to Kansas a couple days ago."

"They left you alone?"

"Oh, no. They left me—"

Who *had* they left him with?

With Uncle Leon.

Uncle Leon.

Who *was* Uncle Leon?

"—they left me alone."

278

"Anybody to check in on you?"

"I took care of myself."

"Near the river."

"That's right."

"You know, Bobby, that's a funny thing, you living over by the river."

"What do you mean?"

"River goes right through the middle of town. Bus station's on the east side, so's the train station. Airport's up north by the lake."

"So?" Bobby said, suddenly wary.

"So what are we doing eating spaghetti over here on the *west* side of town?"

Bobby was silent, his head down.

"You hitchhiking all that way?"

"My father said hitchhiking is too dangerous."

It finally dawned on Tony DiPaolo.

"You telling me you're going to *walk* to Kansas?"

Bobby nodded.

"Pal, you can't walk to Kansas. What'd you do with the money your parents gave you for a ticket?"

"They didn't tell me to buy a ticket."

"I don't know what kind of parents you got, pal, but I just don't buy they're gonna let you walk to Kansas. Wasn't there *anybody* in the house who tried to stop you?"

Bobby said nothing.

"No offense, pal, but you don't look more'n eleven years old."

"Eleven and a half," Bobby said.

The policeman said, "Tell you what, pal. You come with me, tell me a little more about Kansas. I'd like to know. Car's right around the corner. I'll even let you work the radio."

279

Bobby still said nothing.

The policeman squatted down on his haunches so his eyes were level with Bobby's.

"You scared?" the policeman asked. "Don't be scared. Trust me. I just want to talk with you."

That's what Uncle Leon said. Don't be scared. Trust me. I just want to talk with you.

"You all right, son? You look a little shaky."

"I'm all right. Where's the bathroom?"

"Past that end booth. Go ahead. I'll settle up with Lucky, meet you back here."

The bathroom smelled of disinfectant and urine. Bobby looked for windows and found none. Then he opened the door of the single stall and secured it behind him. There was a ventilation window up above the toilet. He clambered up onto the toilet tank, pushed the window open as far as it would go, grabbed the window sill, and hauled himself up. Cold, evil-smelling air hit his face. Below him outside was darkness. He hoped the drop wouldn't be too bad.

He struggled through the open window and dropped to the ground. It was farther than he had thought. His right ankle gave way with an audible wrench. His eyes exploded with tears, but he didn't cry.

His eyes adjusted to the darkness. He was in a garbage-strewn alley that opened at both ends onto traffic-filled streets. To his left was Main Street where he had stood in front of the diner window. He picked himself up and hobbled to his right until he came out onto Hopewell Street. It was only then that he realized he'd left his knapsack behind, but it was too late to go back for it now. He was already getting cold, but at least his shoulders wouldn't hurt so badly. He turned left and resumed his long journey westward, toward his parents and Uncle Harry and Aunt Melissa, who all waited for him in Kansas.

"Tell me about the night Uncle Harry rescued Aunt Melissa from the fire," Bobby would say.

And his father, Timothy, would say, "That was a bad one, all right. They almost didn't get to be your Uncle Harry and Aunt Melissa.

"Saturdays, Uncle Harry used to ride over in the buckboard after supper to see your Aunt Melissa, and they'd go for a ride or sit out on the front porch making eyes at each other. That was how people went out in those days. At least, that's all they'll ever admit to. Courting, they called it.

"Uncle Harry and his brother Luke had a chestnut mare named Sassafras due to foal late one Saturday afternoon. Uncle Harry and Uncle Luke thought the little fella inside was scared or something, because he wasn't coming out. Then when Sassafras started rolling around and sweating like she'd been drenched with a firehose, they figured out the foal wasn't coming out because he was in the breach."

"You mean he was turned backward and couldn't come out?"

"That's what I mean. When a mare drops a foal normal the forelegs come out first, clear the way for the nose to come through and start breathing. In the breach a foal can suffocate. So Uncle Luke started sweet-talking Sassafras up front, and your Uncle Harry got behind her and rolled up his sleeves and just went in there after the foal."

"He just went *in* there? How did he do that?"

"Well, he just *reached* in there. It's something you learn how to do on a farm."

"Where was the vet?"

His father talked faster now.

"Vet was three counties away up against a break-out of hoof 'n' mouth. You couldn't always count on a vet getting there in time in those days, and there had to be somebody else around who knew what to do if things went bad. And your Uncle Harry, he always had good hands."

"Oh."

"So he reached in there and eased the foal around, a little at a time, coaxed the little fella to come out. Spindly, quivering, feisty little thing. Tried to get up on those long, wobbly legs and fell down and tried again anyway."

"Meanwhile at Aunt Melissa's—"

"Don't rush me. After your Uncle Harry helped Sassafras drop the foal, and Sassafras was mothering it and gentling it and licking it clean and all, Uncle Harry got cleaned up and hitched up his other horse, a palomino named Corn Tassel, to the buckboard and drove over to Aunt Melissa's. Her parents had died a ways back and left her the farm. But Uncle Harry wasn't hardly past his own gate when he could see the sky all lit up in the east like the sun rising on Easter morning. Only it was eight o'clock at night and he knew it wasn't the sun, and the only other thing it could be was a fire. Now, your Uncle Harry was not what you might call a God-fearing man."

"Until that night?"

"Until that night. He didn't like to whip horses, either, but he whipped old Corn Tassel that night to make him run faster than he really could, and the whole way Uncle Harry prayed to God to keep Aunt Melissa safe.

"Years later he told me that hardly anything ever filled him with more joy than the sight of Aunt Melissa leading a big brown draft horse out of that burning barn. And he said nothing ever scared him more than when Aunt Melissa tied the horse to a fence post, dunked herself in the water trough, and ran back into the fire."

And Bobby, who had heard the story a hundred times before, would still say, "Didn't he try to stop her?"

And his father would say, the words spilling out now like corn from a ripped-open feed sack, "Of *course* he tried to stop her. He yelled at her from the front gate across the barnyard, but she couldn't hear because of the noise from the fire and all the animals outside going crazy, and she was back in the barn before he could get to her. She would have gone back in even if she *had* heard Uncle Harry. That's just the way she was.

"Well, Uncle Harry only stopped to quick dunk himself in the water trough and he went in after her, and he said the smoke and the heat was so bad it was like being in the middle of a fiery furnace, but finally he could see Aunt Melissa, pinned down by a timber burning on one end. Her dress was smoking but she was yelling at Uncle Harry to try to save the one last horse, a strawberry roan screaming like the devil, because it didn't look like she, Aunt Melissa, could get out from underneath that timber.

"There was no way your Uncle Harry was going to leave that barn without Aunt Melissa. Flaming hunks of wood fell all around him, and a few fell on him, but he just picked up a pitchfork and gave a yell and flipped that burning timber right off her.

Then he grabbed her with one hand, and with his other hand he even managed to grab that strawberry roan, and they made it out just before the whole flaming thing came crashing down.

"After that there were only two things for Uncle Harry and Aunt Melissa to do, and that was rebuild the barn and get married. So they invited everybody in three counties for a barn raising and a wedding all rolled into one. What a shindig. Years later when I spent my summers out there, people were still talking about that day."

And Bobby would say, "Tell me again about summers in Kansas."

And his father would say, "When people say they don't believe in heaven, I tell 'em they've never been to Kansas. Every morning we were up before dawn for one of Aunt Melissa's breakfasts of sausage and eggs and biscuits flaky as a cloud and dripping with fresh butter. Then it was out to the fields with the sun just starting to peek up over the horizon and fill up the land and the sky with light. By the time I got out to Kansas the fields had been all plowed and planted with corn and wheat. And as the summer rolled on, why, the wheat would be waving in the wind, looking as soft and as golden as a high school girl's hair, and the corn—"

"Was over your head?"

"Got to be *way* over my head. You hardly dared go into those fields alone for fear of losing your way. When it got toward the end of the summer we would harvest our crop along with everyone else in Kansas, and there'd be dances and celebrations to take your breath away. Then I'd have to come back east to school, and sometimes I'd have to work extra hard because I'd missed the beginning of the term. But I always got caught up because I didn't want anything to keep me from going to Kansas the next summer."

Bobby would say, "Promise we'll go there someday. Promise we'll go see Uncle Harry and Aunt Melissa."

"I promise, Bobby."

"And Mom will come too. We'll have a great time there, all of us together. I just know we will."

And his father would shake his head. "Somehow I don't think your mother is ever going to be much interested in Kansas."

"Kansas?" said Bobby's mother, Jennifer, one Saturday morning. Two frozen waffles popped up in the toaster. Jennifer put the waffles on Bobby's plate and passed the red plastic tub of margarine.

"Wouldn't it be great, Mom? You and Dad and me and Uncle Harry and Aunt Melissa? Just like when Dad lived out there."

"I don't think we'll be going to Kansas for a while," his mother said. She was a thin, nervous woman. Bobby thought she was still pretty if he looked at her just right. She poured a cup of coffee from the battered drip coffeepot on the stove and sat across from Bobby at the breakfast table. "It's a long time before I get a vacation, and your father just started his new job with the insurance company."

Lately it seemed like his mother always referred to Timothy as "your father." It also seemed like there wasn't ever much else for breakfast these days besides frozen waffles.

Bobby spread margarine on his waffles. "Dad sure has had a lot of different jobs. He must know a lot of stuff."

"That's for sure," his mother said.

"Why did he quit at the furniture store? I thought he was going to be the manager."

"Assistant manager. I think, under the circumstances, your father thought he had more of a future with the insurance company."

"Pass the syrup, please. Hey, couldn't Dad work for an insurance company in Kansas?"

"What would I do?"

"You could be a word processor like you are now. They must need word processors in Kansas. Miss Jackson says they need word processors all over the place. Dad must know someone you could work for out there."

"Why don't you ask him?" She stifled a yawn.

"How come you're tired all the time, Mom?"

"I haven't been sleeping well. You want me to put another waffle in the toaster?"

"No, thanks."

Bobby chewed.

"Hey, Mom? Why don't we get up early tomorrow and make real waffles?"

His mother started to cry.

Bobby knew he had said something terribly wrong. He went to his mother, threw his arms around her neck, and gave her a syrupy kiss.

"I'm sorry, Mom. Frozen waffles are just fine. I love frozen waffles. Put some more in the toaster."

"No, honey," his mother said. She hugged Bobby close and rocked him back and forth. "We'll get up early some morning and make waffles. Some morning real soon. I promise." She cried until she got the hiccups. Then she cried some more.

Later, in the living room, while Bobby and his father watched Kansas score three touchdowns against

Kansas State, Bobby asked, "Why is Mom sad all the time?"

"She's not sad. She's just tired."

"She sure is tired a lot."

"She works pretty hard at the office."

"You work hard and you don't get tired."

"I get tired."

"Not that tired."

"I think I read somewhere that working in front of a computer screen all day makes you really tired."

"If she's so tired, how come she can't sleep?"

"That's the thing about computer screens. They make you so tired you can't sleep."

"Why doesn't she get another job, then?"

"It's a long story. Look. Kansas just scored another touchdown."

Late one Thursday afternoon Bobby was up in his room reading a *Farm Life* magazine his father had bought him. He heard the front door open below. It would be his mother, home from another day in front of the computer screen. She would go into the living room, kick off her shoes, and lie down on the couch.

Bobby thought he would go and ask her if she wanted a soda or something. He was halfway down the stairs when the front door burst open. His father stormed through the door and up the stairs, yanking off his tie as he passed Bobby.

"Dad?" Bobby said. He wanted to tell his father that Miss Jackson had assigned him to prepare an oral report on one of the farm states. There was only one state that Bobby wanted to report on, and he thought his father would be eager to help. But his father had that wild-eyed look about him that he got whenever he'd quit another job. There was an extra edge to it now. Bobby didn't know what it was, but it was scary. The report would have to wait.

A bedroom door slammed. Before Bobby could move, his mother was on the way up the stairs. "Not again," she murmured as she trudged past Bobby. From his position halfway up the stairs, Bobby could hear his mother open the bedroom door and close it behind her.

Bobby knew what was coming. He wanted to go down to the basement, or outside, or anywhere.

Instead he stood rooted to the stairs, paralyzed.

It was going to be a bad one.

"You were really going to try this time," his mother said.

"What's the use? It's a racket like all the others. I deserve better." Something crashed and shattered.

"Bobby and I deserve better than to see you like this."

"You'll have better, I promise. More money than you'll ever need. I know how to provide for my family. I've done it before."

"Not Leon?"

"What do you mean, 'Not Leon'? Leon took good care of us."

"That was before Bobby."

"We don't need money for Bobby?"

"Not that kind of money. We promised each other we were finished with it."

"We'll never be finished with it. You knew that when we tried to quit before. Leon's called in my markers and we need cash."

"Tim, let's run away. Get a fresh start, away from Leon. Oh *please*, Tim." She was crying again.

"Where can we run?" his father said.

Bobby wondered what they were talking about. Why did his mother think they needed to run away?

And if they did need to run away, why had his father said there was no place to run? They'd all be safe in Kansas, wouldn't they?

Wouldn't they?

After Bobby's father went to work for Leon, he spent less and less time at home.

"How come you're never home?" Bobby asked late one Saturday afternoon while he and his father played catch with a scuffed football in the backyard.

"I'm on the road a lot for Leon. He runs the company and I sell his stuff. I used to work for him a long time ago and now I've got my job back."

"What do you sell?"

"Chemicals, pharmaceuticals, stuff like that."

"Farma-what? You mean stuff you use on a farm?"

"Some of it you could use on a farm. Fertilizers, weed killers. But that's just a part of it. You know when your mom gets a headache from the computer screen?"

"Sure. She takes aspirin."

"I sell the ingredients."

"Oh."

"Or like when she wraps your sandwiches in that plastic wrap stuff?"

"What does that have to do with aspirin?"

"I sell the ingredients for the wrap like I do for the aspirin. And stuff for swimming pools, keeping food fresh, you name it. People have to buy the chemicals from somebody, so they buy from me."

They tossed the ball back and forth as they talked.

It got darker earlier now, and it was hard to see the ball.

"Why did you quit?" Bobby asked. He threw the ball back.

"I didn't like the insurance business. You have to talk to a lot of young married couples about how sooner or later one of them is going to die so the other one better have enough money."

"No, I mean with Leon. You said you worked with him before. Why'd you quit your job with him to take those other jobs?"

"Leon had to leave the country for a while. He wanted me to go with him but that's just about the time you came along. I wanted you to be raised right here. Go long."

Bobby took off toward the neighbors' swing set and hauled in his father's long spiral. He returned to his own yard and threw the ball back to his father.

"Do you like your job with Leon?"

"It's paying the bills."

"It just seems different from the other jobs you've had."

"What do you mean? Selling is selling."

"When you were working for the furniture store you always left when I left for school, and you always came home at five o'clock. Then when you were selling insurance, you were gone at night a lot. Now you've got this new job with Leon, you're never home." He threw the ball back to his father. It fell short.

His father retrieved the ball. "I'm home now," he said.

"Almost never. We don't do stuff like we used to."

"You've got to understand, it's a different kind of business. See, these people that I sell to keep their factories going all the time. Twenty-four hours a day. They work a different schedule from what you and I are used to. If I'm going to make a sale, I have to get used to their crazy hours."

"No wonder you quit before."

"Sure. How could I work those crazy hours when I knew you were coming and your mother was going to need help?"

"She looks like she could use some help now."

"You're more grown-up now. I depend on you to help her. Down and out."

Bobby ran fifteen steps away from his father and cut sharply to the right. The ball went over his head and Bobby had to chase it down.

"Does she like you working with Leon?"

"You've been around her when I'm out of a job. Which do you think she likes better?"

"I think she doesn't like your working with Leon."

"Of course she does."

"When you worked at the furniture store she'd always say, 'Sell any furniture today?' And when you were selling insurance she'd ask about that. But she never asks you about your farmsuits."

"Pharmaceuticals."

"Yeah. And when you do say something about Leon, Mom acts all funny."

Bobby threw the ball.

His father dropped it.

"Funny?"

"Yeah, funny. She looks like she's really busy stirring the soup or reading a book like she's pretending she can't hear you."

"I don't think she likes the crazy hours either. You wait. Things will get better. Before you know it I'll take over that company and Leon will be working for me. Then he can work the crazy hours. We better go in."

"One more pass, Dad."

"Better not. It's getting dark."

Things didn't get better. Bobby's father would now be gone for two or three days at a time. Then for a week. He said it was because Leon was expanding his territory. When Timothy returned, his clothes were disheveled and he needed a shave.

And he smelled bad.

"Where's my best girl," he would say when he came through the front door after one of his absences. And if Bobby's mother was near, Timothy would try to embrace her and kiss her, but she would turn away.

One Friday night after his father had returned from another long absence, Bobby lay awake trying not to listen to his parents argue in their bedroom.

But he couldn't help but listen.

"I told you I didn't want you bringing that thing back in the house," his mother said. "Bobby could find it and get hurt."

"I'll keep it in the basement, then," his father said. "Just one more run and I'll be through with it."

"We'll never be through with it," his mother cried. "You said so yourself. You're in so deep now Leon would never let you go. I can't take it anymore. I'm going to my sister's and I'm taking Bobby."

"You might as well go to Kansas."

"Don't talk to me any more about Kansas. I'm sick of hearing about Kansas."

"Just wait, Jenny. One more time—"

"It's *always* one more time."

"But this is different. I've figured out a plan."

"Oh *God*. A *plan*. You can't even figure out how to take a *bath* any more. Now you've got a *plan*."

"I do, Jenny. You'll see. You'll just have to be ready to move fast. I'll pick you and Bobby up at midnight."

Bobby couldn't believe what he was hearing. It was finally going to happen. He knew it. His father was going to take them to Kansas.

The next morning Bobby hoped his father would tell him more, but when Bobby got up, his father was gone.

"Where's Dad?" he asked his mother at the breakfast table. She was very pale and there were great dark circles under her eyes.

"He's gone to work and he won't be back until late. Then we're going on a trip."

"All of us, Mom?"

"All of us."

"But why are we going so late?"

"I told you. Your father has to work. Please don't ask so many questions. I didn't sleep much last night. I'll help you pack after breakfast."

"But what about—"

"Eat your breakfast."

He was unable to choke down even one frozen waffle.

After he had helped his mother clear the table, he ran upstairs and pulled a battered imitation-leather suitcase from his closet. Then from his dresser he removed all the clean underwear and socks, all of his T-shirts, and three pairs of blue jeans. He laid the clothes out on the bed. Then he went around the room and gathered up all of his old *Farm Life* magazines.

He went back to his closet for the hiking boots with the rubberized soles that his father had given him the previous Christmas. They would be just right for walking around the farm with his father and Uncle Harry.

The boots weren't in the closet.

"Mom," he called out, "where are my boots?"

"Don't yell," his mother said at the bedroom door.

"I didn't know you were there."

His mother gestured toward the clothes on the bed.

"You won't have room for all that."

"Yes I will. You're a great packer, Mom. If I need more room I'll use my knapsack. Where are my boots?"

"I think you left them in the basement a couple weeks ago after you came in all muddy. Your knapsack is down there, too."

"I'll be right back," he said, and raced from the room.

"Be careful going down the basement stairs," his mother called after him.

In the kitchen, Bobby opened the basement door, felt for the light switch, and descended into the clammy depths. He had to force himself to walk slowly down the basement stairs. His mother was always after his father to fix the railing.

The boots were in the far corner of the basement where he had left them by the sump pump. He slapped each mud-caked boot against the floor to loosen the chunks of dried mud. He knew he should rinse off the rubber soles and polish the leather uppers. He went through the drawers of his father's workbench and looked for shoe polish.

He found nails and screws of all different sizes, airplane glue, fishing line, several small wrenches, and a pocket knife that had rusted shut, but no shoe polish. He pulled open the last drawer.

The gun lay there, blue tinted and smelling of oil. Bobby picked it up. It felt cold.

His father had never owned a gun.

Had he?

What was his father doing with a gun?

Did his mother know about it?

Did the gun have anything to do with why they were running to Kansas?

"Bobby?" his mother called.

"I'm looking for shoe polish."

"It's up here under the sink. It's cold down there. Come back upstairs."

"Coming."

He put the gun back in the drawer. He decided not to tell his mother what he'd found. But his father would tell him when he had a chance. Bobby knew he would. He picked up the boots and grabbed his knapsack from a nail next to the workbench.

The rest of the day was the longest of Bobby's life. It didn't take long to polish his boots. He was unable to muster any interest in the cartoons on television, or the monster movies, or the football games, or even his old *Farm Life* magazines.

He wondered about the gun.

"I'm going for a walk," he told his mother late in the afternoon. It was already dark out.

"Stay in the house."

"But, Mom—"

"Please, Bobby."

Bobby stayed in the house.

Dinner was tomato soup and peanut-butter-and-jelly sandwiches. Bobby still had little appetite. The sandwiches lay untouched on a paper plate in front of him.

"Don't you even want an Oreo?" his mother said.

"I'm not hungry."

His mother wrapped the sandwiches in plastic wrap. "In case you get hungry later," she said. "Why don't you put these and the cookies into your knapsack?"

Bobby put the sandwiches in his olive green knapsack. As he reached for the package of Oreo cookies, his mother called, "Could you help me with the suitcases?" He left the cookies and the knapsack on the kitchen table, and then he helped his mother struggle with the luggage until all three suitcases were posted like sentinels by the front door.

It got to be nine o'clock. Then ten o'clock. His mother would thumb through the pages of a magazine, get up, pace around the living room, and then sit down and try to read again.

At half past eleven, Bobby started to ask questions about Kansas.

"Did you ever go out there to visit Uncle Harry and Aunt Melissa?"

Her eyes were shut as she gently massaged her temples with her fingertips.

"Never," she said. "I just heard your father tell stories."

"How come we never went out to Kansas before?"

"You'll have to ask your father."

"Didn't you ever wonder what it was really like out there?"

"I never did. I'm going to lie down for a few minutes until your father gets here."

"I sure wish we were there now."

His mother said nothing.

"Mom, do we have any old pictures of the farm in Kansas?"

"I don't think so. My head really hurts."

"Want me to get you an aspirin?"

"That's all right. I just need to lie quietly for a while."

"Aren't there any old pictures somewhere?"

"No, Bobby."

"Or some letters? Hey, Mom?"

"Bobby, please."

"How come we never got any Christmas cards from Uncle Harry?"

"I don't *know*, Bobby. My head hurts terribly. Can't you be quiet a little while longer? I can never sleep in the car and it's a long way to Montreal—"

She brought her hand to her mouth but the words were already out.

"Montreal?"

"Yes, Bobby. When your father gets home, we're going to Montreal."

"But we're going to *Kansas*."

"No, Bobby. We're going to Montreal. We never said anything about Kansas."

"Dad did."

"He told you we were going to Kansas?"

"Sure. Lots of times."

"And you thought we were going tonight?"

"Where *else* could we be going? Who do we know in Montreal?"

"We don't know anybody in Montreal. That's what we're counting on. Your father is in a lot of trouble."

"What kind of trouble?" Bobby asked. He thought about the gun.

"Bad trouble. It's not safe for us around here any more."

"We'd be safe in *Kansas*. Uncle *Harry* is there. He'd keep us safe. Dad must have made a mistake. We're going to see Uncle Harry and Aunt Melissa in Kansas."

"For God's *sake*, Bobby, will you stop all of this talk about *Kansas*?"

"I won't! I won't! I want to go to Kansas! I want—"

His mother's hand flashed out like a rattlesnake. Bobby's cheek burned.

His mother pulled Bobby close and hugged him. "I'm sorry," she cried. "I'm so sorry."

"Don't cry, Mom," Bobby pleaded. But he was crying too.

They were still crying when Bobby's father got home.

"I got the money," he said. "I just have to go down to the basement. Then we can—"

"I told him," his mother managed. There was a tremor in her voice.

"Is it true, Dad? We're going to Montreal?"

"It's true."

"But what about Uncle Harry? What about *Kansas*?"

"I wanted to wait to tell you until we were on the road."

"Tell me what?"

Timothy Benjamin let out a long sigh, and his shoulders slumped. He looked like an old man who had found out he was going to die.

"There is no Uncle Harry."

"Dad?"

"There is no Uncle Harry. And there is no Aunt Melissa. I've never been to Kansas."

This time Bobby's voice was softer.

"Dad?"

"I've never been west of Cleveland."

"But the stories, Dad."

"That's all they were. Just stories."

"But why?"

Timothy dropped down on the couch. He tried to pull Bobby down next to him.

"C'mere," he said. Bobby tried to pull away.

"I said *c'mere*," Timothy said. He pulled Bobby down next to him.

"You, too," he said to Jennifer.

"We haven't got time, Tim."

"Yes, we do. I'm a half hour ahead of schedule."

Jennifer settled on the couch.

"When I was in high school," Timothy said as he pulled Bobby close, "a friend of mine used to tell about going out to Kansas in the summertime to see his Uncle Harry. My parents drank too much and fought all the time, so Kansas sounded like heaven. Then I married your mother and you came along. When you were old enough you started to ask for me to tell you stories. You never liked my stories about genies and pirates, so one night I made up a story about this guy's Uncle Harry. You liked it so much I made up another one. They were the stories you always begged for. After a while I almost believed them myself. I always needed a place to run away, and whenever I lost another job or had a fight with your mother, Kansas seemed as good a place as any."

"You mean there wasn't any Sassafras with a foal?"

"I read about it in a magazine."

"There wasn't any fire?"

"Saw it in a movie."

"But what about—"

"Tim," Jennifer said. "*Please* let's get out of here."

"Your mother's right," Timothy said. "We've got a long drive ahead of us. I'll tell you more in the car. I just need to get something from the basement."

"No, Tim," Jennifer said.

"But we need—"

"We need to put all that behind us. Leave it."

"All right. Let's just get out of here."

They got up from the couch. They each took a suitcase. Bobby opened the front door.

"Going somewhere?" said a tall, skinny man with straw-colored hair that was thinning in front and hung long at the sides and down the back of his neck. He wore a baby-blue suit and a pink shirt open at the neck. He held a gun twice the size of the one Bobby had found in the basement.

Jennifer screamed.

"Oh, now, what's the fuss?" said the skinny man. He sounded like he was from the south. "Aren't you glad to see me? I'd have felt real bad if you'd gone and left without saying good-bye."

"Who is he, Dad?" Bobby said.

The skinny man's face lit up like a jack-o'-lantern.

"You don't know me," he said, "but I sure know you. I guess it's about time we met. I'm your Uncle Leon."

"He's not your uncle," Timothy said after Leon had motioned them back inside the living room.

"Oh, I'm not what you call a blood relation," Leon said easily, "but I'm just like part of the family, ain't I, Timmy boy?"

"No part of *my* family," Timothy said.

"Now is that any way to be? After all I've done for you? You ever tell young Bobby here how far you and me go back? He ever tell you, son?"

Bobby clung to his father's side.

"What's the matter, boy? Cat got your tongue? Didn't your daddy tell you about our business relationship?"

"He said he worked for you and sold pharmaceuticals."

Leon burst out laughing.

"Pharmaceuticals? That what he tell you, boy? That's rich. I never thought of my little drugstore chain quite like that. Pharmaceuticals. My, my."

"What do you want?" Jennifer said.

"Jenny, I don't believe I've said hello to you proper. You're still a pretty little thing. Lost some weight, ain't you? Have to put a little more meat on your bones. You been sleepin' okay? You look a little tense. You always did need to learn to relax. Uncle Leon could teach you to relax just fine. Yes, indeed."

"You pig," she said.

"Honest to goodness, you folks just don't seem to be very friendly at all tonight. Rushin' away without sayin' good-bye, callin' me names. I believe someone's gonna have to teach you some manners."

"Leave my family alone," Timothy said. His voice was tight.

Leon looked heavenward in exasperation. "Who said anything about hurtin' anybody?" he complained. "I just figure to help you act more polite like. But first we got some business to transact. Where's my money?"

"What money?" Timothy said.

"Now, Timmy boy, I'm starting to get a mite perturbed. You don't treat me with any manners and you don't treat me like I'm any too bright. You thought I was down in Binghamton and you could go into business for yourself. You been actin' funny for a couple weeks now, and I've had my eye on you. Never did make it down to Binghamton. Much more educational followin' you around. I'll take that money now."

With his right hand, Timothy reached across his body into the folds of his coat.

"Careful," Leon said quickly. He raised his gun a little higher. "Easy does it there, Timmy boy. No sense bein' in a hurry now, is there? I don't like surprises. Just ease it out real slow."

Timothy pulled out a large packet of bills wrapped in rubber bands. It was more money than Bobby had ever seen.

"Well, now, if that's not a tidy little bundle. I'd almost forgot what a loyal clientele we got. Lot more money than in the old days, huh?"

Timothy started forward.

"Whoa," Leon said. "You just stay put there, Timmy boy. Give it to that sweet young wife of yours. She can bring it over and we can get better acquainted."

"You want your money, you get it from me," Timothy said.

"Don't make him angry, Tim," Bobby's mother pleaded. "Give me the money."

"Do it," Leon said.

Jennifer took the money.

"That's better," Leon said, friendly again. "Now come on over here."

Jennifer approached slowly until she stood in front of Leon.

"Now drop that money into my jacket pocket. No, the inside one. That's right. Mmm, you got a nice, light touch, Jenny. Now turn around."

She turned and started back toward Timothy and Bobby.

"Hold on," Leon said. "Don't you be goin' anywhere. I told you, you got to learn to relax. Back up a little."

She took a step backward.

"Closer, Jenny. Back right up to me."

She obeyed.

"That's it. Just lean back now. Mmm, doesn't your hair smell good? My, my."

"I'll kill you," Timothy said.

"Not right now you won't," Leon said. "Pay attention now, Timmy boy. I want to show you how to help Jenny here relax." The gun was in his right hand. He brought his left hand around in front of Bobby's mother and started running it up and down the front of her blouse.

"You got a little more there than I thought," Leon said.

Timothy took another step.

"Don't try anything, Tim," Jennifer said. "Please. I'm all right."

"There, you see?" Leon said. "She just wants to

be friendly. Why, look what I found, Jenny. How does that feel right there?"

Timothy rushed them.

"Run, Bobby," he shouted.

Bobby stood, transfixed.

The gun roared.

An invisible giant fist knocked Timothy backward to the carpet.

Jennifer grabbed Leon's gun hand and bit down hard.

Leon bellowed and knocked Jennifer away.

"Run," Jennifer shouted.

Bobby ran to the kitchen and yanked open the basement door.

He heard the gun roar again.

He hurried down the basement steps. The light from the kitchen spilled into a pool of illumination at the bottom of the stairs. When he reached the bottom of the stairs, he stepped out of the light and into the darkness toward the workbench.

When he reached the workbench he felt for the drawers on the bench top. He fumbled for the bottom drawer. It was stuck.

"Bobby?" called Leon.

Bobby tugged at the drawer but it wouldn't budge.

"Bobby, this is your Uncle Leon."

Bobby remembered that there were two clusters of drawers on the bench top, one on the left, straight ahead from the stairs, and the other on the right, farther into the shadows. Which side of the bench was he on? The drawer had been much easier to open that morning. Maybe he had the wrong drawer. He felt his way to the right along the bench top until he came to the other cluster of drawers. His eyes adjusted to the darkness. He located the bottom drawer and slid it open on the first try. He took out the gun.

"Bobby, you down there?"

The gun felt colder than it had that morning.

"Bobby, now, we got to have a little talk, man to man."

Bobby gripped the gun and felt along the top for the hammer and pulled it back. It locked into place with a loud click.

He worked his way over to the foot of the stairs, just outside the puddle of light spilling down from the kitchen.

The puddle all but disappeared as a dark shadow moved into the doorway and loomed at the top of the stairs.

Bobby raised the gun with both hands and pointed at the middle of the shadow.

His stomach felt like it was falling out. The way it did sometimes when he went up in an elevator, only worse. Much worse.

He felt for the trigger.

"Don't be scared, Bobby. Trust me. I just want to talk with you."

Bobby fired.

That first night he had reached a park where he fell asleep on a bench. He had awakened the next morning, cold and stiff, and had made his way farther west. By nightfall he had reached Lucky's Diner, where Tony DiPaolo had found him.

Now on his third night away from home, cold, hungry, and almost delirious from the pain in his ankle, Bobby tried to sleep under a covering of old newspapers at the back of an alley. He knew he'd need all his strength for the next day, and all the days after that, but the pain in his ankle made sleep almost impossible.

Then, just as he was about to drift into unconsciousness, a vision would come to him. A strange-looking man, unrecognizable but somehow familiar, beckoned to him from some great, dark, frozen depth. Bobby would awake from this vision with a jolt, soaked in sweat, and then try to sleep again. But the vision of the strange man would come to him again and Bobby would cry out loud.

He wished his parents had waited for him before they had left for Kansas. He couldn't remember what they had said to him, or when they had left, but he remembered that suddenly there he was in the kitchen, taking what was left of his mother's grocery money from the glass jar next to the breadbox. Then he had put on his knapsack, which he'd left on the kitchen table. He had started for the living room, but something made him decide not to leave the house that way. Instead he went out the back door, down the back-porch steps, and back up the driveway until he reached the street. Then he turned left, to the west. His father had often told him that if he turned in that direction and walked for a thousand miles, more or less, he would reach Kansas.

In the hours after he'd left Lucky's Diner, people had given him strange looks as he hobbled through the city. He could have sworn he'd seen his own picture looking back at him from a group of television sets in an appliance-store window. He knew that the policeman was probably looking for him. Uncle Leon would be looking too. Bobby wished he could remember who Uncle Leon was. Whoever he was, it made Bobby feel bad to think about him. But he didn't know why.

Instead he thought about his parents and Uncle Harry and Aunt Melissa. Right now they were probably sitting around the kitchen table in the farmhouse wondering where he was, and when he was going to get there, and if he was all right. Soon he would be asleep in the big feather bed in the bedroom that looked out onto the barnyard. The next morning he would awaken to the smell of one of Aunt Melissa's breakfasts. He could almost taste the sausage and eggs and biscuits flaky as a cloud. . . .

The next morning when Officer Tony DiPaolo found him sleeping in the alley and scooped him up into his arms, Bobby was still dreaming of Kansas.

Purple Prose

JULIANN EVANS

Juliann Evans has published a mystery story, a story in *Woman's World*, and several true-crime stories. She is at work on a mystery novel, *Flower Death*, with a female private detective. "Purple Prose," based on a real murder in New York City, demonstrates the logic of a serial killer's compulsion.

Would the purple speak to him today?

"Charles, do you want more coffee?"

Six words. He nodded and watched his mother pour the hot liquid into the cup. It was a delicate bone china with roses splattered on the sides. There was a small chip on the edge.

He added the sugar, one teaspoon, and the creamer, two teaspoons, stirring them ten times exactly. One-two-three-four-five-six-seven-eight-nine-ten.

His mother sat down heavily on the cracked vinyl chair across from him. "I see that girl down the hall got married. I thought she'd be a nice girl for you."

Eighteen words. He didn't answer. He thought his mother didn't really expect an answer. He sipped his coffee, his tongue carefully touching the chip in the cup. After two swallows, he set the cup carefully on the table. He always put the cup there after two swallows. Otherwise everything was invalid, and he had to start over again. Fourteen sips, seven times to a cup, unless she filled it too full.

He pushed his chair back and put on his jacket. She always told him to wear a jacket. He had lost count of the number of times she said that, but he knew it was somewhere in the hundreds. This time she didn't say anything but continued reading her paper.

"Thanks for breakfast. See you tonight," he said. Six words. He allotted himself 200 each day. He had worked his system out carefully. Two hundred words each day or less. The total couldn't carry over to the next day.

Words possessed colors for him: red, yellow, or green. If asked, he had just spoken in blue. Blue words were for his mother. She used yellow for him.

He closed the door to the apartment and looked at his watch. Exactly on time, as usual: 7:40 A.M. Ten minutes to walk to the subway. He counted his steps, paying so much attention to the numbers that he didn't see the red light. A taxi almost hit him.

"Hey, stupid, look out."

Four red words. He smiled an apology but didn't waste words on the angry taxi driver.

Into the subway and down the stairs with the rest of the moving feet. He shuddered as arms and legs touched him. He tried to avoid them every morning, but they pushed him up against the railing. He felt the metal cut into his leg. He refused to look at them. He held himself rigidly.

He didn't like going underground. It smelled bad. And if one of the overhead lights burned out, he couldn't see, and that made him uneasy. He didn't like being in the dark. He always felt dirty down here. The smell of garbage and cigarettes suffocated him. One man clutching a brown paper bag to his chest breathed heavy, rancid air in his face. He tried to turn away. The choking began as it did each morning. He put his hand to his throat. I must breathe slowly, he thought, counting one-two-three.

The choking subsided. He focused on looking at the walls. This might be the day. Purple might speak to him today.

Words were printed unevenly across the walls in black, blue, and a vivid red. He read the names of people, most of them unfamiliar to him. The subway cars pulled in. They were covered with black-and-blue words. No one else heard the words as he heard them. Occasionally he dared to glance into the blank faces, but there was no sign they heard the colors.

He scanned the words. Nothing. Every day he looked, but nothing, not since the last time. He stood for a while in the car, clinging to a pole, keeping his eyes on the walls of the car. Once it lurched, and he nearly fell into the lap of a young girl. He looked at her for the first time. "I'm sorry," he said. Two words. What color? He couldn't decide. He felt confused.

"That's okay." She smiled, and he could see her even white teeth. Does she also brush her teeth twenty-five times morning and night, he wondered. She shifted in her seat, and he realized that he was staring at her. He looked away, searching the graffiti again.

His head swiveled slowly as he read the walls. Nothing. He began to smell her perfume. It smelled like flowers, not like the smells of the subway. It always reeked of the grave. After all, it was a hole in the ground, a place for worms. That was another word for snake, and he knew who the snake served. But he would escape with the sign.

He left the car, letting the young woman step in front of him, as his mother had taught him. "Be polite. Make the girls like you." His mother wanted him to get married. He smelled the girl's hair. Roses, and not too strong. He forced himself to search the walls of the station, walking slowly, looking. It had only been twelve hours since he had been here the day before. The message could have been left in that time.

He wasn't sure if the message would be left for him. He didn't know how many others looked for the purple and how many others heard the color speak to them.

The girl stopped in front of him next to a pillar, and Charles stepped around her. It was then that he saw it. The purple. The words didn't matter. All that mattered was that they were written in purple. Splashed across the wall behind the girl, the purple spoke to him.

He moved his eyes and saw her again. She smiled at him. He looked away. He knew what he had to do.

He waited until the crowd pushed by them and the two of them were alone. The cars pulled out. He waited on the other side of the metal pillar. She must be waiting for another car, he thought.

He looked at her from behind the pillar. Her makeup was carefully applied. She was a nice girl, the kind his mother wanted him to marry. He stiffened.

It was so easy. She never knew that he was behind her. As the other shiny cars came gliding near the platform, he stepped out and shoved her onto the tracks. He closed his eyes as she fell and tried not to hear her screams or the sound of the brakes. He could smell the brakes burning. He couldn't look. She had been so nice, not like the other, the old, crippled woman.

But rules were rules. He couldn't make exceptions. He had received the sign, and the next person he saw was the one. He had to obey. He couldn't substitute. He had to redeem himself and escape from the tomb.

The purple had spoken.

The White Cat

JOYCE CAROL OATES

The most recent book by Joyce Carol Oates is
On Boxing, published by Dolphin-Doubleday. Her
most recent novel, *You Must Remember This*,
features a boxer, who prompted her research into
the sport. "The White Cat" demonstrates the
mysterious allure of feline/female behavior.

There was a gentleman of independent means who,
at about the age of fifty-six, conceived of a passionate
hatred for his much-younger wife's white Persian cat.

His hatred for the cat was all the more ironic, and
puzzling, in that he himself had given the cat to his
wife as a kitten, years ago, when they were first married. And he himself had named her—Miranda—
after his favorite Shakespearean heroine.

It was ironic, too, in that he was hardly a man
given to irrational sweeps of emotion. Except for his
wife (whom he'd married late—his first marriage, her
second) he did not love anyone very much, and would
have thought it beneath his dignity to hate anyone.
For who should he take that seriously? Being a
gentleman of independent means allowed him that
independence of spirit unknown to the majority of
men.

Julius Muir was of slender build, with deep-set,
somber eyes of no distinctive color; thinning, graying, baby-fine hair; and a narrow, lined face to which

the adjective *lapidary* had once been applied, with no vulgar intention of mere flattery. Being of old American stock he was susceptible to none of the fashionable tugs and sways of "identity": He knew who he was, who his ancestors were, and thought the subject of no great interest. His studies both in America and abroad had been undertaken with a dilettante's rather than a scholar's pleasure, but he would not have wished to make too much of them. Life, after all, is a man's primary study.

Fluent in several languages, Mr. Muir had a habit of phrasing his words with inordinate care, as if he were translating them into a common vernacular. He carried himself with an air of discreet self-consciousness that had nothing in it of vanity, or pride, yet did not bespeak a pointless humility. He was a collector (primarily of rare books and coins), but he was certainly not an obsessive collector; he looked upon the fanaticism of certain of his fellows with a bemused disdain. So his rather quickly blossoming hatred for his wife's beautiful white cat surprised him, and for a time amused him. Or did it frighten him? Certainly he didn't know what to make of it!

The animosity began as an innocent sort of domestic irritation, a half-conscious sense that being so respected in public—so recognized as the person of quality and importance he assuredly was—he should warrant that sort of treatment at home. Not that he was naively ignorant of the fact that cats have a way of making their preferences known that lacks the subtlety and tact devised by human beings. But as the cat grew older and more spoiled and ever more choosy it became evident that she did not, for affection, choose *him*. Alissa was her favorite, of course;

then one or another of the help; but it was not uncommon for a stranger, visiting the Muirs for the first time, to win or to appear to win Miranda's capricious heart. "Miranda! Come here!" Mr. Muir might call—gently enough, yet forcibly, treating the animal in fact with a silly sort of deference—but at such times Miranda was likely to regard him with indifferent, unblinking eyes and make no move in his direction. What a fool, she seemed to be saying, to court someone who cares so little for you!

If he tried to lift her in his arms—if he tried, with a show of playfulness, to subdue her—in true cat fashion she struggled to get down with as much violence as if a stranger had seized her. Once as she squirmed out of his grasp, she accidentally raked the back of his hand and drew blood that left a faint stain on the sleeve of his dinner jacket. "Julius, dear, are you hurt?" Alissa asked. "Not at all," Mr. Muir said, dabbing at the scratches with a handkerchief. "I think Miranda is excited because of the company," Alissa said. "You know how sensitive she is." "Indeed I do," Mr. Muir said mildly, winking at their guests. But a pulse beat hard in his head and he was thinking he would like to strangle the cat with his bare hands—were he the kind of man who was capable of such an act.

More annoying still was the routine nature of the cat's aversion to him. When he and Alissa sat together in the evening, reading, each at an end of their sofa, Miranda would frequently leap unbidden into Alissa's lap—but shrink fastidiously from Mr. Muir's very touch. He professed to be hurt. He professed to be amused. "I'm afraid Miranda doesn't like me any longer," he said sadly. (Though in truth he could no longer remember if there'd been a time the creature *had* liked him. When she'd been a kitten, perhaps, and utterly indiscriminate in her affections?) Alissa laughed and said apologetically, "Of course she likes you, Julius," as the cat purred loudly and sensuously in her lap. "But—you know how cats are."

"Indeed, I am learning," Mr. Muir said with a stiff little smile.

And he felt he *was* learning—something to which he could give no name.

What first gave him the idea—the fancy, really—of killing Miranda, he could not have afterward said. One day, watching her rubbing about the ankles of a director-friend of his wife's, observing how wantonly she presented herself to an admiring little circle of guests (even people with a general aversion to cats could not resist exclaiming over Miranda—petting her, scratching her behind the ears, cooing over her like idiots), Mr. Muir found himself thinking that, as he had brought the cat into his household of his own volition and had paid a fair amount of money for her, she was his to dispose of as he wished. It was true that the full-blooded Persian was one of the prize possessions of the household—a household in which possessions were not acquired casually or cheaply—and it was true that Alissa adored her. But ultimately she belonged to Mr. Muir. And he alone had the power of life or death over her, did he not?

"What a beautiful animal! Is it a male or a female?"

Mr. Muir was being addressed by one of his guests (in truth, one of Alissa's guests; since returning to her theatrical career she had a new, wide, rather promiscuous circle of acquaintances) and for a moment he could not think how to answer. The question lodged deep in him as if it were a riddle: *Is it a male or a female?*

"Female, of course," Mr. Muir said pleasantly. "Its name after all is Miranda."

He wondered: Should he wait until Alissa began rehearsals for her new play—or should he act quickly, before his resolution faded? (Alissa, a minor but well-regarded actress, was to be an understudy for the female lead in a Broadway play opening in September.) And how should he do it? He could not strangle the cat—could not bring himself to act with such direct and unmitigated brutality—nor was it likely that he could run over her, as if accidentally, with the car. (Though *that* would have been fortuitous, indeed.) One midsummer evening when sly, silky Miranda insinuated herself onto the lap of Alissa's new friend Alban (actor, writer, director; his talents were evidently lavish) the conversation turned to notorious murder cases—to poisons—and Mr. Muir thought simply, *Of course. Poison.*

Next morning he poked about in the gardener's shed and found the remains of a ten-pound sack of grainy white "rodent" poison. The previous autumn they'd had a serious problem with mice, and their gardener had set out poison traps in the attic and basement of the house. (With excellent results, Mr. Muir surmised. At any rate, the mice had certainly disappeared.) What was ingenious about the poison was that it induced extreme thirst—so that after having devoured the bait the poisoned creature was driven to seek water, leaving the house and dying outside. Whether the poison was "merciful" or not, Mr. Muir did not know.

He was able to take advantage of the servants' Sunday night off—for as it turned out, though rehearsals for her play had not yet begun, Alissa was spending several days in the city. So Mr. Muir himself fed Miranda in a corner of the kitchen where she customarily ate—having mashed a generous teaspoon of the poison in with her usual food. (How spoiled the creature was! From the very first, when she was a seven-weeks' kitten, Miranda had been fed a special high-protein, high-vitamin cat food, supplemented by raw chopped liver, chicken giblets, and God knows what all else. Though as he ruefully had to admit, Mr. Muir had had a hand in spoiling her, too.)

Miranda ate the food with her usual finicky greed, not at all conscious of, or grateful for, her master's presence. He might have been one of the servants; he might have been no one at all. If she sensed something out of the ordinary—the fact that her water dish was taken away and not returned, for instance— like a true aristocrat she gave no sign. Had there ever been any creature of his acquaintance, human or otherwise, so supremely complacent as this white Persian cat?

Mr. Muir watched Miranda methodically poison herself with an air not of elation as he'd anticipated, not even with a sense of satisfaction in a wrong being righted, in justice being (however ambiguously) exacted—but with an air of profound regret. That the spoiled creature deserved to die he did not doubt; for after all, what incalculable cruelties, over a lifetime, must a cat afflict on birds, mice, rabbits! But it struck him as a melancholy thing, that *he*, Julius Muir—who had paid so much for her, and who in fact had shared in the pride of her—should find himself out of necessity in the role of executioner. But it was something that had to be done, and though he had perhaps forgotten why it had to be done, he knew that he and he alone was destined to do it.

The other evening a number of guests had come to dinner, and as they were seated on the terrace Miranda leapt whitely up out of nowhere to make her way along the garden wall—plumelike tail erect, silky ruff floating about her high-held head, golden eyes gleaming—quite as if on cue, as Alissa said. "This is Miranda, come to say hello to you! *Isn't* she beautiful!" Alissa happily exclaimed. (For she seemed never to tire of remarking upon her cat's beauty—an innocent sort of narcissism, Mr. Muir supposed.) The usual praise, or flattery, was aired; the cat preened herself—fully conscious of being the center of attention—then leapt away with a violent sort of grace and disappeared down the steep stone steps to the river embankment. Mr. Muir thought then that he understood why Miranda was so uncannily *interesting* as a phenomenon: She represented a beauty that was both purposeless and necessary; a beauty that was (considering her pedigree) completely an artifice, and yet (considering she *was* a thing of flesh and blood) completely natural: Nature.

Though was Nature always and invariably—*natural*?

Now, as the white cat finished her meal (leaving a good quarter of it in the dish, as usual) Mr. Muir said aloud, in a tone in which infinite regret and satisfaction were commingled, "But beauty won't save you."

The cat paused to look up at him with her flat, unblinking gaze. He felt an instant's terror: Did she know? Did she know—already? It seemed to him that she had never looked more splendid: fur so purely, silkily white; ruff full as if recently brushed; the petulant pug face; wide, stiff whiskers; finely shaped ears so intelligently erect. And, of course, the eyes. . . .

He'd always been fascinated by Miranda's eyes, which were a tawny golden hue, for they had the mysterious capacity to flare up, as if at will. Seen at night, of course—by way of the moon's reflection, or the headlights of the Muirs' own homebound car— they were lustrous as small beams of light. "Is that Miranda, do you think?" Alissa would ask, seeing the twin flashes of light in the tall grass bordering the road. "Possibly," Mr. Muir would say. "Ah, she's waiting for us! Isn't that sweet! She's waiting for us to come home!" Alissa would exclaim with childlike excitement. Mr. Muir—who doubted that the cat had even been aware of their absence, let alone eagerly awaited their return—said nothing.

Another thing about the cat's eyes that had always seemed to Mr. Muir somehow perverse was the fact that, while the human eyeball is uniformly white and the iris colored, a cat eyeball is colored and the iris purely black. Green, yellow, gray, even blue—the entire eyeball! And the iris so magically responsive to gradations of light or excitation, contracting to razor-thin slits, dilating blackly to fill almost the entire eye. . . . As she stared up at him now her eyes were so dilated their color was nearly eclipsed.

"No, beauty can't save you. It isn't enough," Mr.

Muir said quietly. With trembling fingers he opened the screen door to let the cat out into the night. As she passed him—perverse creature, indeed!—she rubbed lightly against his leg as she had not done for many months. Or had it been years?

Alissa was twenty years Mr. Muir's junior but looked even younger: a petite woman with very large, very pretty brown eyes; shoulder-length blond hair; the upbeat if sometimes rather frenetic manner of a well-practiced ingenue. She was a minor actress with a minor ambition—as she freely acknowledged—for after all, serious professional acting is brutally hard work, even if one somehow manages to survive the competition.

"And then, of course, Julius takes such good care of me," she would say, linking her arm through his or resting her head for a moment against his shoulder. "I have everything I want, really, right here . . ." By which she meant the country place Mr. Muir had bought for her when they were married. (Of course they also kept an apartment in Manhattan, two hours to the south. But Mr. Muir had grown to dislike the city—it abraded his nerves like a cat's claws raking against a screen—and rarely made the journey in any longer.) Under her maiden name, Howth, Alissa had been employed intermittently for eight years before marrying Mr. Muir; her first marriage—contracted at the age of nineteen to a well-known (and notorious) Hollywood actor, since deceased—had been a disaster of which she cared not to speak in any detail. (Nor did Mr. Muir care to question her about those years. It was as if, for him, they had not existed.)

At the time of their meeting Alissa was in temporary retreat, as she called it, from her career. She'd had a small success on Broadway but the success had not taken hold. And was it worth it, really, to keep going, to keep trying? Season after season, the grinding round of auditions, the competition with new faces, "promising" new talents. . . . Her first marriage had ended badly and she'd had a number of love affairs of varying degrees of worth (precisely how many Mr. Muir was never to learn), and now perhaps it was time to ease into private life. And there was Julius Muir: not young, not particularly charming, but well-to-do, and well-bred, and besotted with love for her, and—*there*.

Of course Mr. Muir was dazzled by her; and he had the time and the resources to court her more assiduously than any man had ever courted her. He seemed to see in her qualities no one else saw; his imagination, for so reticent and subdued a man, was rich, lively to the point of fever, immensely flattering. And he did not mind, he extravagantly insisted, that he loved her more than she loved him—even as Alissa protested she *did* love him—would she consent to marry him otherwise?

For a few years they spoke vaguely of "starting a family," but nothing came of it. Alissa was too busy, or wasn't in ideal health; or they were traveling; or Mr. Muir worried about the unknown effect a child would have upon their marriage. (Alissa would have less time for him, surely?) As time passed he vexed himself with the thought that he'd have no heir when he died—that is, no child of his own—but there was nothing to be done.

They had a rich social life; they were wonderfully

busy people. And they had, after all, their gorgeous white Persian cat. "Miranda would be traumatized if there was a baby in the household," Alissa said. "We really couldn't do that to her."

"Indeed we couldn't," Mr. Muir agreed.

And then, abruptly, Alissa decided to return to acting. To her "career" as she gravely called it—as if it were a phenomenon apart from her, a force not to be resisted. And Mr. Muir was happy for her— very happy for her. He took pride in his wife's professionalism, and he wasn't at all jealous of her ever- widening circle of friends, acquaintances, associates. He wasn't jealous of her fellow actors and actresses— Rikka, Mario, Robin, Sibyl, Emile, each in turn— and now Alban of the damp dark shiny eyes and quick sweet smile; nor was he jealous of the time she spent away from home; nor, if home, of the time she spent sequestered away in the room they called her studio, deeply absorbed in her work. In her ma- turity Alissa Howth had acquired a robust sort of good-heartedness that gave her more stage presence even as it relegated her to certain sorts of roles—the roles inevitable, in any case, for older actresses, re- gardless of their physical beauty. And she'd become a far better, far more subtle actress—as everyone said.

Indeed, Mr. Muir *was* proud of her, and happy for her. And if he felt, now and then, a faint re- sentment—or, if not quite resentment, a tinge of regret at the way their life had diverged into lives— he was too much a gentleman to show it.

"Where is Miranda? Have you seen Miranda today?"

It was noon, it was four o'clock, it was nearly dusk,

and Miranda had not returned. For much of the day Alissa had been preoccupied with telephone calls—the phone seemed always to be ringing—and only gradually had she become aware of the cat's prolonged absence. She went outside to call her; she sent the servants out to look for her. And Mr. Muir, of course, gave his assistance, wandering about the grounds and for some distance into the woods, his hands cupped to his mouth and his voice high-pitched and tremulous: "*Kitty-kitty-kitty-kitty-kitty! Kitty-kitty-kitty*—" How pathetic, how foolish—how futile! Yet it had to be performed since it was what, in innocent circumstances, *would* be performed. Julius Muir, that most solicitous of husbands, tramping through the underbrush looking for his wife's Persian cat. . . .

Poor Alissa! he thought. She'll be heartbroken for days—or would it be weeks?

And he, too, would miss Miranda—as a household presence at the very least. They would have had her, after all, for ten years this autumn.

Dinner that night was subdued, rather leaden. Not simply because Miranda was missing (and Alissa did seem inordinately and genuinely worried), but because Mr. Muir and his wife were dining alone; the table, set for two, seemed almost aesthetically wrong. And how unnatural, the quiet. . . . Mr. Muir tried to make conversation but his voice soon trailed off into a guilty silence. Midmeal Alissa rose to accept a telephone call (from Manhattan, of course—her agent, or her director, or Alban, or a female friend—an urgent call, for otherwise Mrs. Muir did not accept calls at this intimate hour) and Mr. Muir—crestfallen, hurt—finished his solitary meal in a kind of trance, tasting nothing. He recalled the night before—the

324

pungent-smelling cat food, the grainy white poison, the way the shrewd animal had looked up at him, and the way she'd brushed against his leg in a belated gesture of . . . was it affection? Reproach? Mockery? He felt a renewed stab of guilt, and an even more powerful stab of visceral satisfaction. Then, glancing up, he chanced to see something white making its careful way along the top of the garden wall. . . .

Of course it was Miranda come home.

He stared, appalled. He stared, speechless—waiting for the apparition to vanish.

Slowly, in a daze, he rose to his feet. In a voice meant to be jubilant he called out the news to Alissa in the adjoining room: "Miranda's come home!"

He called out: "Alissa! Darling! Miranda's come home!"

And there Miranda was, indeed; indeed it *was* Miranda, peering into the dining room from the terrace, her eyes glowing tawny gold. Mr. Muir was trembling, but his brain worked swiftly to absorb the fact, and to construe a logic to accommodate it. She'd vomited up the poison, no doubt. Ah, no doubt! Or, after a cold, damp winter in the gardener's shed, the poison had lost its efficacy.

He had yet to bestir himself, to hurry to unlatch the sliding door and let the white cat in, but his voice fairly quavered with excitement: "Alissa! Good news! Miranda's come home!"

Alissa's joy was so extreme and his own initial relief so genuine that Mr. Muir—stroking Miranda's plume of a tail as Alissa hugged the cat ecstatically in her arms—thought he'd acted cruelly, selfishly—certainly he'd acted out of character—and decided that Miranda, having escaped death at her master's hands, should be granted life. He would *not* try another time.

Before his marriage at the age of forty-six Julius Muir, like most never-married men and women of a certain temperament—introverted, self-conscious; observers of life rather than participants—had believed that the marital state was unconditionally *marital*; he'd thought that husband and wife were one flesh in more than merely the metaphorical sense of that term. Yet it happened that his own marriage was a marriage of a decidedly diminished sort. Marital relations had all but ceased, and there seemed little likelihood of their being resumed. He would shortly be fifty-seven years old, after all. (Though sometimes he wondered: Was that truly *old*?)

During the first two or three years of their marriage (when Alissa's theatrical career was, as she called it, in eclipse), they had shared a double bed like any married couple—or so Mr. Muir assumed. (For his own marriage had not enlightened him to what "marriage" in a generic sense meant.) With the passage of time, however, Alissa began to complain gently of being unable to sleep because of Mr. Muir's nocturnal "agitation"—twitching, kicking, thrashing about, exclaiming aloud, sometimes even shouting in terror. Wakened by her he would scarcely know, for a moment or two, where he was; he would then apologize profusely and shamefully, and creep away into another bedroom to sleep, if he could, for the rest of the night. Though unhappy with the situation, Mr. Muir was fully sympathetic with Alissa; he even had reason to believe that the poor woman (whose nerves were unusually sensitive) had suffered many a sleepless night on his account without telling him. It was like her to be so considerate; so loath to hurt another's feelings.

As a consequence they developed a cozy routine in which Mr. Muir spent a half-hour or so with Alissa when they first retired for the night; then, taking care not to disturb her, he would tiptoe quietly away into another room, where he might sleep undisturbed. (If, indeed, his occasional nightmares allowed him undisturbed sleep. He rather thought the worst ones, however, were the ones that failed to wake him.)

Yet a further consequence had developed in recent years: Alissa had acquired the habit of staying awake late—reading in bed, or watching television, or even, from time to time, chatting on the telephone—so it was most practical for Mr. Muir simply to kiss her good-night without getting in bed beside her, and then to go off to his own bedroom. Sometimes in his sleep he imagined Alissa was calling him back—awakened, he would hurry out into the darkened corridor to stand by her door for a minute or two, eager and hopeful. At such times he dared not raise his voice above a whisper: "Alissa? Alissa, dearest? Did you call me?"

Just as unpredictable and capricious as Mr. Muir's bad dreams were the nighttime habits of Miranda, who at times would cozily curl up at the foot of Alissa's bed and sleep peacefully through to dawn, but at other times would insist upon being let outside, no matter that Alissa loved her to sleep on the bed. There was comfort of a kind—childish, Alissa granted—in knowing the white Persian was there through the night, and feeling at her feet the cat's warm, solid weight atop the satin coverlet.

But of course, as Alissa acknowledged, a cat can't be forced to do anything against her will. "It seems almost to be a law of nature," she said solemnly.

A few days after the abortive poisoning Mr. Muir was driving home in the early dusk when, perhaps a mile from his estate, he caught sight of the white cat in the road ahead—motionless in the other lane, as if frozen by the car's headlights. Unbidden, the thought came to him: *This is just to frighten her*—and he turned his wheel and headed in her direction. The golden eyes flared up in a blaze of blank surprise—or perhaps it was terror, or recognition—*This is just to redress the balance*, Mr. Muir thought as he pressed down harder on the accelerator and drove directly at the white Persian—and struck her, just as she started to bolt toward the ditch, with the front left wheel of his car. There was a thud and a cat's yowling, incredulous scream—and it was done.

My God! It *was* done!

Dry mouthed, shaking, Mr. Muir saw in his rearview mirror the broken white form in the road; saw a patch of liquid crimson blossoming out around it. He had not meant to kill Miranda, and yet he had actually done it this time—without premeditation, and therefore without guilt.

And now the deed was done forever.

"And no amount of remorse can undo it," he said in a slow, wondering voice.

Mr. Muir had driven to the village to pick up a prescription for Alissa at the drugstore—she'd been in the city on theater matters; had returned home late on a crowded commuter train and gone at once to lie down with what threatened to be a migraine headache. Now he felt rather a hypocrite, a brute, presenting headache tablets to his wife with the guilty knowledge that if she knew what he'd done, the severity of her migraine would be tenfold. Yet how could he have explained to her that he had not meant to kill Miranda this time, but the steering wheel of his car had seemed to act of its own volition, wresting itself from his grip? For so Mr. Muir—speeding home, still trembling and excited as though he himself had come close to violent death—remembered the incident.

He remembered too the cat's hideous scream, cut off almost at once by the impact of the collision— but not quite at once.

And was there a dent in the fender of the handsome, English-built car? There was not.

And were there bloodstains on the left front tire? There were not.

Was there in fact any sign of a mishap, even of the mildest, most innocent sort? There was not.

"No proof! No proof!" Mr. Muir told himself happily, taking the stairs to Alissa's room two at a time. It was a matter of some relief as well when he raised his hand to knock at the door to hear that Alissa was evidently feeling better. She was on the telephone, talking animatedly with someone; even laughing in her light, silvery way that reminded him of nothing so much as wind chimes on a mild summer's night. His heart swelled with love and gratitude. "Dear Alissa—we will be so happy from now on!"

Then it happened, incredibly, that at about bedtime the white cat showed up again. *She had not died after all.*

Mr. Muir, who was sharing a late-night brandy with Alissa in her bedroom, was the first to see Miranda: She had climbed up onto the roof—by way, probably, of a rose trellis she often climbed for that purpose—and now her pug face appeared at one of the windows in a hideous repetition of the scene some nights ago. Mr. Muir sat paralyzed with shock, and it was Alissa who jumped out of bed to let the cat in.

"Miranda! What a trick! What *are* you up to?"

Certainly the cat had not been missing for any worrisome period of time, yet Alissa greeted her with as much enthusiasm as if she had. And Mr. Muir—his heart pounding in his chest and his very soul convulsed with loathing—was obliged to go along with the charade. He hoped Alissa would not notice the sick terror that surely shone in his eyes.

The cat he'd struck with his car must have been another cat, not Miranda. . . . Obviously it had not been Miranda. Another white Persian with tawny eyes, and not his own.

Alissa cooed over the creature, and petted her, and encouraged her to settle down on the bed for the night, but after a few minutes Miranda jumped down and scratched to be let out the door: She'd missed her supper; she was hungry; she'd had enough of her mistress's affection. Not so much as a glance had she given her master, who was staring at her with revulsion. He knew now that he *must* kill her—if only to prove he could do it.

Following this episode the cat shrewdly avoided Mr. Muir—not out of lazy indifference, as in the past, but out of a sharp sense of their altered relations.

She could not be conscious, he knew, of the fact that he had tried to kill her—but she must have been able to sense it. Perhaps she had been hiding in the bushes by the road and had seen him aim his car at her unfortunate doppelgänger, and run it down. . . .

This was unlikely, Mr. Muir knew. Indeed, it was highly improbable. But how otherwise to account for the creature's behavior in his presence—her demonstration, or simulation, of animal fear? Leaping atop a cabinet when he entered a room, as if to get out of his way; leaping atop a fireplace mantel (and sending, it seemed deliberately, one of his carved jade figurines to the hearth, where it shattered into a dozen pieces); skittering gracelessly through a doorway, her sharp toenails clicking against the hardwood floor. When, without intending to, he approached her out-of-doors, she was likely to scamper noisily up one of the rose trellises, or the grape arbor, or a tree; or run off into the shrubbery like a wild creature. If Alissa happened to be present she was invariably astonished, for the cat's behavior *was* senseless. "Do you think Miranda is ill?" she asked. "Should we take her to the veterinarian?" Mr. Muir said uneasily that he doubted they would be able to catch her for such a purpose—at least, he doubted *he* could.

He had an impulse to confess his crime, or his attempted crime, to Alissa. He had killed the hateful creature—*and she had not died.*

One night at the very end of August Mr. Muir dreamt of glaring, disembodied eyes. And in their centers those black, black irises like old-fashioned keyholes: slots opening into the Void. He could not move to protect himself. A warm, furry weight settled luxuriantly upon his chest . . . upon his very face! The cat's whiskery white muzzle pressed against his mouth in a hellish kiss and in an instant the breath was being sucked from him. . . .

"Oh, no! Save me! Dear God—"

The damp muzzle against his mouth, sucking his life's breath from him, and he could not move to tear it away—his arms, leaden at his sides; his entire body struck dumb, paralyzed. . . .

"Save me . . . *save me!*"

His shouting, his panicked thrashing about in the bedclothes, woke him. Though he realized at once it had been only a dream, his breath still came in rapid, shallow gasps, and his heart hammered so violently he was in terror of dying: Had not his doctor only the other week spoken gravely to him of imminent heart disease, the possibility of heart failure? And how mysterious it was, his blood pressure being so very much higher than ever before in his life. . . .

Mr. Muir threw himself out of the damp, tangled bedclothes and switched on a lamp with trembling fingers. Thank God he was alone and Alissa had not witnessed this latest display of nerves!

"Miranda?" he whispered. "Are you in here?"

He switched on an overhead light. The bedroom shimmered with shadows and did not seem, for an instant, any room he knew.

"Miranda . . . ?"

The sly, wicked creature! The malevolent beast! To think that cat's muzzle had touched his very lips, the muzzle of an animal that devoured mice, rats— any sort of foul filthy thing out in the woods! Mr. Muir went into his bathroom and rinsed out his mouth even as he told himself calmly that the dream had been only a dream, and the cat only a phantasm, and that of course Miranda was *not* in his room.

Still, she had settled her warm, furry, unmistakable weight on his chest. She had attempted to suck his breath from him, to choke him, suffocate him, stop his poor heart. *It was within her power.* "Only a dream," Mr. Muir said aloud, smiling shakily at his reflection in the mirror. (Oh! To think that pale, haggard apparition was indeed *his*. . . .) Mr. Muir raised his voice with scholarly precision. "A foolish dream. A child's dream. A woman's dream."

Back in his room he had the fleeting sense that something—a vague white shape—had just now scampered beneath his bed. But when he got down on his hands and knees to look, of course there was nothing.

He did, however, discover in the deep-pile carpet a number of cat hairs. White, rather stiff—quite clearly Miranda's. Ah, quite clearly. "Here's the evidence!" he said excitedly. He found a light scattering of them on the carpet near the door and, nearer his bed, a good deal more—as if the creature had lain there for a while and had even rolled over (as Miranda commonly did out on the terrace in the sun) and stretched her graceful limbs in an attitude of utterly pleasurable abandon. Mr. Muir had often been struck by the cat's remarkable *luxuriance* at such times: a joy of flesh (and fur) he could not begin to imagine. Even before relations between them had deteriorated, he had felt the impulse to hurry to the cat and bring the heel of his shoe down hard on that tender, exposed, pinkish-pale belly. . . .

"Miranda? Where are you? Are you still in here?"

Mr. Muir said. He was breathless, excited. He'd been squatting on his haunches for some minutes, and when he tried to straighten up his legs ached.

Mr. Muir searched the room, but it was clear that the white cat had gone. He went out onto his balcony, leaned against the railing, blinked into the dimly moonlit darkness, but could see nothing—in his fright he'd forgotten to put on his glasses. For some minutes he breathed in the rather humid, sluggish night air in an attempt to calm himself, but it soon became apparent that something was wrong. Some vague murmurous undertone of—was it a voice? Voices?

Then he saw it: the ghostly white shape down in the shrubbery. Mr. Muir blinked and stared, but his vision was unreliable. "Miranda . . . ?" A scuttling noise rustled above him and he turned to see another white shape on the sharp-slanted roof making its rapid way over the top. He stood absolutely motionless— whether out of terror or cunning, he could not have said. That there was more than one white cat, more than one white Persian—more, in fact, than *merely one Miranda*—was a possibility he had not considered! "Yet perhaps that explains it," he said. He was badly frightened, but his brain functioned as clearly as ever.

It was not so very late, scarcely 1:00 A.M. The undertone Mr. Muir heard was Alissa's voice, punctuated now and then by her light, silvery laughter. One might almost think there was someone in the bedroom with her—but of course she was merely having a late-night telephone conversation, very likely with Alban—they would be chatting companionably, with an innocent sort of malice, about their co-actors and -actresses, mutual friends and acquaintances. Alissa's balcony opened out onto the same side of the house that Mr. Muir's did, which accounted for her voice (or *was* it voices? Mr. Muir listened, bemused) carrying so clearly. No light irradiated from her room; she must have been having her telephone conversation in the dark.

Mr. Muir waited another few minutes, but the white shape down in the shrubbery had vanished. And the slate-covered roof overhead was empty, reflecting moonlight in dull, uneven patches. He was alone. He decided to go back to bed but before doing so he checked carefully to see that he *was* alone. He locked all the windows, and the door, and slept with the lights on—but so deeply and with such grateful abandon that in the morning, it was Alissa's rapping on the door that woke him. "Julius? Julius? Is something wrong, dear?" she cried. He saw with astonishment that it was *nearly noon*: He'd slept four hours past his usual rising time!

Alissa said good-bye to him hurriedly. A limousine was coming to carry her to the city; she was to be away for several nights in succession; she was concerned about him, about his health, and hoped there was nothing wrong. . . . "Of course there is nothing wrong," Mr. Muir said irritably. Having slept so late in the day left him feeling sluggish and confused; it had not at all refreshed him. When Alissa kissed him good-bye he seemed rather to suffer the kiss than to participate in it, and after she had gone he had to resist an impulse to wipe his mouth with the back of his hand.

"God help us!" he whispered.

By degrees, as a consequence of his troubled mind, Mr. Muir had lost interest in collecting. When an antiquarian bookdealer offered him a rare octavo edition of the *Directorium Inquisitorum* he felt only the mildest tinge of excitement, and allowed the treasure to be snatched up by a rival collector. Only a few days afterward he responded with even less enthusiasm when offered the chance to bid on a quarto Gothic edition of Machiavelli's *Belfagor*. "Is something wrong, Mr. Muir?" the dealer asked him. (They had been doing business together for a quarter of a century.) Mr. Muir said ironically, "*Is* something wrong?" and broke off the telephone connection. He was never to speak to the man again.

Yet more decisively, Mr. Muir had lost interest in financial affairs. He would not accept telephone calls from the various Wall Street gentlemen who managed his money; it was quite enough for him to know that the money was there and would always be there. Details regarding it struck him as tiresome and vulgar.

In the third week of September the play in which Alissa was an understudy opened to superlative reviews, which meant a good, long run. Though the female lead was in excellent health and showed little likelihood of ever missing a performance, Alissa felt obliged to remain in the city a good deal, sometimes for a full week at a time. (What she did there, how she busied herself day after day, evening after evening, Mr. Muir did not know and was too proud to ask.) When she invited him to join her for a weekend (why didn't he visit some of his antiquarian dealers, as he used to do with such pleasure?) Mr. Muir said simply, "But why, when I have all I require for happiness here in the country?"

Since the night of the attempted suffocation Mr. Muir and Miranda were yet more keenly aware of each other. No longer did the white cat flee his presence; rather, as if in mockery of him, she held her ground when he entered a room. If he approached her she eluded him only at the last possible instant, often flattening herself close against the floor and scampering, snakelike, away. He cursed her; she bared her teeth and hissed. He laughed loudly to show her how very little he cared; she leapt atop a cabinet, out of his reach, and settled into a cat's blissful sleep. Each evening Alissa called at an appointed hour; each evening she inquired after Miranda, and Mr. Muir would say, "Beautiful and healthy as ever! A pity you can't see her!"

With the passage of time Miranda grew bolder and more reckless—misjudging, perhaps, the quickness of her master's reflexes. She sometimes appeared underfoot, nearly tripping him on the stairs or as he left the house; she dared approach him as he stood with a potential weapon in hand—a carving knife, a poker, a heavy, leatherbound book. Once or twice, as Mr. Muir sat dreaming through one of his solitary meals, she even leapt onto his lap and scampered across the dining room table, upsetting dishes and glasses. "Devil!" he shrieked, swiping in her wake with his fists. "What do you want of me!"

He wondered what tales the servants told of him, whispered backstairs. He wondered if any were being relayed to Alissa in the city.

One night, however, Miranda made a tactical error, and Mr. Muir did catch hold of her. She had slipped into his study—where he sat examining some of his rarest and most valuable coins (Mesopotamian, Etruscan) by lamplight—having calculated, evidently, on making her escape by way of the door.

But Mr. Muir, leaping from his chair with extraordinary, almost feline swiftness, managed to kick the door shut. And now what a chase! What a struggle! What a mad frolic! Mr. Muir caught hold of the animal, lost her, caught hold of her again, lost her; she raked him viciously on the backs of both hands and on his face; he managed to catch hold of her again, slamming her against the wall and closing his bleeding fingers around her throat. He squeezed, he squeezed! He had her now and no force on earth could make him release her! As the cat screamed and clawed and kicked and thrashed and seemed to be suffering the convulsions of death, Mr. Muir crouched over her with eyes bulging and mad as her own. The arteries in his forehead visibly throbbed. "Now! Now I have you! Now!" he cried. And at that very moment when, surely, the white Persian was on the verge of extinction, the door to Mr. Muir's study was flung open and one of the servants appeared, white faced and incredulous: "Mr. Muir? What is it? We heard such—" the fool was saying; and of course Miranda slipped from Mr. Muir's loosened grasp and bolted from the room.

After that incident Mr. Muir seemed resigned to the knowledge that he would never have such an opportunity again. The end was swiftly approaching.

It happened quite suddenly, in the second week of November, that Alissa returned home.

She had quit the play; she had quit the "professional stage"; she did not even intend, as she told her husband vehemently, to visit New York City for a long time.

He saw to his astonishment that she'd been crying.

Her eyes were unnaturally bright and seemed smaller than he recalled. And her prettiness looked worn, as if another face—harder, of smaller dimensions—were pushing through. Poor Alissa! She had gone away with such hope! When Mr. Muir moved to embrace her, however, meaning to comfort her, she drew away from him; her very nostrils pinched as if she found the smell of him offensive. "Please," she said, not looking him in the eye. "I don't feel well. What I want most is to be alone . . . just to be alone."

She retired to her room, to her bed. For several days she remained sequestered there, admitting only one of the female servants and, of course, her beloved Miranda, when Miranda condescended to visit the house. (To his immense relief Mr. Muir observed that the white cat showed no sign of their recent struggle. His own lacerated hands and face were slow to heal, but in her own grief and self-absorption, Alissa seemed not to have noticed.)

In her room, behind her locked door, Alissa made a number of telephone calls to New York City. Often she seemed to be weeping over the phone. But so far as Mr. Muir could determine—being forced, under these special circumstances, to eavesdrop on the line—none of her conversations were with Alban.

Which meant . . . ? He had to confess he had no idea; nor could he ask Alissa. For that would give away the fact that he'd been eavesdropping, and she would be deeply shocked.

Mr. Muir sent small bouquets of autumn flowers to Alissa's sickroom; bought her chocolates and bonbons, slender volumes of poetry, a new diamond bracelet. Several times he presented himself at her door, ever the eager suitor, but she explained that she was not prepared to see him just yet—not just yet. Her voice was shrill and edged with a metallic tone Mr. Muir had not heard before.

"Don't you love me, Alissa?" he cried suddenly.

There was a moment's embarrassed silence. Then: "Of course I do. But please go away and leave me alone."

So worried was Mr. Muir about Alissa that he could no longer sleep for more than an hour or two at a time, and these hours were characterized by tumultuous dreams. The white cat! The hideous smothering weight! Fur in his very mouth! Yet awake he thought only of Alissa and of how, though she had come home to him, it was not in fact to *him*.

He lay alone in his solitary bed, amidst the tangled bedclothes, weeping hoarsely. One morning he stroked his chin and touched bristles: He'd neglected to shave for several days.

From his balcony he chanced to see the white cat preening atop the garden wall, a larger creature than he recalled. She had fully recovered from his attack. (If, indeed, she had been injured by it. If, indeed, the cat on the garden wall was the selfsame cat that had blundered into his study.) Her white fur very nearly blazed in the sun; her eyes were miniature golden-glowing coals set deep in her skull. Mr. Muir felt a mild shock seeing her: What a beautiful creature!

Though in the next instant, of course, he realized what she was.

One rainy, gusty evening in late November Mr. Muir was driving on the narrow blacktop road above the river, Alissa silent at his side—stubbornly silent, he thought. She wore a black cashmere cloak and a hat of soft black felt that fitted her head tightly, covering most of her hair. These were items of clothing Mr. Muir had not seen before, and in their stylish austerity they suggested the growing distance between them. When he had helped her into the car she'd murmured "thank you" in a tone that indicated "Oh! Must you touch me?" And Mr. Muir had made a mocking little bow, standing bareheaded in the rain.

And I had loved you so much.

Now she did not speak. Sat with her lovely profile turned from him. As if she were fascinated by the lashing rain, the river pocked and heaving below, the gusts of wind that rocked the English-built car as Mr. Muir pressed his foot ever harder on the gas pedal. "It will be better this way, my dear wife," Mr. Muir said quietly. "Even if you love no other man, it is painfully clear that you do not love me." At these solemn words Alissa started guiltily, but still would not face him. "My dear? Do you understand? It will be better this way—do not be frightened." As Mr. Muir drove faster, as the car rocked more violently in the wind, Alissa pressed her hands against her mouth as if to stifle any protest; she was staring transfixed—as Mr. Muir stared transfixed—at the rushing pavement.

Only when Mr. Muir bravely turned the car's front wheels in the direction of a guard railing did her resolve break: She emitted a series of breathless little screams, shrinking back against the seat, but made no effort to seize his arm or the wheel. And in an instant all was over, in any case—the car crashed through the railing, seemed to spin in midair, dropped to the rock-strewn hillside and bursting into flame, turned end over end. . . .

He was seated in a chair with wheels—a wheeled chair! It seemed to him a remarkable invention and he wondered whose ingenuity lay behind it.

Though he had not the capacity, being almost totally paralyzed, to propel it of his own volition.

And, being blind, he had no volition in any case! He was quite content to stay where he was, so long as it was out of the draft. (The invisible room in which he now resided was, for the most part, cozily heated—his wife had seen to that—but there yet remained unpredictable currents of cold air that assailed him from time to time. His bodily temperature, he feared, could not maintain its integrity against any sustained onslaught.)

He had forgotten the names for many things and felt no great grief. Indeed, not knowing *names* relaxes one's desire for the *things* that, ghostlike, forever unattainable, dwell behind them. And of course his blindness had much to do with this—for which he was grateful! Quite grateful!

Blind, yet not wholly blind: for he could see (indeed, could not *not* see) washes of white, gradations of white, astonishing subtleties of white like rivulets in a stream perpetually breaking and falling about his head, not distinguished by any form or outline or vulgar suggestion of an object in space. . . .

He had had, evidently, a number of operations. How many he did not know; nor did he care to know. In recent weeks they had spoken earnestly to him of the possibility of yet another operation on his brain, the (hypothetical) object being, if he understood cor-

rectly, the restoration of his ability to move some of
the toes on his left foot. Had he the capacity to laugh
he would have laughed, but perhaps his dignified
silence was preferable.

Alissa's sweet voice joined with the others in a
chorus of bleak enthusiasm, but so far as he knew
the operation had never taken place. Or if it had, it
had not been a conspicuous success. The toes of his
left foot were as remote and lost to him as all the
other parts of his body.

Driving alone in a violent thunderstorm on the narrow road high above the river embankment, losing
control of his car, plunging through the guardrail and
over the side, "miraculously" being thrown clear of
the burning car albeit with two-thirds of the bones
in his body broken, his skull severely fractured, his
spinal column smashed, a lung pierced. . . . So the
story of how he had come to this place emerged, in
fragments shattered and haphazard as those of a
smashed windshield.

By a stroke of good fortune (as the story continued), another car had come by within minutes. So
an ambulance was called and his life saved. He did
not believe that any irony was intended by such kindly
words as *good fortune* and *saved*, though it was not
a very happy story, as even Alissa acknowledged.

Yet it was not an entirely tragic story—as Alissa
insisted with that effort of resolute cheerfulness for
which others in this place (he had heard them) whispered praise of her in her absence—since there was
always the possibility of some of his vision being
restored. And then, so long as he lived and maintained his courage there was always the possibility

of new medical technology, new neurological discoveries that might alleviate some of the paralysis.

Sometimes when Alissa came to visit she brought a certain furry, warm creature with her, and he'd begun to look forward to—and even to a degree anticipate—these rare occasions. Awaking from his doze he would feel a weight lowered into his lap: soft, yet heavy; heated, yet not unpleasantly so; initially a bit restless (as a cat must circle fussily about, trying to determine the ideal position before she settles herself down), yet within a few minutes quite wonderfully relaxed, kneading her claws gently against his limbs and purring as she drifted into a companionable sleep. He would have liked to see, beyond the shimmering watery whiteness of his vision, her particular whiteness; certainly he would have liked to feel once again the softness, the astonishing silkiness, of that fur. But he could hear the deep-throated melodic purring. He could feel, to a degree, her warmly pulsing weight, the wonder of her mysterious *livingness* against his—for which he was infinitely grateful.